DATE DUE

GAYLORD		PRINTED IN U.S.A.

SOCIAL EXCLUSION IN GREAT BRITAIN

Social Exclusion in Great Britain
An Empirical Investigation and Comparison with the EU

MATT BARNES
National Centre for Social Research, UK

ASHGATE

Published by
Ashgate Publishing Limited
Gower House
Croft Road
Aldershot
Hampshire GU11 3HR
England

Ashgate Publishing Company
Suite 420
101 Cherry Street
Burlington, VT 05401-4405
USA

Ashgate website: http://www.ashgate.com

British Library Cataloguing in Publication Data
Barnes, Matt
    Social exclusion in Great Britain : an empirical
    investigation and comparison with the EU. - (Studies in
    cash & care)
    1. Marginality, Social - Great Britain - History - 20th
    century 2. Marginality, Social - Great Britain -
    Longitudinal studies
    I. Title
    305.5'6'0941

Library of Congress Cataloging-in-Publication Data
Barnes, Matt.
    Social exclusion in Great Britain : an empirical investigation and comparison with
the EU / by Matt Barnes.
        p. cm. -- (Studies in cash & care)
    Includes bibliographical references and index.
    ISBN 0-7546-4209-7
  1. Marginality, Social--Great Britain--Longitudinal studies. 2. People with social
disabilities--Great Britain-- Longitudinal studies. 3. Social indicators--Great
Britain. 4. Household surveys--Great Britain. 5. Great Britain--Social policy--1979-
6. Marginality, Social--European Union countries. I. Title. II. Series: Cash &
care.

    HN400. M26B37 2005
    305.5'6'0941--dc22

                                                                        2005007478

ISBN 0 7546 4209 7

Printed and bound in Great Britain by MPG Books Ltd, Bodmin, Cornwall

Contents

List of Figures

List of Tables

About the Author

Matt Barnes is a Senior Researcher at the National Centre for Social Research, London, UK (m.barnes@natcen.ac.uk). His research interests are the conceptualization and measurement of poverty and social exclusion, and issues of work-life balance.

Preface

This book builds upon theoretical discussions of social exclusion to construct an empirical model, using quantitative survey data, to investigate the nature and extent of social exclusion in Great Britain. This investigation of social exclusion is also taken to a European level by comparing findings for Great Britain with other European Union (EU) Member States. The crux of the investigation, the operationalization and measurement of social exclusion, is achieved through the use of quantitative research methods involving secondary analysis of two complex longitudinal datasets – the British Household Panel Survey (BHPS) and the European Community Household Panel (ECHP) survey.

The theoretical foundation of the book is a clarification of the conceptual properties that are crucial to the notion of social exclusion. Two of the most important theoretical properties of social exclusion are that it incorporates the use of information on a range of disadvantage domains and that it uses the concept of time to identify the most disadvantaged individuals. The operationalization of social exclusion is carried out through the use of quantitative techniques to construct binary outcome indicators of separate domains of social exclusion: financial situation (income poverty), material possessions, housing circumstance, neighbourhood perception, social relations, physical health and mental health. The indicators are used in various ways – independently and concurrently, and, at a point in time and longitudinally – to provide an in-depth investigation of the multi-dimensional and longitudinal nature of social exclusion. Thus a multi-dimensional and longitudinal model of social exclusion is constructed to identify the prevalence of social exclusion in Great Britain and to distinguish socio-demographic characteristics of individuals associated with an increased likelihood of such experiences.

The empirical model of social exclusion is then used in a comparative manner to place the experiences of Great Britain in a European context. This is achieved by comparing and contrasting the prevalence and nature of social exclusion in Great Britain with other EU Member States. The book concludes by summarising the theoretical and policy implications of operationalizing social exclusion in this way, including a discussion for developments to the government's indicators of poverty and social exclusion detailed in the *Opportunity for all* report.

Acknowledgements

This book is based on work I undertook at the University of Bath and, in particular, research for my Ph.D. thesis. Hence I am indebted to my Ph.D. supervisor, Professor Jane Millar, for the assistance and support she provided. I am also thankful to colleagues on the European Commission funded Targeted Socio-Economic Research project, in particular Professor Chris Heady with whom I spent many hours discussing issues of social exclusion and the intricacies of the ECHP dataset. I must also thank Karl Ashworth for advice on constructing patterns of disadvantage used in Chapter 5. On a more logistical note, I am grateful to Eric Marlier at Eurostat for providing access to the ECHP dataset and to the Data Archive at the University of Essex for providing access to the BHPS dataset.

Finally I would like to thank my family and friends for the endless encouragement they have given me during my Ph.D. research and in preparation for this book. I apologise if I have neglected them in any way during this time and only hope I can be as generous if they ever call on me for support.

List of Abbreviations

BHPS	British Household Panel Study
DSS	Department of Social Security
DWP	Department of Work and Pensions
ECHP	European Community Household Panel (survey)
EU	European Union
EU-12	The 12 European Union Member States present in the first three waves of the ECHP survey (Belgium, Denmark, France, Germany, Greece, Ireland, Italy, Luxembourg, the Netherlands, Portugal, Spain and the United Kingdom)
FWLS	Family and Working Lives Survey
GHS	General Household Survey
HED	Household Economic Deprivation
ONS	Office for National Statistics
PCE	Personal Civic Exclusion
PDI	Proportional Disadvantage Index
PHE	Personal Health Exclusion
PSE	Poverty and Social Exclusion Survey
PSEI	Proportional Social Exclusion Index
RPI	Retail Price Index
UK	United Kingdom
UN	United Nations

Chapter 1

Towards An Empirical Operationalization of Social Exclusion

Existing definitions of poverty and deprivation are sufficiently broad to incorporate attention to a range of dimensions, to take a longitudinal view, and to allow for causes of disadvantage other than low income, but most research has not reflected all these elements (Burchardt, 2000, p. 388).

Introduction

New Labour has embraced the notion of social exclusion, describing it as 'the greatest social crisis in our times' (Peter Mandelson, 1997) and has placed the reduction of social exclusion at the forefront of Government social policy. Despite such well-intentioned commitments there is a lack of clarity, within both academic and political circles, about what the notion of social exclusion actually captures and this is something that can seriously undermine policy making. One of the reasons for this ambiguity is the limited extent of attempts to operationalize and understand social exclusion empirically. The aim of the book therefore is to build upon theoretical discussions of social exclusion to construct an empirical model, using quantitative survey data, to investigate the nature and extent of social exclusion in Great Britain. This investigation of social exclusion is also taken to a European level by comparing findings for Great Britain with other European Union (EU) Member States.[1]

The notion of social exclusion incorporates much of the most influential conceptual and methodological contributions of over a century of theoretical research into disadvantage. Hence, the theoretical foundation of the book is a clarification of the conceptual properties that are crucial to the notion of social exclusion (as compared with those that are associated with other popular notions of disadvantage in society, such as 'poverty' and 'deprivation'). Two of the most important theoretical properties of social exclusion are that it incorporates the use of information on a range of disadvantage domains and that it uses the concept of time to identify the most disadvantaged individuals (see Room, Ed. 1995, 1998, 2000). Thus a multi-dimensional and longitudinal model of social exclusion is

---

[1] The 11 other EU Member States are those in the first three waves of the European Community Household Panel (ECHP) survey dataset: Belgium, Denmark, France, Germany, Greece, Ireland, Italy, Luxembourg, the Netherlands, Portugal and Spain. In the ECHP dataset information is not provided for Great Britain but instead for the UK.

constructed here to identify the prevalence of social exclusion in Great Britain and to distinguish socio-demographic characteristics of individuals associated with an increased likelihood of such experiences.

This empirical model of social exclusion is also used in a comparative manner to place the experiences of Great Britain in a European context by comparing and contrasting the prevalence and nature of social exclusion in Great Britain with other EU Member States. This analysis contributes to the methodological advances of the cross-country analysis of social exclusion by applying multi-dimensional and longitudinal techniques, of which there are very few attempts to do so in current European empirical research.[2]

At the end of the book, the results of the empirical investigations are used to discuss the theoretical and policy implications of operationalizing social exclusion. This discussion includes an assessment of the contribution an empirical model of social exclusion offers the research and policy process over and above more commonly used, less complex models of disadvantage (such as poverty and deprivation). These comparisons will contribute to an assessment of the importance of the conceptualization and operationalization of social exclusion and the role social exclusion has in the advancement of theoretical research and in policy making aimed at improving the situation of the most disadvantaged members of society.

Objectives

In order to operationalize and investigate social exclusion empirically a number of research objectives have to be successfully accomplished. These objectives are:

- To clarify the conceptual properties of social exclusion;
- To operationalize this notion of social exclusion using empirical models based on quantitative survey data;
- To examine in detail the nature of social exclusion in Great Britain, in particular its multi-dimensional and longitudinal characteristics;
- To identify the prevalence of social exclusion in Great Britain and the socio-demographic characteristics associated with increased odds of social exclusion;
- To compare the extent of social exclusion and the characteristics of the socially excluded in Great Britain with other EU Member States;
- To discuss the theoretical and policy implications of operationalizing social exclusion in this way.

These objectives will be attempted sequentially to build towards the operationalization of social exclusion, the identification of the extent and nature of social exclusion in Great Britain and Europe and a discussion of resultant theoretical and policy implications.

---

[2] For an example of those that do exist see Gallie and Paugam (Eds, 2000), Mejer and Linden (2000), Barnes et al (2002) and Aspori and Millar (Eds, 2002).

Outline of research methods

The theoretical foundation of the book is based on over a century of academic work on disadvantage, particularly contemporary debates on the notion of social exclusion. A review of this literature is necessary to clarify the conceptual properties crucial to the operationalization and measurement of social exclusion. The crux of the book, an empirical measurement of social exclusion, is achieved through use of quantitative research methods that involve the analysis of secondary survey data. Investigations of social exclusion are made possible through the use of two complex longitudinal datasets – the British Household Panel Survey (BHPS) and the European Community Household Panel (ECHP) survey. Both datasets contain information on a wide-range of social exclusion related topics, including income, the possession of durable items, housing quality, social relationships and health. Both datasets are also longitudinal; meaning that they contain information routinely collected for the same individuals for annually repeated waves of the survey.

The BHPS dataset is appropriate for an in-depth investigation into the multi-dimensional and longitudinal nature of social exclusion for a number of reasons. The BHPS contains information on various aspects of British society crucial to an understanding of social exclusion. The BHPS has been conducted since 1991 and at the time of writing nine waves of data are available to the researcher. This allows for an extensive analysis of the longitudinal nature of disadvantage, including an examination of patterns of duration for almost the whole of the 1990s (1991-1999).[3]

The ECHP survey on the other hand provides the most appropriate dataset for a comparative analysis of social exclusion in Europe (the ECHP was in fact devised for such purposes). The ECHP contains information for the same individuals for each annual wave of the survey across participating EU Member States. This information is collected using a harmonized questionnaire, making comparable data easy to collect and ensuring that concepts are analogous across countries. The survey is designed specifically to collect information on social exclusion in Europe; meaning recent methodological advances in the collection of such data are incorporated into the questionnaire. Although at the time of writing only three waves of data (1994-1996) are available to the researcher, this still allows for the identification of longitudinal aspects of social exclusion, particularly persistent disadvantage (disadvantage experienced in three consecutive waves).

The unit of analysis in panel surveys such as the BHPS and ECHP is the individual, as it is these who are followed over time (households cannot be followed over time as by definition they change, and hence are different entities, as members enter and exit the household). Individuals, therefore, are the unit of analysis in this research.[4] However, instead of focussing on social exclusion as it

---

[3] For ease of presentation, the period 1991-1999 will be referred to throughout the book as the 1990s.

[4] It is in fact individuals who live in private households that are the focus of the research, as the coverage of households surveys does not include segments of the population such as the

affects all members of society, the study concentrates on the experiences of working-age adults only. There are two main reasons for this focus. First, there are some methodological constraints. The majority of information supplied in both surveys refers only to adults 16 years of age and over (in other words there is a distinct lack of information on children). Secondly, much of recent government welfare policy in relation to social exclusion, particularly labour market policy, is aimed specifically at working-age adults. It is therefore justifiable to omit individuals of retirement age and over from this investigation.[5]

The operationalization of social exclusion is carried out through the use of quantitative techniques to construct binary outcome indicators of separate domains of social exclusion. These indicators are constructed in an identical way in each wave of the survey to enable valid longitudinal analysis to be performed.[6] These indicators are used in various ways – independently and concurrently, and, at a point in time and longitudinally – to provide an in-depth investigation of the multi-dimensional and longitudinal nature of social exclusion. As well as determining the prevalence of social exclusion in society, analysis examines which groups of individuals are at particular risk of such experiences. Multivariate analysis, using logistic regression techniques, is used to predict the occurrence of social exclusion (in the form of odds ratios) based on individual and household socio-demographic and economic characteristics.

Chapter outline

Chapter 2 attempts to clarify the conceptual and methodological properties of social exclusion by reviewing and evaluating theoretical work on disadvantage. The discussion draws out the main conceptual and measurement issues from key studies of poverty, deprivation and social exclusion. This provides the foundation on which to create four summary models to be used in the development of empirical work to operationalize social exclusion:

---

homeless and those living in institutions. The implications of this coverage are included in a discussion of limitations of the research in Chapter 8.
[5] An investigation of children and individuals over state-retirement age would raise different issues regarding both the measurement of social exclusion and resulting policy implications, something that is beyond the scope of this book.
[6] Even though the same domains of social exclusion are used when constructing indicators from the BHPS and ECHP datasets, the BHPS indicators are not identical to the ECHP indicators. This is because the two surveys contain slightly different information as a consequence of asking slightly different questions. Comparisons of findings for Great Britain/United Kingdom from the two surveys can be found in Appendix D. Regardless of any differences between the two surveys, the BHPS dataset is used specifically to investigate the multi-dimensional and particularly, given the nine available waves of data, the longitudinal nature of social exclusion in Great Britain, whereas the ECHP is used specifically to compare social exclusion across Europe.

- Current one-dimensional disadvantage, used to investigate disadvantage on each of a range of domains, including the traditional notion of income poverty, at a point in time.
- Current multi-dimensional disadvantage, used to investigate simultaneous disadvantage on a number of domains at a point in time.
- Longitudinal one-dimensional disadvantage, used to investigate disadvantage on each of a range of domains over a period of time.
- Longitudinal multi-dimensional disadvantage, used to investigate disadvantage on a number of domains over a period of time.

It is the development of these models that will be used to operationalize social exclusion and to identify individuals experiencing the most widespread and enduring forms of disadvantage in society.

The core of the book is an empirical investigation of social exclusion. This is dealt with over a number of chapters. The first objective of this investigation is to operationalize social exclusion using empirical models. This is performed on data for Great Britain using nine waves of the BHPS. The first stage of this analysis (Chapter 3) constructs indicators of social exclusion at a cross-sectional level, ensuring they can also be used for multi-dimensional and longitudinal analysis. The indicators cover seven dimensions of social exclusion: financial situation, ownership of durable goods, quality of housing, neighbourhood perception, personal social relationships, physical health and psychological well-being. The different dimensions of social exclusion are used to assess how, even at a relatively simplistic level, each measure can reveal a different 'face' of disadvantage.

The second objective is to examine the nature of social exclusion in Great Britain, in particular its multi-dimensional and longitudinal characteristics. Chapter 4 concentrates on the multi-dimensional nature of social exclusion (building on the work of, amongst others, Nolan and Whelan, 1996, Burchardt, 1999 and Layte et al, 2000). The chapter begins with a brief exploration of current one-dimensional disadvantage. The main body of the chapter investigates the relationships between the separate indicators at a cross-sectional level, using a range of analytical techniques and from this a model of current multi-dimensional disadvantage is constructed.

Much recent research into income poverty has identified the differences between the experience of poverty at one particular time and the experience over a period of time (Bane and Ellwood, 1986; Jarvis and Jenkins, 1996). Chapter 5 introduces a longitudinal aspect to the investigation of social exclusion in Great Britain. A panel sample of working-age adults present in all nine waves of the survey is selected to allow an investigation of the duration and stability of various dimensions of social exclusion using models of longitudinal one-dimensional disadvantage. This chapter includes an examination of longitudinal patterns of non-monetary indicators of social exclusion – investigations seldom touched upon in previous studies.

Chapter 6 constructs a model to operationalize social exclusion in Great Britain, using a model of longitudinal multi-dimensional disadvantage, drawing on the main findings of the previous two chapters. The model identifies the most widespread and enduring forms of disadvantage amongst the working-age population. The main part of the chapter is an identification of the prevalence of social exclusion amongst working-age adults in British society during the 1990s. Analysis also determines the socio-demographic characteristics of individuals associated with increased odds of social exclusion. This helps to identify particular risk groups at which related policy would be advised to focus on.

The final analysis chapter (Chapter 7) investigates social exclusion across the EU using the first three waves of ECHP survey. There are two main reasons for extending the investigation to a European level. The first reason is to compare and contrast the prevalence and risk of social exclusion in Great Britain with other countries. This type of analysis opens the way to explore how different policy assumptions translate into different standards of living for working-age individuals. The second reason is to contribute to the methodological advances of the cross-country analysis of social exclusion across Europe. Before the recent introduction of the ECHP, information on the nature of social exclusion in Europe was limited by the lack of truly comparative multi-dimensional and longitudinal data on disadvantage.

Chapter 7 thus builds on the methodology of Chapter 3 in order to construct multi-dimensional and longitudinal indicators of social exclusion for the 12 Member States included in all three waves of the ECHP. The multi-dimensional component of the social exclusion model uses a composite index – commonly understood as the combination of a variety of aggregate-level indicators – to absorb the features of the individual indicators. The index employs a weighting procedure according to the proportion of individuals excluded on each indicator in each country, to create a relative measure of disadvantage – ideal for the cross-country analysis of social exclusion. Although only three waves of the ECHP survey are available, the analysis considers the longitudinal aspects of disadvantage, focussing on a measure of persistent disadvantage, in an attempt to investigate the most enduring and widespread forms of social exclusion in Member States across the EU Analysis is also used to identify patterns of social exclusion across Europe, clustering countries into groups according to the prevalence of persistent disadvantage. These groups are contrasted and compared with groups from other comparative studies that cluster countries according to poverty rates and welfare regimes (Gallie and Paugam, Eds. 2000).

The final chapter (Chapter 8) assembles the main methodological and substantive findings from the book and discusses the implications of operationalizing social exclusion for research and policy. The chapter begins with a succinct account of the key empirical findings. It then moves on to discuss the context in which these findings should be regarded, concentrating in particular on methodological considerations and the limitations of survey data. There follows a discussion of the significance of the main findings for policy analysis and policy making, with particular reference to recommendations for improvements to the government's *Opportunity for all* indicators. The chapter concludes with a final reflection on the implications for defining and measuring social exclusion in this manner and themes for future research.

Chapter 2

The Operationalization of Social Exclusion: Theoretical and Policy Approaches

I suggest that the concept of social exclusion has two distinct connotations: its comprehensiveness and its dynamic character. Together these connotations make it a difficult, but at the same time, a very useful concept (Berghman, 1995, p. 16).

Introduction

Despite various attempts to conceptualize disadvantage over the last 100 years, it is generally agreed that no unique and universally accepted definition exists, nor is ever likely to. Instead various notions of disadvantage have been used in theoretical and policy discourse, including 'poverty', 'hardship', 'destitution' and 'deprivation'. Each notion brings to the investigation of disadvantage a slightly different basis for the process of operationalization and measurement. This results in an often conflicting and confusing array of concepts and measures. The recent introduction of 'social exclusion' has added fresh impetus to the study of disadvantage and provides an opportunity to elucidate a theory and empirical model of disadvantage useful for both academic and political use.

The aim of this research is to construct an empirical model, using quantitative survey data, to investigate the nature and extent of social exclusion in Great Britain, and then to compare findings for Great Britain with other European Union Member States. In order to be able to investigate social exclusion effectively the notion needs to be appropriately conceptualized and accurately measured. This chapter outlines the rationale for the conceptualization and measurement of social exclusion to be used in this research.

Attempts to operationalize social exclusion need to be based on a strong conceptual basis. The chapter begins with a review of previous, often contested, theoretical and political attempts to define a range of concepts linked to disadvantage, from the more simplistic notions of (income) poverty and (economic) deprivation to more complex notions of persistent multi-dimensional disadvantage and social exclusion. The conceptualization of social exclusion used in this research is not new and instead draws on the main elements of existing theories.

Just as various, albeit limited, notions of social exclusion exist in the current literature, so do attempts at measurement. The chapter moves on to detail previous attempts to operationalize social exclusion, and other forms of disadvantage, and again draws on the main elements of the most influential research to outline methods that will be used to investigate social exclusion in this research.

Most quantitative research on disadvantage uses one, or a range of, measures or indicators as a basis for investigation. The same is true for this research, which is based on data for Great Britain using the British Household Panel Survey and for Europe using the European Community Household Panel survey. The chapter discusses a framework for the design of indicators of social exclusion, in relation to the conceptual and measurement issues outlined earlier. In order to investigate the nature of social exclusion fully, four empirical models are outlined that draw on two of its main conceptual properties – scope and time. These models will be used in later chapters for separate investigations of the multi-dimensional and longitudinal nature of social exclusion, before being combined to identify longitudinal measures of multi-dimensional disadvantage aimed at identifying the prevalence of social exclusion and the characteristics of individuals most likely to face such experiences.

The conceptualization of social exclusion

In a paper given by Room (1998) at a conference on the future of the welfare state he commented that despite the British government making much reference to social exclusion, and many in the research community launching investigations into the problems of exclusion, there is no clear statement of what the concept actually means. In particular, he points out, there is a need to distinguish 'social exclusion' from 'poverty' as a point of reference for research and policy. These comments are especially relevant for this research, as without a distinct concept of social exclusion on which to build empirical investigations, attempts at operationalization are likely to be severely flawed.

This section outlines the conceptualization of social exclusion to be used in this research. As there have been relatively few previous attempts to conceptualize social exclusion the main developments from a history of academic research into disadvantage are drawn upon, including discussions of notions of poverty and deprivation. The final part of this section presents the definition of social exclusion to be used in this research, a summary of its main conceptual properties and how these properties differ from other more commonly used concepts of disadvantage. The aim of this is to clarify some of the ambiguities and confusion associated with concepts of disadvantage and to create a theoretical framework from which to construct suitable measures of social exclusion later in the book.

Theoretical and political approaches

Given that the term social exclusion has only recently emerged in work on disadvantage, a discussion of how to conceptualize the concept cannot take place without recognition of over a century of studies on poverty. This discussion is therefore split into two sub-sections, one that deals with work on poverty and another that relates the developments in poverty work with attempts to conceptualize social exclusion.[1]

Poverty

Virtually all investigations of disadvantage focus on a notion of want and misery, and that the moral obligation of discovering such existence is that something must be done to eliminate it. It is only when attempts are made to define what such want and misery constitutes that such notions become ambiguous. The most common terminology used to describe these experiences is 'poverty'. There is an abundance of studies attempting to define what is meant by the term poverty (for a summary see Saunders, 1994 and Kangas and Ritakallio, 1998). Indeed in his work on *Understanding poverty* Alcock stated that 'there is no one correct, scientific agreed definition because poverty is inevitably a political concept, and thus inherently a contested one' (Alcock, 1993, p. 3).

Traditionally, the intellectual understanding of poverty has focussed upon distributional issues: the lack of resources at the disposal of an individual or household to ensure a suitable standard of subsistence or living. In 1899 Rowntree defined an absolute measure of poverty (Rowntree, 1901) in terms of minimum standards based on a person's biological needs for food, water, clothing and shelter.

> My primary poverty line represented the minimum sum on which physical efficiency could be maintained. It was a bare standard of *subsistence* rather than *living* ... (Rowntree, 1941, p. 102).

Absolute definitions of poverty attempt to define minimum standards scientifically. They are criticized for a number of reasons. First, it is generally agreed that it is very difficult to define the minimum on which physical efficiency can be maintained. Secondly, even if this was possible, levels of subsistence change between individuals, cultures, societies and, importantly, over time. Thirdly, absolute definitions such as Rowntree's[2] determine sufficient resources at the level of physical needs and not on broader social and cultural needs. This final point has relevance for the usefulness of an absolute measure of subsistence in cross-country analysis. An absolute definition of physical subsistence is clearly of critical relevance for much of the world's population but for the more developed countries is of less use, given that most of the population has acceptable levels of nutrition, clothing and housing.

In the latter half of the twentieth century, various experts worked on developing a more sophisticated approach to the definition of poverty. Peter Townsend's definitive work on poverty in the UK (Townsend, 1979) went beyond

---

[1] This discussion focuses on Great Britain. For a European level discussion see the chapter on an investigation of social exclusion in Europe (Chapter 7).
[2] There is some debate whether Rowntree's definition of poverty really was absolute given his inclusion of some inappropriate items, for example tea, in a minimum standard of biological need (for more information see Veit-Wilson, 1986 and Alcock, 1993).

an absolute definition based on physical needs, to view poverty in relation to a generally accepted standard of living, in a specific society, at a particular time.

> Individuals ... can be said to be in poverty when they lack the resources to obtain the types of diet, participate in the activities and have the living conditions and amenities which are customary, or at least widely encouraged or approved, in the societies to which they belong. Their resources are so seriously below those commanded by the average individual or family that they are, in effect, excluded from the ordinary living patterns, customs and activities (Townsend, 1979, p. 31).

Rather than simply concentrating on a level of subsistence, Townsend's definition focuses on the distribution and level of resources that individuals need to participate in ordinary living patterns, customs and activities. Townsend's work became the foundations on which much contemporary poverty debates were built.

As with the seminal work of Rowntree, Townsend's approach received various well-levelled criticisms. Sen (1983) criticized Townsend's purely relativist notions of poverty, arguing that there is an irreducible absolutist core in the idea of poverty. Sen argued that in certain cases, for example starvation or hunger, the relative picture has to take a back seat behind the possibly dominating absolutist consideration. In other words, if there is starvation or hunger, then no matter what the relative picture looks like; there clearly is poverty (for further information see the debate of Sen and Townsend in *Oxford Economic Papers*; Townsend, 1985). Other authors criticized Townsend's attempt to define a society's customary resources and participation activities. Much debate focussed on the validity of the researcher deciding what is customary levels of living standards and the role choice plays in individual's decision of what resources and participation activities to go without (Piachaud, 1987).[3]

More recently, theories have been developed to explain the role time plays in the understanding of poverty (Leisering and Walker, Eds. 1998). Introducing a longitudinal element to theories of poverty has enabled distinctions to be made between individuals according to the duration of their low-income experience. Understandably particular focus has been paid to the long-term poor, most notably in relation to the immediate alleviation of poverty and the identification of risk factors that can contribute to preventative policies.

As well as including the role time has in the notion of poverty, recent research has seen the growth of theories of multi-dimensional disadvantage. Concerns about different domains of disadvantage have led to the development of theories of 'deprivation' (Townsend, 1979; Mack and Lansley, 1985; Ringen, 1988; Nolan and Whelan, 1996). These studies continued to focus on the economic forms of disadvantage but moved away from the initial focus on low income to incorporate other aspects of disadvantage such as housing quality and lack of

---

[3] Whereas Townsend's notion of poverty centres on exclusion from society due to lack of resources, for others concern about poverty is related more directly to actual levels of living. Consequently people have focussed on individual's rights for minimum standards, relative to place and time, on a whole host of living standard domains, including health (Department of Health, 1998), housing (Ginsburg, 1997), the labour market (Gallie and Paugam, Eds. 2000), and social relationships (Perri 6, 1997).

household items. Authors suggested that to identify the most disadvantaged in society it is necessary to consider those that are suffering from a multitude of disadvantage simultaneously at any one time. By this conjecture someone who has low income *and* is suffering from other forms of disadvantage (such as bad housing) is experiencing more acute disadvantage than someone just experiencing low income, even if these income levels are roughly similar.

Bradshaw and Finch (2001) investigated the notion of poverty from a multi-dimensional perspective in their paper on core poverty. They defined 'core poverty', or 'real need', according to four notions of need: 'normative need', a lack of socially perceived necessities; 'felt need', subjective feelings of being poor; 'expressed need', a reliance on means-tested benefits and 'comparative need', a low income in relation to the rest of the population. The authors recommended a cumulative approach that assumes that a person who is poor on all measures is more likely to be core poor than a person poor on less than all measures, rather than an approach that treats particular dimensions as meriting more attention than others.

Despite the abundance of theoretical work in the conceptualization of poverty, relatively little of this research has been used to inform British government policy. Indeed, unlike some other countries, notably the US (see Fisher, 1992) and Ireland (see National Anti-Poverty Strategy, 1997), Great Britain has never had an official poverty line. Despite this, there is still some evidence of where the theoretical conceptualization of poverty has had an impact on government opinion and policy applications.

Although the current (and previous) British government has no official definition of poverty, Great Britain has signed treaties and agreements at a European level that define poverty (EEC, 1981, 1985). The British government has also made a global commitment to the eradication of poverty and to drawing up national poverty-alleviation plans (UN, 1995). The Copenhagen World Summit on Social Development in 1995 recommended a two-tier measure of 'absolute' and 'overall' poverty to be applied to every country. Here absolute poverty was defined in terms of:

> a condition characterized by severe deprivation of basic human needs, including food, safe drinking water, sanitation facilities, health, shelter, education and information. It depends not only on income but also on access to services (UN, 1995, p. 57).

Overall poverty was defined as a wider measure than can take various forms including:

> lack of income and productive resources to ensure sustainable livelihoods; hunger and malnutrition; ill health; limited or lack of access to education and other basic services; increased morbidity and mortality from illness; homelessness and inadequate housing; unsafe environments and social discrimination and exclusion. It is also characterized by lack of participation in decision-making and in civil, social and cultural life. It occurs in all countries; as mass poverty in many developing countries, pockets of poverty amid wealth in developed countries, loss of livelihoods as a result of economic recession, sudden poverty as a result of disaster or conflict, the poverty of low-wage workers, and the utter destitution of people who fall outside family support systems, social institutions and safety nets (UN, 1995, p. 57).

In Great Britain, the most widely used 'official' conceptualization of poverty is provided in the government published annual series of statistics called *Households Below Average Income* (*HBAI*), first published in 1988[4] (for the latest version see the DSS, 2001b). The concept of poverty used in the *HBAI* series is regarded primarily according to living standards. The *HBAI* series presents 'attempts to measures people's potential living as determined by disposable income' (DSS, 2001a, p. 8). Some of the theoretical criticisms of the income-resource concept of poverty were outlined in a review of the *HBAI* series in 1996 (DSS, 1996). The report acknowledged that income was not always a complete reflection of actual or potential living standards and hence incorporated household possession of consumer durables in a notion of poverty. A more recent government discussion of poverty appears in the *Opportunity for all* report (DSS, 1999a) but no distinct definition of poverty is given (see further discussion of *Opportunity for all* below).

Social exclusion

Recent conceptual and empirical developments in the debate about poverty and deprivation have been enhanced by the introduction of the term 'social exclusion'. The process of elucidating a precise concept of social exclusion is still in its early stages but many believe it derives from notions of 'solidarity' (Spicker, 1991, Levitas 1998). Solidarity is what people adopt within certain societal networks in the form of support of those around them – whether from the family, the workplace, the community in general or the state. Social exclusion is therefore used to refer to the process that leads to a breakdown of the relationship between society and the individual.

As with other concepts of disadvantage, there are alternative notions of social exclusion. Social exclusion has also been developed as a term that emphasizes the non-realization of civil, political and social rights, and to the failure of the various social systems that underpin modern life (Berghman, 1995). Social exclusion may, therefore, be seen as the denial of the rights of citizenship (Marshall, 1950).

Graham Room has been influential in the conceptualization of social exclusion,[5] particularly at a European level. He argues that much of what is claimed as new in the analysis of social exclusion can also be found in the existing poverty and deprivation literature (Room, Ed. 1995, 1998, 2000). Nevertheless he regards social exclusion as an important concept in the study of disadvantage and distinguishes five main elements in what he sees as the conceptual reconfiguration from poverty to social exclusion.

---

[4] Prior to the HBAI series the government produced the Low Income Families (LIF) statistics, which concentrated on showing the numbers of people living on, below and up to 140 per cent of supplementary benefit/income support.
[5] The Centre for Analysis of Social Exclusion (CASE), a research centre at the London School of Economics (LSE), has also produced a number of innovative discussion papers on various aspects of social exclusion (see http://sticerd.lse.ac.uk/Case for details).

1. Social exclusion implies a conceptual shift from financial to multi-dimensional disadvantage.
2. Social exclusion implies a conceptual shift from static to dynamic analysis.
3. Social exclusion implies a conceptual shift from concentration on the individual or household to the local neighbourhood.
4. Social exclusion implies a conceptual shift from a distributional to a relational focus.
5. Finally, social exclusion implies the connotation of separation and permanence from wider society.

Room has argued that, by themselves, none of these elements are particularly new to disadvantage research. As illustrated above, many of the classic studies of poverty and deprivation were already aware of the multi-dimensional and dynamic nature of disadvantage. Similarly, there has been a long tradition of studies of disadvantaged local communities (Home Office, 1977) and of the government using local area indicators in their programmes of resource allocation (Robson, 1995). However, according to Room, what is new is that the concept of social exclusion implies an integration and consolidation of all these five elements. Social exclusion therefore entails 'the connotation of separation and permanence: a catastrophic discontinuity in relationships with the rest of society' (Room, 1998, p. 16).

Just as research has started to focus more on social exclusion, rather than income poverty, so has the political and policy agenda. From a political viewpoint, until recently the notion of poverty has been regarded as the dominant ideology in the area of disadvantage. When Labour came to power in May 1996 a marked shift in emphasis on poverty was observed. The New Labour government encompassed the discourse and notion of social exclusion, whilst still retaining a focus on poverty, and made tackling poverty and social exclusion one of their highest priorities.

In 1997 the Social Exclusion Unit (SEU) was set up to enhance understanding of the key characteristics of social exclusion and to cover the impact of government policy. The SEU chose to define social exclusion as:

> ... a shorthand term for what can happen when people or areas suffer from a combination of linked problems such as unemployment, poor skills, low incomes, poor housing, high crime environments, bad health and family breakdown (Social Exclusion Unit, 2000b).

Although the SEU definition of social exclusion represents a marked shift in political discourse, it incorporates only some of the ideas outlined in the theoretical conceptualization of social exclusion discussed above. For example, although the SEU definition focuses on the notion of multi-dimensional disadvantage there is no justification for the selection of the array of linked problems. Of the list of problems included in the definition, there is no specific mention of the social and relational aspect of social exclusion, although family breakdown may allude to it. There is also no mention of the dynamic process of social exclusion.

Similar issues arise in respect of monitoring government policies in this area. In September 1999 the government displayed its commitment to tackling disadvantage and its causes by producing *Opportunity for all* (DSS, 1999a, DSS 1999b), a report that outlined initiatives and plans to combat poverty and social exclusion.[6] Many applauded the proposal of a national programme of policy priorities to tackle poverty and social exclusion (for example see Bradshaw, 2001), commending a commitment to improving the living standards of the poorest in society and of monitoring attempts to do so. However from a theoretical perspective the report failed to incorporate many of the conceptual advances discussed throughout this chapter.

First, there appears to be a lack of consideration of how to define, and consequently how to operationalize, the notions of disadvantage alluded to in the report – that of poverty and social exclusion. The report suggests that poverty encompasses 'lack of income, access to good-quality health, education, housing and the quality of the local environment' (DSS, 1999a, p. 23) whilst social exclusion is 'a short-hand label for what can happen when individuals suffer from a combination of linked problems such as unemployment, poor skills, low incomes, poor housing, high crime environments, bad health and family breakdown' (DSS, 1999a, p. 23). The definitions appear rather confused and no theoretical rationale for their selection is provided. The report acknowledges that the concepts are different whilst admitting that 'social exclusion and poverty are terms that are often used interchangeably' (DSS, 1999a, p. 23). However the report makes no attempt to describe their differences.

Secondly, although *Opportunity for all* does move away from a traditional income-based concept of poverty to an understanding of the 'complex, multi-dimensional problems' of social exclusion (DSS, 1999a, p. viii), that can 'build up over long periods' (DSS, 1999a, p. 2), there is little attempt to explain the multi-dimensional or longitudinal nature of disadvantage. For example, the report suggests that 'social exclusion occurs where different factors combine to trap individuals and areas in a spiral of disadvantage' (DSS, 1999a, p. 23) – yet there is no explanation of which factors must combine, and for what duration, to suggest poverty and social exclusion has in fact occurred.

Aside from the *Opportunity for all* report there is other evidence, albeit limited, that the notion of social exclusion is beginning to be incorporated into the mindset of government policy makers. The Prime Minister has argued that in order to deal with social exclusion the government needs to work across disciplinary and departmental boundaries. Policies are therefore concerned with a much wider range of aims than simply supplementing income. They also involve attempts to connect

---

[6] *Opportunity for all* was modelled on a previous independent report on poverty and social exclusion undertaken by researchers at the New Policy Institute (NPI) in the hope of creating the basis for an official report on poverty and social exclusion. The NPI report identified trends in poverty and social exclusion in the UK using 46 different indicators collected from a variety of sources, including official statistics on income, work, health, education and housing. The NPI has now published a number of annual reports (Howarth et al, 1998, Howarth et al, 1999, Rahman et al, 2000 and Rahman et al, 2001).

people back into the labour market, a particular focus of the New Labour government, and to give people access to social resources, family support, social networks and community services. The New Deal for example represents an important shift from thinking about social security as about financial support only, to designing it also as an incentive for employment.

Discourse has also begun to view disadvantage from a dynamic perspective. The Prime Minister has claimed it essential that policy becomes more preventative and more about long-term investment, rather than trying to solve problems once they have become established (Mulgan, 1998). Particular focus has been given to policy that advocates the accumulation of assets – not only income and capital, but also others such as employment, social and psychological skills and education[7] – to help protect against hardship and misfortune (HM Treasury, 2001). However as the introduction of the notion of social exclusion into the political arena is relatively recent, the influence on political reasoning is still at an early stage.

Defining social exclusion

The concept of social exclusion to be used in this research draws on important theoretical elements that appear repeatedly in the discussion above, and especially on the work of Room (1995, 1998, 2000). In particular the multi-dimensional and longitudinal nature of social exclusion will be emphasized, as there is a lack of empirical work, and therefore understanding, in this area. This implies that the research has to consider a range of dimensions of social exclusion other than low income, and how these dimensions relate to each other, as well as the consequence of including time in the definition. The definition of social exclusion to be used in this research is therefore summarized as follows:

- *Social exclusion* refers to the multi-dimensional and dynamic process of being shut out, fully or partially, from the economic, social and cultural systems that determine the social integration of a person in society (developed from a definition proposed by Walker, 1997, p. 8).

The research will retain a distinction between poverty (and deprivation) and social exclusion. When notions of poverty (and deprivation) are specified in the book, they take the following definitions:

- *Poverty* is a lack of financial resources (primarily income) necessary to achieve a minimum standard of physical subsistence in society, measured at a point in time.
- *Deprivation* is a lack of financial resources (primarily income) and other economic non-income material resources (such as household amenities and quality of housing) necessary to achieve a minimum standard of physical subsistence and living standard in society, measured at a point in time.

---

[7] Room (2000) refers to these as 'buffers'.

Figure 2.1 corroborates the conceptual properties of social exclusion, and how these differ from the other main concepts of disadvantage outlined above.

Poverty	Deprivation	Social exclusion
One-dimensional	Multi-dimensional	Multi-dimensional
Physical needs	Physical needs, Material needs	Physical needs, Material needs, Societal participation
Distributional	Distributional	Distributional, Relational
Static	Static	Dynamic
Individual, Household	Individual, Household	Individual, Household, Community

Figure 2.1   Main properties of the conceptualization of poverty, deprivation and social exclusion[8]

As Room has mentioned, there is a need to distinguish 'social exclusion' from 'poverty' as a point of reference for research and policy. The most simplistic concept of disadvantage, that of poverty, suggests a one-dimensional notion of resources required to achieve a minimum physical level of subsistence at a point in time. At the other end of the scale, the concept of social exclusion is much more complex. It evokes a multi-dimensional notion of participation in society, involving a combination of physical, material, relational and societal needs, over a period of time. Between these most basic and most complex concepts lay notions that utilize elements of multi-dimensional, physical, material, relational and societal needs and longitudinal aspects of disadvantage, but not a combination of each and every one.

The measurement of social exclusion

Not only is there a lack of clarity concerning the conceptualization of social exclusion, there is also no widely accepted approach to its measurement. However, just as efforts to conceptualize social exclusion, and other forms of disadvantage, have developed over the previous century, so have attempts to construct valid measures. The following discussion moves towards a measure of social exclusion

---

[8] This figure is an adaptation of the figure included in *Social exclusion and the life course* (Barnes et al, 2002).

to be used in this research and details a framework for an empirical quantitative analysis of national level household data sets.

Theoretical and political approaches

This section details the main quantitative approaches to measuring disadvantage, from the traditional resource-based notion of poverty and deprivation to the more recent, albeit somewhat limited, attempts to operationalize social exclusion. Core elements of measurement will be highlighted during the review and retained for means of operationalizing the concept of social exclusion to be used in this research. Again, as research into poverty has dominated the empirical investigation of disadvantage to date, the discussion is split between attempts to measure poverty and more recent attempts to measure social exclusion.

Poverty

The early work on measuring disadvantage, pioneered by Rowntree's (1901) work on poverty at the turn of the twentieth century, emphasized the role of income in the operationalization of a lack of resources. Rowntree used a low-income threshold as an indicator of resources unable to achieve a minimum level of subsistence. Income is still used as the primary indicator of resources in contemporary research for a number of reasons. Income is a resource that individuals, and households, have a reasonable amount of control over how to use and, although perhaps to a lesser degree, to acquire. It is also a resource that governments, usually through the workings of the welfare state, can administer to individuals and households in an attempt to maintain reasonable levels of subsistence in the population.[9]

Critics of the income measure argue that it is problematic to determine what is meant by a minimum level of subsistence, or living standards, and to equate this with a sum of money from which this can be achieved (Gordon et al, 2000). Others point to the many other factors beside income that provide resources, including the ability to borrow money and participation in the informal economy (Ringen, 1985). Even amongst those that agree that income is an adequate indicator of resources, there are many who note the measurement of income is fraught with problems, including what to count as income and what not, and the fact that particular sources of income are likely to face differential measurement error in surveys (Taylor et al, 1994). There has also been much research that has questioned the way in which income measures generally account for needs of households by assuming income is shared amongst household members (for example Millar and Glendinning, 1989 and Middleton et al, 1997).

---

[9] Another way of looking at poverty is through expenditure rather than income. Both income and expenditure reveal different aspects of poverty and each has its own strengths and weaknesses. Atkinson (1989) argues that an income measure is about a right to a minimum level of resources, while expenditure is about a standard of living that can be achieved.

Rowntree's first poverty study not only relied on income as an indicator of subsistence but it also attempted to define the level of income that represented a minimum subsistence level. The poverty line was determined by calculating the cost of minimum needs according to items in a basket of minimum subsistence. This approach to measuring poverty is still in use. The Family Budget Unit (Bradshaw, 1993; Parker, Ed. 1998) adopted the approach to define and cost the basic needs of families. Items were included in a 'modest but adequate' budget based on opinions of a panel of experts and consumer groups. Items included in the budget were mass manufactured furniture, basic clothing, basic jewellery and a second-hand car (also included were other non-material items such as a holiday and other more social activities). Critics of this approach (Piachaud, 1987) question the choice of items to be included and also point out that individuals tend to not allocate their expenditure in as an optimum way as experts suggest.

Relating poverty lines to subsistence benefit levels is another commonly used approach to measuring poverty. The rate of support provided by the social welfare system is therefore regarded as an 'official poverty line'. Abel-Smith and Townsend carried out the first major reassessment of poverty in the British welfare state, comparing the income of poor households to the basic National Assistance scale (Abel-Smith and Townsend, 1965). However there are obvious problems with this approach. Social welfare rates are not designed as a poverty threshold, but instead reflect a number of influences including the state of public finances and the objectives of the welfare system (Veit-Wilson, 1998). Moreover an increase in social welfare rates could lead to a rise in measured poverty since the poverty lines also rises.

Probably the most common method of measuring poverty according to income levels is through the construction of purely relative poverty lines. In this approach those who fall a certain distance below the average income level are understood to live in income poverty. Relative income levels are particularly relevant for cross-country comparisons or for measuring poverty over time for a particular country. [10] However the method discounts improvements in living standards of low-income groups that are shared by the rest of the population or differences in average living conditions across countries (Callan and Nolan, 1994). Veit-Wilson (1998) argues that relative income poverty lines represent nothing more than an abstract statistical construct that have no independent validity as an empirical indicator of poverty.

Townsend's work on poverty according to participation in various lifestyles also defined an income poverty line, to reflect the point at which individuals are unable to participate fully in the life of the society in which they live. Rather than focusing only on physical subsistence Townsend chose indicators of deprivation to score individuals according to their ownership of socially perceived necessary items. Relating deprivation scores to household income, he suggested that there was an income threshold below which deprivation scores escalated disproportionately and that this should be taken as the poverty line. Ringen (1985,

---

[10] See Chapter 7 for more details and for an empirical investigation of social exclusion in the European Union.

1988) has argued that there is a theoretical inconsistency in using an indirect measure of resources – income – to measure a direct concept of deprivation. He argues that to understand the notion of poverty it is necessary to focus on a range of resources, not simply income, and so using an income poverty line to summarize such deprivation is conceptually and empirically flawed.

Critics of Townsend's approach question the methodology for calculating the income threshold from deprivation scores and his selection of deprivation indicators (Piachaud, 1981). Some see an improvement on Townsend's methodology of selecting deprivation indicators in the consensual approach to poverty. This uses social analysis to decide what a decent minimum standard of living really means. The Breadline Britain studies (Mack and Lansley, 1985; Gordon and Pantazis, Eds. 1997, Gordon et al, 2000) surveyed the general population in order to derive a consensual view of the necessities of life in current British society. Items that were perceived as 'necessary' by over half the population were defined as 'socially perceived necessities'. Households that could not afford these items were adjudged to be in poverty according to 'an enforced lack of socially perceived necessities' (for a similar methodology see Hallerod, 1995). A slightly alternative method takes the common patterns of observed consumption in society to decide minimum standards (Desai and Shah, 1988).

Much research has shown that the relationship between income and deprivation is rather looser than would be expected *a priori* (Mack and Lansley, 1985; Callan, Nolan and Whelan, 1993). These studies have shown that there are substantial proportions of households with relatively large incomes that are nevertheless lacking in terms of non-monetary indicators of deprivation. And, in the other direction, a majority of those in low-income groups do not suffer from deprivation, as measured by absence of particular items, because of lack of resources (Nolan, 1999).

The supposed inconsistent relationship between deprivation and income has been challenged through the use of longitudinal research techniques. The use of panel data has enabled researchers to distinguish between the income-poor deprived and the income-poor non-deprived according to their location on paths into and out of disadvantage, and the length of time they have been living on low income. The dynamic approach to poverty is not new and was in fact pioneered in Rowntree's (1901) study in the form of the life-cycle theory of poverty. However, the use of longitudinal methods in empirical investigations is a relatively recent phenomenon, despite the groundbreaking work by Bane and Elwood (1986) on poverty dynamics in the mid-1980s. Indeed, most methodological advances have been made in the study of income dynamics, where studies have investigated in great detail the nature of short- and long-term income poverty (Ashworth and Walker, 1994; Walker and Ashworth, 1994; Jarvis and Jenkins, 1995, 1996, 1998a, 2000a, 2000b; Jenkins and Rigg, 2001).

Moving away from theoretical attempts to measure poverty, there are a few, albeit relatively limited, examples of publicly available measures of low income in Great Britain. These measures include general social statistics – defined as an ad hoc collection of statistics relating to social phenomena (Carley, 1981) – for publicizing information on poverty, and social indicators – defined as a more systematically designed set of statistics with an integral, usually political, structure and rationale (Carley, 1981) – specifically produced for policy use. These are produced by a number of different organizations and used to a varying degree by the government, local authorities, policy makers and other professionals.

Probably the most well known government published information on poverty is the *HBAI* series, which presents tables of statistics on the distribution of income in the British population. In terms of policy indicators of income poverty, although Great Britain does not have an official poverty line, the *HBAI* statistics do present the prevalence and socio-demographic make-up of individuals below certain proportions of average income. The *HBAI* series includes statistics on the proportion of individuals living in households with income below 60 per cent of the median, the European Union income-poverty standard, which is often used as an unofficial measure of income poverty in Great Britain. In fact, this measures the household level income position of the individual in relation to the rest of the population, so criticisms of relative measures apply (see discussion above).

The theoretical movement to measure poverty from a longitudinal perspective has led to only limited developments in the area of social statistics, although the *HBAI* series has recently included an analysis of income dynamics. This analysis, based on data from the British Household Panel Survey, presents longitudinal income information relating to the 1990s, focussing on an investigation of how the incomes of those at the bottom of the income distribution change over time.

Social exclusion

Given the complex notion of social exclusion it is clear that measurement involves more than simply information on income. As highlighted in Figure 2.1 above, the investigation of social exclusion requires a detailed analysis of income and other resources, of the relationship between indicators of exclusion and of issues of duration. In essence it combines much of the methodological developments of previous research into disadvantage. To date there have been very few studies that concentrate on the measurement of social exclusion. A handful of studies have used secondary data sources to create indicators of social exclusion and to examine the relationship between such indicators, and over time, but such investigations are at a relatively early stage with only very simplistic multi-dimensional and longitudinal analysis achieved.

Of the limited amount of previous academic studies Burchardt et al (1999) performed research most relevant to the identification of social exclusion in Great Britain. They used data from the British Household Panel Survey to identify five components of social exclusion that leads to non-participation in the 'normal activities of citizens in that society': a low standard of living, lack of security, lack of engagement in an activity valued by others, lack of decision-making power and a lack of support from or contact with friends, family and the wider community. The study explored the nature of social exclusion over a five-year period, albeit only at a summary level, and concluded that there is little evidence of an abundance of persistent multi-dimensional disadvantage in British society.

Gordon et al (2000) performed what has been described as 'the most comprehensive survey of poverty and social exclusion ever undertaken in Great Britain' (Barclay, 2000, p. 5). The survey extended the approach used in the Breadline Britain Surveys of 1983 and 1990 (Mack and Lansley, 1985; Gordon and Pantazis, Eds. 1997) but included specific attempts to operationalize the concept of social exclusion. Empirical analysis focussed in particular on exclusion from social relations, an area that is often neglected in approaches that rely on proxy indicators. However as the study relied on data from a cross-sectional survey, no true longitudinal analysis was performed, crucial to the notion of social exclusion. Also, the survey report included very little multi-dimensional analysis although separately published subsequent analyses should provide an insight into this equally important aspect of social exclusion.

A more comprehensive study of multi-dimensional disadvantage and social exclusion, performed by Barnes et al (2002) and Aspori and Millar (Eds, 2002), used data for six countries, including the UK, from the European Community Household Panel survey. The study focussed on four 'high risk' subsets of the population – young adults, lone parents, people experiencing sickness or disability and people retiring from employment – and examined the relationships between social exclusion, labour market participation and family structures in different national contexts. Indicators of the outcomes and risk factors of social exclusion were constructed at a multi-dimensional and dynamic level, covering income, non-monetary deprivation, health and social participation.

In general, advances in the production of publicly disseminated social statistics of social exclusion have lagged behind theoretical innovations. There is an abundance of statistics produced to measure forms of disadvantage other than low income, but very few are produced to present a notion of social exclusion. In particular there are no regular and generally available statistics that illustrate both the multi-dimensional and longitudinal nature of social exclusion.

The Office for National Statistics (ONS) is responsible for producing a variety of social indicators on 13 areas of national life (for more information see the ONS website www.statistics.gov.uk). The ONS also produce *Social Trends*, which draws together social and economic data from a wide range of government departments and other organizations to paint a broad picture of British society (for the latest edition see ONS, 2001b). However no attempt is made to investigate the relationship between these indicators or how they behave over time. Recent *HBAI* series have included statistics on non-monetary forms of economic disadvantage, in the form of ownership of consumer durable items such as a television, telephone and freezer. In general however, these statistics receive much less media and political coverage than the *HBAI* estimates of low income. There are very few, if any, statistics produced on social relationships, community cohesion or political participation for example, partly because these aspects of disadvantage are only recently being introduced into national household surveys.

Until very recently the picture for social, policy-focussed, indicators of social exclusion was similar. In 1998 the government produced a Green Paper (DSS, 1998) that outlined a range of success measures in the area of welfare, covering subjects such as literacy, housing and unemployment. However, the report failed to explicitly mention outcomes of poverty and social exclusion, in particular a level of income the government regards as inadequate to achieve a minimum standard of living. In 1999 the government produced a set of indicators in an attempt to measure 'quality of life' (DETR, 1999). These indicators were designed to judge performance in improving the economy, the environment and social welfare. However poverty and social exclusion were again left out of the set of indicators. Anyway, the indicators have received very little attention, either politically or from the media, and their contribution to social policy appears minimal.

The breakthrough in terms of the official measurement of social exclusion was the introduction of *Opportunity for all* (DSS, 1998) and in particular the Government's commitment to annually monitor the state of poverty and social exclusion through a set of quantitative social indicators. The introduction of an annually updated, official set of quantitative social indicators to understand and monitor the complexities of poverty and social exclusion represented a new step in bringing together information on the disadvantaged aspects of British society.

The *Opportunity for all* report presented 32 'indicators of success' that relate directly to measurable aspects of the Government's policy priorities aimed at tackling poverty and social exclusion.[11] The indicators are grouped by policy priority according to three sub-groups of the population (children and young people, people of working age and older people) and communities. Many of the indicators focus on the integration of individuals, households and communities through work, the central theme of New Labour's welfare programme. However, the indicators by no means exclude other strands of the poverty and social exclusion debate. The report includes indicators of low income, access to services, health, education and social isolation. The total list of indicators, according to the different policy priorities,[12] is presented in Figure 2.2.

---

[11] One year after the publication of the first *Opportunity for all* report the Government published *Opportunity for all: One year on, making a difference* (DSS, 2000a). The indicators published in the first report, set to a baseline of 1997 where possible, were updated, some by a year and some to the year of publication, in an attempt to see the impact of policies introduced since the Government came to power. For these and subsequent *Opportunity for all* reports see (http://www.dwp.gov.uk/).

[12] Not all of the policy priorities and indicators of success are relevant to the UK as a whole. The devolution of national administrations means that countries can develop indicators and policies to reflect their particular circumstances and institutions.

Children and young people

Ensuring that all children get a high-quality education wherever they go to school and providing additional help to children in the crucial pre-school years.
- An increase in the proportion of seven-year-old Sure Start children achieving level 1 or above in the Key Stage 1 English and maths tests.
- Health outcomes in Sure Start areas:
- A reduction in the proportion of low birth-weight babies in Sure Start areas; and
  a) A reduction in the rate of hospital admissions as a result of serious injury in Sure Start areas.
  b) An increase in the proportion of those aged 11 achieving level 4 or above in the key stage 2 tests for literacy and numeracy.
- A reduction in the proportion of truancies and exclusions from school.
- An increase in the proportion of 19-year-olds with at least a level 2 qualification or equivalent.

Combating family poverty and social exclusion through policies to tackle worklessness, increasing financial support for families and improving the environment in which children grow up.
- A reduction in the proportion of children living in workless households, for households of a given size, over the economic cycle.
- Low-income indicators:
  a) A reduction in the proportion of working age people in households with relatively low incomes;
  b) A reduction in the proportion of working age people in households with low incomes in an absolute sense; and
  c) A reduction in the proportion of working age people with persistently low incomes.
- A reduction in the proportion of children living in poor housing.
- A reduction in the proportion of households with children experiencing fuel poverty.
- A reduction in the rate at which children are admitted to hospital as a result of unintentional injury resulting in a hospital stay of longer than three days.

Supporting vulnerable young people, especially in the difficult transition from childhood to adult life.
- A reduction in the proportion of 16 to 18-year-olds not in education or training.
- An improvement in the educational attainment of children looked after by local authorities.
- Teenage pregnancy: a reduction in the rate of conceptions for those aged under 18 and an increase in the proportion of those who are teenage parents, in education, employment or training.

Figure 2.2   (continued)

People of working age

Building a proactive welfare system to help people into work.
- An increase in the proportion of working age people in employment, over the economic cycle.
- A reduction in the proportion of working age people living in workless households, for households of a given size, over the economic cycle.
- A reduction in the number of working age people living in families claiming Income Support or income-based Job Seekers Allowance who have been claiming these benefits for long periods of time.
- An increase in the employment rates of disadvantaged groups – people with disabilities, lone parents, ethnic minorities and the over 50s – and a reduction in the difference between their employment rates and the overall rate.

Making work pay.
- Low-income indicators:
  a) A reduction in the proportion of working age people in households with relatively low incomes;
  b) A reduction in the proportion of working age people in households with low incomes in an absolute sense; and
  c) A reduction in the proportion of working age people with persistently low incomes.

Promoting lifelong learning to ensure people have the skills and education to respond to the modern labour market.
- An increase in the proportion of working age people with a qualification.

Supporting vulnerable groups and those most at risk of discrimination and disadvantage.
- A reduction in the number of people sleeping rough.
- A reduction in cocaine and heroin use by young people.
- A reduction in adult smoking rates in all social classes.
- A reduction in the death rates from suicide and undetermined injury.

Older people

Ensuring that more of tomorrow's pensioners can retire on a decent income.
- An increase in the proportion of working age people contributing to a non-state pension.
- An increase in the amount contributed to non-state pensions.
- An increase in the proportion of working age individuals who have contributed to a non-state pension in at least three years out of the last four.

Figure 2.2   (continued)

Tackling the problems of low income and social exclusion among today's pensioners.
- Low-income indicators:
  a) A reduction in the proportion of older people in households with relatively low incomes;
  b) A reduction in the proportion of older people in households with low incomes in an absolute sense; and
  c) A reduction in the proportion of older people with persistently low incomes.
- A reduction in the proportion of elderly households experiencing fuel poverty.

Improving opportunities for older people to live secure, fulfilling and active lives.
- A reduction in the proportion of older people whose lives are affected by fear of crime.
- An increase in healthy life expectancy at age 65.
- A reduction in the proportion of households containing at least one person aged 75 or more living in poor housing.
- An increase in the proportion of older people being helped to live independently.

Communities[13]

Narrowing the gap between the poorest neighbourhoods and the rest of the country.
- A reduction in the difference between employment rates in the most deprived local authority districts and the overall employment rate.
- A reduction in the national rate of domestic burglary and a reduction in the difference between the rates in the most deprived local authority areas and the national average.
- A reduction in the number of families living in a home that falls below the set standard of decency.

Figure 2.2   The *Opportunity for all* policy objectives (bold text) **and indicators**

Despite such advances, the *Opportunity for all* report still falls behind theoretical efforts to measure social exclusion. The conceptual inadequacies of the report have been outlined above and it is because of these failings that the list of indicators in *Opportunity for all* appears rather unstructured and incomplete. This

---

[13] The indicators of success for Communities were introduced in the Second Annual Report. The Social Exclusion Unit's Policy Action Team is still developing a number of new indicators in this area (Social Exclusion Unit, 2000a).

has led to a number of criticisms of the selection of indicators and their utilization in attempts to understand social exclusion in Great Britain. Four of the most significant criticisms are discussed below.

First, there is a particular need for a theoretical explanation for the selection of indicators for the different sub-groups in the report. For example, the chosen indicators for young adults cover health and well-being, economic circumstances and barriers to work, whilst for adults aged 25 years to retirement age the indicators cover exclusion from work, disadvantage at work and health. Although there is no doubt that these indicators are important and relevant for the respective age groups, most relate to both groups. Also there are other key subjects crucial to a notion of poverty and social exclusion, such as social and neighbourhood participation that are not included in the list.

Secondly, it is questionable whether some indicators actually relate to poverty and social exclusion at all. For example, an indicator of cocaine and heroin use amongst young working age adults may be more likely to capture those who use such drugs for recreational purposes rather than those suffering from deprivation-led drug abuse. Similarly, smoking is not necessarily an indicator of poverty and social exclusion, although it is a habit disproportionately embraced by the poor and deprived (Townsend, 1995).

The third, and one of the most pertinent, criticisms of the *Opportunity for all* indicators comes from Bradshaw (2001) who argues that the report does not adequately differentiate between risk factors and output indicators of poverty and social exclusion. The need to distinguish risk factors from output indicators is crucial to an understanding of the causes and effects of poverty and social exclusion, particularly from a policy perspective. It is outcome indicators that should be used to operationalize poverty and social exclusion, as they capture the effects of the phenomena. Signs of lack of material possessions, poor mental health and low quality accommodation, for example, reflect the nature and extent of poverty and social exclusion. If the outcomes of poverty and social exclusion are to be tackled, policies should aim at an improvement in the quality of life of individuals that have to endure such experiences. Risk factors on the other hand are characteristics (or events) that can differentially influence (or trigger a change in) the likelihood of experiencing such outcomes. Having a low education is one factor that may increase the chances of being unemployed or having a low self-esteem, whilst taking a training-course may increase the chances of experiencing an improvement in such poverty and social exclusion related outcomes. If the aim of policy is to reduce the likelihood of experiencing poverty and social exclusion, it is at these risk factors that policies should be focussed.

According to technical information supplied in an annex to the second *Opportunity for all* report, the indicators 'fall into two main categories: indicators that focus on the current aspects of poverty and social exclusion, such as health, housing and low income ["*outcome indicators*"]; and indicators that capture factors that increase the risk of experiencing deprivation later in life, such as school truancy, teenage pregnancy and not having a non-state pension' ['*risk factors*']14

---

14 Words in italics added by author.

(DSS, 2000b, p. 1). Although this annex does appear to acknowledge the difference between outcome indicators and risk factors, the choice of indicators and the interpretation in the main report fails to adequately differentiate between them. For example, for working-age adults the report includes as 'indicators of success'; the proportion of adults in employment, the proportion of adults with low incomes and the number of adults sleeping rough – a confusing mix of outcome indicators and risk factors of poverty and social exclusion. However, it should be noted that one of the complexities surrounding the notions of poverty and social exclusion is that risk factors and outcomes are often difficult to tell apart.

Finally, although the *Opportunity for all* indicators are useful for presenting an overall, if somewhat limited, picture of poverty and social exclusion, the report can not claim to reveal a true understanding of the multi-dimensional and dynamic nature of the phenomena. The indicators come from different data sources and relate to different subjects, reference points and time scales. This means that they are not designed to allow dynamic and multi-dimensional analysis, crucial to an understanding of the complexities surrounding poverty and social exclusion, to take place.[15] One of the objectives of this research is to investigate in detail the multi-dimensional and longitudinal nature of social exclusion using data from household panel surveys.[16]

Other than the *Opportunity for all* report, there are very few examples of information on the prevalence and nature of multi-dimensional disadvantage. The most commonly used government indicators of multi-dimensional disadvantage are those that identify the geography of deprivation and help target policies and funding more effectively to needy areas. The Government's official measure of deprivation is the Index of Local Conditions (ILC), more recently updated by the Department of the Environment, Transport and the regions (DETR) as the Index of Local Deprivation (ILD) (for a discussion of such indices see Robson, 1995). The indicators combine a number of deprivation measures, such as overcrowded housing, households lacking amenities, children in low earning households and unemployment, to identify the most deprived areas in the country. Other multi-dimensional deprivation indicators that are in use include the Townsend Material Deprivation Score (Townsend et al, 1988), the Jarman Underprivileged Area Score (Jarman, 1984) and the material deprivation (MATDEP) and social deprivation (SOCDEP) indices (Forrest and Gordon, 1993). The Townsend Score – based on four variables originally taken from the 1981 Census: unemployment, overcrowding, lack of owner occupied accommodation and lack of car ownership – is probably the most popular tool and often used by Health Authorities.

---

[15] The few examples of dynamic analysis in the report come from analysis of income poverty from the British Household Panel Survey.
[16] Another objective is to discuss the policy implications of operationalizing social exclusion. A part of this discussion includes recommendations for development of the *Opportunity for all* indicators (see Chapter 8).

Indicators that incorporate the longitudinal nature of social exclusion are more difficult to locate. As already mentioned, there are generally very few statistics produced at longitudinal level. Those that are produced at regular intervals usually only provide the potential for an analysis of aggregate trends rather than for information to be presented dynamically at the level of the individual.

This discussion has highlighted the fact that there is a dearth of official information on the multi-dimensional and longitudinal aspects of social exclusion in Great Britain. In particular, despite an acceptance that social exclusion is a complex, multi-dimensional and longitudinal problem, and that polices should be designed accordingly, there is a distinct lack of empirical evidence of the prevalence and nature of social exclusion in Great Britain. Great Britain still has a less sophisticated debate about disadvantage in general than many other countries – for example compare the multi-dimensional analyses of human development and well-being that are used in the third world (de Haan and Maxwell, 1998) with the static, distributional income poverty statistics of the *HBAI* reports. Such primitive statistics and indicators not only severely limit policy makers' attempts to understand the nature of social exclusion, but they also hinder efforts to identify the individuals most at risk of the most serious, enduring, multifaceted forms of disadvantage. Information on both these issues is crucial to the formulation of efficient policies designed to prevent and alleviate social exclusion in society. Hence, the following section outlines a methodological framework to guide the operationalization of social exclusion.

A framework for the design of indicators of social exclusion

This section details a methodological framework for an investigation into social exclusion. The investigation is based on a transformation of the conceptualization of social exclusion into quantitative social indicators, constructed on data from two national level datasets, the British Household Panel Survey and the European Community Household Panel survey.

The framework for this study incorporates three features essential to the design of valid and robust indicators of social exclusion. The first details the *functional* rationale for the choice of indicators – that is to ensure the indicators are designed in relation to a specific purpose, in this case to contribute to the existing knowledge on social exclusion for both academic- and policy-related reasons. The second details the *theoretical* rationale for the choice of indicators – that is to adopt a philosophical foundation on which to base the operationalization of social exclusion and which the indicators must attempt to represent. The third details the *methodological* rationale for the choice of indicators – that is to ensure the indicators have a solid foundation from which to employ practical applications. Figure 2.3 suggests the key criteria for the selection of indicators of social exclusion according to such a framework.

Functional
- The indicators must be able to be utilized to identify the prevalence of social exclusion.
- The indicators should allow for analysis to aid an understanding of the complexities of social exclusion, in particular its multi-dimensional and longitudinal aspects.
- The indicators should be relevant for policy as well as intellectual purposes.

Theoretical
- Each indicator must be able contribute to a theoretical, rather than political, notion of social exclusion.
- Each indicator must represent a distinct and separate domain of social exclusion.
- The indicators should focus on outcomes of social exclusion rather than risk factors.

Methodological
- A range of separate indicators should be constructed, to be used on their own or to allow the design of a composite index, or indices, of social exclusion.
- The indicators must be constructed at least at an individual level, and ideally at a household and community level also.
- The indicators must come from a common data source to allow multi-dimensional and longitudinal analysis to take place.
- The indicators must be valid proxies of the dimensions of social exclusion they intend to represent.
- Each indicator must be unambiguous in interpretation.
- The indicators must be produced regularly, at least annually.
- The indicators must be based on national data.
- The indicators must be able to be broken down by other economic and socio-demographic characteristics to allow an investigation of 'risk factors'.
- Ideally, the indicators should allow for cross-country comparisons.

Figure 2.3   The framework and key criteria for the design of indicators of social exclusion

The framework detailed in Figure 2.3 proposes a range of criteria for the design of indicators of social exclusion. The functional rationale for the selection of the indicators advocates that the indicators must be able to be utilized to identify the prevalence of social exclusion. It is also important that the indicators are flexible enough to enable a through understanding of social exclusion and can be used for both intellectual and policy purposes, crucial to enhancing existing knowledge and contributing to effective policy making.

From a theoretical perspective the indicators must contribute to an intellectual, rather than a political, concept of social exclusion. This is paramount to an understanding of the underlying notion of social exclusion rather than requirements of particular political philosophies. To enable this, the indicators will build on the conceptual notion of social exclusion outlined above. Consequently, the indicators must represent important elements of the concept of social exclusion, such as separate and distinct domains of disadvantage, as well as focusing on outcomes rather than risk factors.

There are various methodological requirements that the indicators must fulfil before they become robust, legitimate and practical measures of social exclusion. Consequently the indicators need to be capable of separate or combined use, over time and at an individual level. Ideally they need to refer to other levels of analysis, such as households or communities, to be able to be broken down by other economic and socio-demographic characteristics (risk factors) to identify the individuals most likely to encounter such experiences, and to be applicable to cross-country analysis.

At an analytical level the indicators need to be able to be utilized to investigate the nature of social exclusion. For the purpose of this research in particular, the indicators need to be able to thoroughly investigate the significance of time in the measurement of social exclusion and its multi-dimensional properties. Four models of disadvantage will be used to ensure the nature of social exclusion is thoroughly investigated. These models are detailed in Figure 2.4.

Extent	*Time*	
	Static	Longitudinal
Singular	Current one-dimensional disadvantage (including notions of poverty)	Persistent one-dimensional disadvantage (including notions of enduring poverty)
Complex	Current multi-dimensional disadvantage (including notions of deprivation)	Persistent multi-dimensional disadvantage (including notions of social exclusion)

Figure 2.4   Operationalizing social exclusion: Measurement models

Figure 2.4 assigns conceptually important properties of social exclusion into four distinct measurement models: current one-dimensional disadvantage, persistent one-dimensional disadvantage, current multi-dimensional disadvantage and persistent multi-dimensional disadvantage. The current one-dimensional model uses aspects derived from a traditional singular, static approach to measuring disadvantage. Investigations using these models focus on just one domain of disadvantage at a point in time. Examples of the models include current low income (often referred to as 'poverty'), the lack of household items (most commonly defined using deprivation indicators) and non-economic measures such as social isolation and poor health. Such models are used to investigate the static nature of disadvantage in its own right as well as to identify individuals at risk of more severe, multifaceted and enduring disadvantage.

The use of complex panel surveys allows a longitudinal approach to complement the cross-sectional snapshots of disadvantage. The persistent one-dimensional disadvantage model is used to investigate the longitudinal nature of each domain of disadvantage separately and to explore the consequence of introducing time into the study of social exclusion.

The current multi-dimensional disadvantage model is used to investigate individuals who experienced simultaneous disadvantage on a number of domains at a point in time (encompassing notions of economic deprivation). This type of analysis has been central to the work of, amongst others, Townsend (1979) and Nolan and Whelan (1996) who define disadvantage according to relative income poverty lines *and* deprivation indicators. The persistent multi-dimensional disadvantage model combines the methodological approaches of the previous models to investigate the longitudinal nature of disadvantage experienced on a number of domains. Very little empirical research has been performed on identifying the individuals that experience the most enduring and multifaceted disadvantage in society (conceptualized in Figure 2.4 as 'social exclusion'). The persistent multi-dimensional disadvantage model is used to investigate the nature of, prevalence of, and risk factors associated with, social exclusion.[17]

Conclusion

Over the past century of British theoretical work on disadvantage there have been many attempts to define 'poverty', 'deprivation' and the more recent concept of 'social exclusion'. Partly because of its recent introduction to disadvantage research and policy planning, the notion of social exclusion has generally been used in a rather loose and inconsistent manner across different studies, and attempts at conceptualization are relatively under-developed between in academic discourse. However it is clear that the introduction of the notion of social exclusion has brought an important methodological contribution to the debate on disadvantage – explicit recognition of the core elements of a century's attempts to define disadvantage, particularly the importance of multi-dimensional and longitudinal aspects. This chapter has clarified a concept of social exclusion that draws in particular on Room's notion of 'catastrophe' and detailed how it fits into the framework of research adopted here.

Just as the conceptualization of social exclusion is hotly contested so is its measurement. There are relatively few attempts to operationalize the social, cultural and communal aspects of disadvantage associated with the concept of

---

[17] Constructing these models also provides the opportunity to assess what a model of social exclusion adds to investigations of disadvantage over less complex models such as poverty and deprivation.

social exclusion. In particular, there has been little effort to measure both the multi-dimensional and longitudinal nature of social exclusion; something that the empirical work of this research will focus upon.

A framework has been outlined that details the functional, theoretical and methodological criteria for a quantitative investigation into social exclusion, using a set of robust and valid social indicators. The investigation will use four distinct models that highlight the important methodological developments of research into social exclusion. These models reflect current one-dimensional research (incorporating the notion of 'poverty'); persistent one-dimensional research; current multi-dimensional research and persistent multi-dimensional research (incorporating the notion of 'social exclusion'). The models will be used to empirically investigate the nature of social exclusion, the latter, relatively underused, model being used to identify the prevalence of social exclusion and the characteristics of individuals most likely to endure such experiences.

Being able to develop complex models to investigate social exclusion using empirical research methods is not straightforward. One of the stumbling blocks to such analysis is the availability of suitable data. Publicly available, regularly collected, longitudinal and multi-dimensional information on social and economic aspects of society is few and far between. Probably the most useful source of such data for Great Britain is the British Household Panel Survey. The following chapter outlines the unique features of the British Household Panel Survey, an as yet under-used source in the investigation of disadvantage, and the construction of indicators which are relevant, both from a theoretical and policy perspective, to an investigation into the extent and nature of social exclusion in Great Britain.

Chapter 3

Developing a Set of Quantitative Indicators of Social Exclusion for Great Britain

Concepts are the building blocks of theory. However, concepts themselves are not measurable directly. Instead, for each concept in the theory there must be a corresponding indicator (Fielding and Gilbert, 2000, p. 11).

Introduction

This chapter is the first of four that investigates the nature of social exclusion in Great Britain in the 1990s. The investigation builds on the conceptualization and measurement issues discussed in Chapter 2 to construct a valid set of social exclusion indicators for Great Britain (Chapter 3), explore in detail the multi-dimensional (Chapter 4) and longitudinal (Chapter 5) properties of social exclusion, and identify the prevalence of social exclusion in Great Britain and the socio-demographic characteristics of working-age adults most likely to encounter such experiences (Chapter 6).

This chapter outlines the design and construction of set of indicators of social exclusion. The chapter begins with a brief description of the British Household Panel Survey – one of few datasets that allow a complex multi-dimensional and longitudinal analysis of social exclusion in Great Britain – the data source that will be employed in this and the following three chapters. This section includes a brief reliability analysis of the sample of working-age adults selected as the focus of this study.[1]

The main part of the chapter details the selection and operationalization of the indicators using data from the BHPS. This section includes a detailed description of indicator construction, including choice of subject domain and indicator threshold. The chapter ends with a concise validation exercise, using internal consistency checks and external comparisons with proven indicators from established data sources.

---

[1] The reasons for focussing on working-age adults were discussed in Chapter 1. In any case, the majority of questions in the BHPS are only asked to adults of 16 years and over.

The British Household Panel Survey

The framework and key criteria for the design of indicators of social exclusion detailed in Figure 2.3 (see Chapter 2) stated that indicators need to be constructed from a reputable, multi-dimensional and longitudinal survey that contains the necessary information for a complex in-depth study of social exclusion. These surveys are far and few between in Great Britain. This section outlines one of the few surveys available for such analysis – the British Household Panel Survey – paying particular attention to its multidimensional and longitudinal design, and the selection and validation of the sample to be used in this study.

Describing the survey

The British Household Panel Survey[2] (BHPS) was established in 1989 to examine social and economic change at the individual and household level in Great Britain and to identify, model and forecast such changes, and their causes and consequences in relation to a range of socio-economic characteristics. The BHPS is a unique source of information for investigating social exclusion in Great Britain because it is both a multi-dimensional and longitudinal survey. Not only does the survey cover a wide range of topics simultaneously, it also adopts a panel design in which information on the same set of individuals is gathered at annual intervals. The BHPS data can therefore be used to generate multi-level data on the condition, duration and frequency of a variety of topics, and how conditions, life events, behaviour and values are linked with each other dynamically over time.

The survey design begins with a nationally representative sample of households. The head of each household[3] is subject to a detailed household interview that covers information on a range of topics such as household demography, tenure of accommodation, housing amenities and costs, possession of durable goods, major sources of income and indicators of the household's financial situation. All household members aged 16 years and over are then given a detailed personal interview. The personal interview again covers a wide range of subjects, including economic activity, personal income, education and training, social relations, health and degree of satisfaction with various aspects of work and life. Information on each of these issues may be less detailed than in single-topic surveys, but the BHPS forms a single micro-date source, on the basis of which inter-relationships between the different fields of disadvantage can be analysed. It is therefore invaluable for research into the multi-dimensional nature of social exclusion.

The longitudinal design of the survey means that many of the questions asked in the first wave are repeated in subsequent waves. However not all topics

---

[2] The BHPS is designed, implemented and disseminated at the Institute for Social and Economic research (ISER) at the University of Essex. For a detailed description of the BHPS see http://www.iser.essex.ac.uk/bhps/.

[3] The head of the household is defined as the person legally or financially responsible for the accommodation, or the elder of two people equally responsible.

are included in every wave of the survey. Topics that are covered at every wave are known as Core Components; these are the heart of the survey and allow researchers to study net changes and trends. Topics covered periodically (i.e. every two or three waves) are known as Rotating Core Components. These topics are addressed only in situations in which large changes over time are not expected. The Non Core Components are 'one-off' questions usually asked only once. These include many questions such as 'What age did you leave school?' and 'Where were you born?'. Figure 3.1 summarizes the range of topics included in the BHPS, along with the regularity of coverage.

Household questionnaire	Individual questionnaire
Core components	*Core components*
Socio-demographic characteristics	Neighbourhood characteristics
Geographic location	Demographic characteristics
Accommodation status	Finances
Household finances	Health and caring
Consumer durables	Employment status
	Employment history
	Values and opinions
Rotating core components	*Rotating core components*
	Health and caring
	Distribution of wealth
Non core components	*Non core components*
	Marital status history
	Fertility and adoption history
	Employment status history
	Values and opinions
	Health and caring
	Neighbourhood and demographics

Figure 3.1   Core components of the BHPS questionnaire

The coverage of topics and frequency of inclusion in the survey is especially important for an analysis of the multi-dimensional nature of disadvantage. The number of topics covered by the BHPS is large, allowing for the construction of various indicators of disadvantage and for an analysis of the relationship between them. However this breadth of coverage is offset by the lack of depth in some areas. In this respect the BHPS does not provide as detailed information on certain topics as provided by other more specialist surveys. For example, BHPS income data is collected in rather less detail than the cross-sectional Family Resources Survey (FRS).[4] Despite the breadth of coverage of the BHPS the survey does not contain

---

[4] For information on the FRS see the ONS website http://www.statistics.gov.uk.

information on every aspect of social exclusion. In particular there is a lack of information on consensual approaches to poverty and deprivation, and on social activities.

The majority of empirical data available to social scientists is based on cross-sectional enquiries, in which a random sample of people is interviewed once at about the same time. This produces a 'snapshot' of the situation at that time – the proportion of people with low income, the extent of poor quality housing and so on. Surveys repeated at intervals can show net changes in these measures, such as widening inequality or a reduction in sub-standard housing. Valuable though these data sources are, they lack the picture of changes in individual experience that contribute to an understanding of social process. Longitudinal data such as that collected in the BHPS offers a 'movie' rather than a 'snapshot'. It allows the possibility of following individuals through time, recording circumstances, attitudes and behaviour from one point in time to the next. Analysis of such data can help to describe, explain and understand social situations and social change.

The BHPS has been collecting a longitudinal sample of respondents since 1991. The survey began by collecting a nationally representative sample of the population of Great Britain living in private households.[5] Households were selected using an equal probability sampling mechanism using a standard design for British household social surveys. Each member of these original households became a 'panel member' and is followed over time at annual intervals. Persons who move or who otherwise form or join new households are followed-up at their new location. Children in the original sample become eligible for the detailed personal interview when they reach 16 years of age, and children born to sample persons are automatically included as part of the survey population.

Given that some panel members will die from one wave to the next, such methods ensure that the sample remains broadly representative of the population of Great Britain as it changes through the years (except for losses due to sample attrition and non-inclusion of households formed purely of new immigrants into the population). This constant renewal of the sample means that in addition to providing longitudinal data, the BHPS is also designed to provide representative cross-sectional pictures of Great Britain over time.

To allow a longitudinal investigation of social exclusion, topics need to be included in as many of the waves selected for analysis as possible. As already mentioned not all topics are included each wave and within topics certain questions do not appear on a regular basis. There are also some slight modifications in question wording and, in a few cases, in the level of specificity in the response categories between waves. Inexact comparability between the waves may result in missing data, either within or across waves that may have consequences for trend and longitudinal analysis.

---

[5] As is common with most surveys the BHPS will not pick up individuals who are homeless or living in institutions, arguably sections of the population most likely to suffer from social exclusion.

Although many of the questions are repeated at every interview, some important information for the analysis of social exclusion is only included intermittently in the survey. For example, information on neighbourhood conditions and personal values and opinions is only included in certain waves of the survey. Data on household consumer durables, often used in an analysis of deprivation, is also included irregularly. Such shortcomings are to be expected from a survey not designed specifically to measure social exclusion. Despite these criticisms the BHPS is a uniquely valuable data source for an investigation of social exclusion in Great Britain.

Selecting and validating the sample

For the purposes of this study a sample of working-age adults is required from the BHPS database. This section details the selection of a cross-sectional sample of working-age adults from the 1996 wave of the survey. It also features an internal and external validation of the sample.

Table 3.1   Cross-sectional sample statistics, BHPS, 1991-1999, frequency[6]

Unit of analysis	Wave of survey[d]								
	1991	1992	1993	1994	1995	1996	1997	1998	1999
Households[a]	4852	4556	4354	4378	4259	4372	4384	4328	4273
Adults[b]	8999	8497	8108	8125	7858	8199	8230	8079	7888
Working-age adults[c]	7041	6669	6412	6412	6186	6520	6541	6411	6251

Notes:
[a] Households where all eligible adults (aged 16 years of age and over) completed a full individual interview and where the household interview was completed in full also.
[b] Adults who completed a full individual interview living in households where all eligible adults completed a full individual interview.
[c] Working age adults are those over 16 years of age and under sex specific retirement age (60 years for women and 65 years for men).
[d] 1997, 1998 and 1999 waves exclude BHPS-Scotland, BHPS-Northern Ireland and ECHP sub-samples (introduced in 1997 wave).

Table 3.1 presents statistics on the number of completed[7] household and individual interviews for nine waves of the BHPS (1991-1999). During these nine waves there have been approximately 4,400 households interviewed annually, providing

---

[6] All tables in this and the following three chapters present own analysis of BHPS data unless indicated otherwise.
[7] All analysis is performed on fully completed interviews only. This minimizes the amount of missing data, crucial to successful multi-dimensional and longitudinal analysis. For an analysis of missing data within fully completed interviews see Appendix B.

on average 8,200 full individual interviews each wave. Table 3.1 also presents the number of completed interviews for adults of working age who lived in households where all adults completed a full interview and where the household questionnaire was completed in full also. It is working-age adults that form the subset of interest for the majority of analysis in this research. In each wave there were on average 6,500 working-age individuals who completed a full individual interview.

As with all sample surveys, the validity with which the BHPS represents the population as a whole is heavily dependent on the respondent response rate. The achieved wave one household sample corresponded to a response rate of approximately 65 per cent of effective sample size (69 per cent if proxy interviews were included). These response rates are much the same as in other British household surveys (Buck, Ermisch and Jenkins, 1995). After data for the first wave of the BHPS was collected, researchers at Essex carried out a comparative analysis with the 1991 Census to assess non-response bias which occurs when households and individuals who fail to respond to the survey are systematically different from those who do respond (Taylor, 1994). The main differences between the BHPS and the Census were that the BHPS under-represented households in rented tenures, those with six plus individuals and those that did not have access to any cars or vans. As a result of this analysis cross-sectional weights, which adjust specific marginal distributions, have been made available for use with the BHPS data.[8]

The Essex analysis compared findings from the whole BHPS sample (representative of the population of Great Britain living in private households) with corresponding statistics from the Census. As the analysis in this study concentrates on just a subset of that sample – adults of working-age – it is important to assess how well the selected BHPS sample represents the population of working-age adults. Table 3.2 compares the BHPS with the Family and Working Lives Survey (FWLS) and the General Household Survey (GHS).[9] The FWLS is a retrospective, longitudinal survey of adults aged 16-69 years in Great Britain, developed to explore how various aspects of people's lives affect their work experience. The GHS is a multi-purpose survey on a sample of the general population resident in private, non-institutional households, providing information on aspects of housing, employment, education, health and social services, health related behaviour, transport, population and social security.

---

[8] As a consequence of only using working-age individuals who have completed a full interview and where the household interview was completed in full also, all BHPS analysis in this and the following three chapters (unless specified otherwise) does not use the cross-sectional and longitudinal weights provided in the BHPS data, since they are designed to be applied to samples of all respondent households. According to Jarvis and Jenkins (1995) not weighting the BHPS data produces no significant attrition biases in the analysis of income poverty and it is assumed that similar conclusions can be drawn from an analysis of social exclusion presented here.

[9] Comparisons are performed on data from the 1994 waves of the BHPS and GHS (both annual surveys), to correspond to the information from the SFWL.

Table 3.2 **Socio-demographic characteristics of working-age adults in the BHPS and a comparison with FWLS and GHS, 1994,** column per cent within category

Socio-demographic Characteristics in 1994	Working-age adults BHPS[a]	Adults aged 16-69 years[10]		
		BHPS[b]	FWLS[c]	GHS[c]
Sex				
Male	50	48	50	49
Female	50	52	50	51
Age group				
16-29 years	34	27	27	26
30-44 years	36	32	33	33
45-69 years	30	41	40	41
Ethnic origin				
White	96	96	94	94
Black – African	<1	1	1	<1
Black – Caribbean	<1	1	1	1
Black – other	<1	<1	<1	N/A
Indian	1	1	2	2
Pakistani	<1	1	1	1
Bangladeshi	<1	<1	1	<1
Other	1	1	1	1
Number of children in household				
None	57	62	67	62
One	22	19	13	17
Two	15	13	14	15
Three	5	4	4	5
Four or more	1	1	2	2
Housing tenure				
Own outright	13	20	16	19
Buying with mortgage or loan	60	54	44	53
Rented or free with job	26	26	39	28
Other	<1	<1	1	<1

[10] Information from the FWLS and GHS was only available for adults aged between 16 and 69 years.

Table 3.2   (continued)

Main activity status				
Employed full-time	63	57	47	48
Employed part-time	5	6	13	16
Unemployed	7	6	8	11
Education	8	6	6	3
Training scheme	1	1	1	1
Looking after home	10	10	9	6
Sick or disabled	4	4	5	4
Retired	2	10	10	9
Base	6412	7078	9139	15679

Notes:
[a] Unweighted analysis.
[b] Weighted analysis using BHPS cross-sectional weights.
[c] FWLS and GHS estimates from McKay et al (1996).

The comparisons presented in Table 3.2 are conducted on adults between the ages of 16 and 69 years, slightly different to the working age definition used in this research but the age range used in the available FWLS and GHS analysis. The BHPS sample of 16 to 69 year-olds shows many similarities to the other two samples. The small differences between the samples are likely to reflect population estimates based on different weighting methodologies (and variable definition in some cases).[11]

The BHPS sample does appear more likely than the comparable surveys to be female, of white ethnic origin, have children living in their household, owner-occupiers and, particularly, to be employed full-time. Some of these differences could be down to the fact that the majority of respondents in the 1994 wave of the BHPS have been panel members for four waves. Despite the influx of new respondents to the survey, the cross-sectional sample is likely to display characteristics of panel attrition (discussed in Chapter 5 below). That is to say, many of the 1994 wave respondents are more likely to represent individuals who wished to remain in the survey or who were more easily contacted.

---

[11] It is possible that some differences could occur because of inflated percentages due to small sample size. To prevent inaccurate reporting of results due to small sample size, cell-size thresholds apply to all cross-sectional analysis of BHPS data presented in tables in this and the following three chapters. The cell-size thresholds adopted replicate those recommended by researchers of longitudinal data at Eurostat, the statistical department of the European Commission (Eurostat, 1999). The thresholds for cross-sectional results are: below 20 observations (unweighted sample), base too small for sensible analysis, results not published, denoted by a *; from 20 to 49 observations (unweighted sample), small base so analysis must be read with caution, results may be published but are to be individually identified, shown in brackets [ ].

That completes a succinct account of the BHPS data to be used in this study.[12] The following section details the selection and construction of indicators of social exclusion using BHPS data.

Constructing a set of indicators of social exclusion with the BHPS[13]

In Chapter 2 key criteria for choosing and constructing indicators for this study were identified (see Figure 2.3). The selection of indicators represents one of the most important stages of operationalizing the concept of social exclusion. This process poses a series of problems that range from deciding on the dimensions of social exclusion to be investigated, to deciding on the variables to be utilized in indicator construction. Overcoming such problems is essential if indicator construction is to go beyond the theoretical stage. This section details the construction of indicators that will be used to investigate social exclusion in Great Britain in this and the following three chapters.

Lazarsfeld (1958) outlines three stages in the approach to the measurement of concepts. First the researcher forms an image from a theoretical domain. From this imagery stage a concept starts to be formed. The second stage involves a development of the concept to establish whether it comprises different aspects or dimensions. The third and final stage of operationalization is the selection of indicators, in which the researcher searches for an indicator, or indicators, of each dimension. Once the indicators have been selected a decision has to be made regarding the evaluation of disadvantage in each domain. This is often achieved through the formation of scales, with a threshold employed to signify disadvantage.

The first stage of measurement was dealt with in Chapter 2 where the theoretical notion of social exclusion was outlined. The following sections detail stages two and three, beginning with the selection of dimensions of social exclusion to be investigated.

Selecting dimensions of social exclusion

Nolan and Whelan (1996) have emphasized the importance of identifying different dimensions of disadvantage, and the relationship between them, to thoroughly understand notions of poverty, deprivation and social exclusion. Establishing such dimensions can be an important step in moving from the complexity and abstractness of a concept to a possible measure (Bryman and Cramer, 1997).

---

[12] The construction of a nine-wave panel sample of working-age adults, to be used in a longitudinal analysis of poverty and social exclusion in Britain, is detailed in Chapter 5.

[13] For presentation purposes the indicators are constructed from the 1996 wave of the BHPS as this corresponds with data from the most recent wave of the ECHP survey used to investigate social exclusion across the EU in Chapter 7. For the longitudinal analysis presented in Chapter 5 the indicator methodology outlined here is replicated for all nine waves of the BHPS data.

A review of previous attempts to operationalize social exclusion (see Chapter 2) suggests that there is a lack of consensus on the number and choice of both dimensions and indicators. Some of the discrepancies between these previous studies are no doubt attributed to differences in theoretical opinions. Such opinions are often subjective choices made by the researcher, usually supported by substantial evidence, but choices that are influenced by unavoidable parameters, such as the availability of data, timescale or cost.[14]

Although attempts to operationalize social exclusion are relatively scarce, various efforts have been made to distinguish its key components. According to Dunn et al (1998) exclusionary processes may arise in four key 'societal systems': civic (democratic participation); economic (labour market); social (welfare state); and interpersonal (social networks of family and friends). The researchers on the *Poverty and Social Exclusion survey* also identified four dimensions of exclusion (Gordon et al, 2000): exclusion from adequate income or resources, labour market exclusion, service exclusion and exclusion from social relations.

Burchardt et al (1999) on the other hand identified five components of social exclusion that leads to non-participation in the 'normal activities of citizens in that society': a low standard of living, lack of security, lack of engagement in an activity valued by others, lack of decision-making power and a lack of support from or contact with friends, family and the wider community. One of the most elaborate attempts at operationalizing social exclusion was performed by Percy-Smith (2000), who identified seven dimensions: economic, social, political, neighbourhood, individual, spatial and group.

It is clear from these studies that, as yet, there is no unanimous decision on the set of dimensions that best portray the notion of social exclusion. The choice of dimensions to be included in this study is derived from the theoretical discussion of social exclusion in Chapter 2, taking account of the capabilities of the BHPS and the framework for the design of indicators in Figure 2.3. In particular, dimensions are selected that encompass the variety of material, social and cultural experiences associated with the notion of social exclusion.

The notion of poverty, and consequent recognition of economic deprivation other than low income, has remained strong in much theoretical work on social exclusion. Room (Ed. 1995, 1998, 2000), amongst others, has acknowledged this, while also identifying the role of the community and the neighbourhood in creating exclusionary experiences and the importance of relational and social factors. A lack of engagement in societal activities can also be severely limited according to health, both physical and mental (Bajekal and Purdon, 2001). Accordingly, and given that capabilities of the BHPS dataset in terms of available, valid and reliable longitudinal information, the following domains of social exclusion are selected.

---

[14] Procedures do exist to minimize researcher bias in these decisions. For example, discussion groups were used in the preparation work for the recent Poverty and Social Exclusion (PSE) survey (Gordon et al, 2000).

- Financial situation.
- Material possessions.
- Housing circumstance.
- Neighbourhood perceptions.
- Social relations.
- Physical health.
- Mental health.

These domains are essential for the empirical work of this study as they encompass a broad range of aspects of disadvantage crucial to the notion of social exclusion. The domains can also be used to operationalize concepts of income poverty (using the financial situation indicator) and deprivation (using the financial situation, material possessions and housing circumstance indicators). This is useful for comparing analysis of different notions of disadvantage and assessing the value of operationalizing social exclusion.

Selecting the indicators of social exclusion and appropriate thresholds

The next stage of operationalization involves selecting indicators to act as proxies of each dimension of social exclusion. For ease of interpretation one indicator for each dimension will be selected. The selection of indicators in disadvantage research is usually somewhat arbitrary (Martinez and Ruiz-Huerta, 1999), but in this case reflects the capability of the BHPS data and the functional, theoretical and methodological criteria for indicators outlined earlier (see Chapter 2, Figure 2.3). In particular the indicators need to be constructed to allow a thorough understanding of both the multi-dimensional and longitudinal nature of social exclusion. Most importantly, the questions used to construct the indicators need to be asked consistently in all nine waves of the survey data used.

The indicators are constructed using information from singular questions in the BHPS or, where possible given the increased validity of intra-method triangulation,[15] by combining information from a number of questions. Implicit to the selection of indicators is the choice of threshold designed to differentiate between the disadvantaged and the non-disadvantaged. At this stage it is necessary to only define a threshold for each indicator separately, rather than a threshold for a combination of indicators to signify multi-dimensional disadvantage (this approach will be used briefly in Chapter 4 and more extensively in cross-national analysis in Chapter 7).

The task of identifying an objective threshold is clearly a difficult one and depends to a certain extent on whether the indicator is measuring a relative or absolute level of disadvantage. Debates about whether the investigation of

---

[15] Intra-method triangulation used in this instance refers to using a number of questions, rather than only one, to identify the disadvantaged on a particular indicator. This method increases the validity of an indicator as it identifies individuals on a number of questions that relate to the particular notion of disadvantage under investigation (for more information on triangulation see Denzin, 1989).

disadvantage should employ absolute or relative measures, or a combination of both, are commonplace and rarely reach agreement (such debates, with particular reference to income poverty, were outlined in Chapter 2).

The approach used in this research adopts the methodology used in the recent *Poverty and Social Exclusion survey* in Great Britain (Gordon et al, 2000). The PSE study used an *absolute* approach to investigate the levels of individual dimensions of disadvantage but also a *relative* approach in the sense that the dimensions reflect the population's judgement on what is essential to have in modern British society. In other words, the research presented in this book attempts to define indicators of social exclusion based on minimum standard of inclusion in society (for individuals of working age) according to the views of the British population as to what these minimum standards, or necessities, are.

The relative component of the methodology used in this research utilizes information from the PSE survey, and other more specialist studies if a particular domain of social exclusion was not included in the PSE that identifies items and activities considered necessary by the majority of the British population. Although the PSE survey was administered in 1999, it is still relevant to the BHPS data used in this study (which refers to the waves 1991-1999). Also, although what the population considers as necessities can change over time, the PSE survey found changes for non-luxury items to be negligible (Gordon et al, 2000). Therefore the consensual opinion of a necessity from 1999 can justifiably be employed in the construction of indicators through all nine waves of the BHPS data.

The absolute component of the methodology used in this research uses thresholds based on those employed in leading studies – the PSE study where possible – designed to investigate the individual dimensions of social exclusion in question. This approach therefore takes into account two of the main flaws of the objective approach. First, it is dubious for experts to decide on minimum acceptable standards and secondly, that social and cultural needs are overlooked. This approach also deals with a popular criticism of the relative approach – that arbitrary thresholds are set which identify inequality rather than disadvantage (these criticisms were discussed in more detail in Chapter 2).

The indicators are constructed as dichotomous variables that represent the possession or lack of a resource or condition, or the participation in or exclusion from a given activity. It is important to note here that the BHPS data is unable to identify why it is that individuals are disadvantaged and is therefore unable to distinguish between 'disadvantage', caused for example by personal preference and life-style, and 'enforced disadvantage', caused for example by lack of resources. This is an unfortunate constraint of the BHPS survey, as a good measure of disadvantage ideally needs to be able to distinguish constraint from choice (Piachaud, 1987). The BHPS information also neglects aspects such as quality or state of repair. However, in this research thresholds of disadvantage have been constructed at such levels that it is reasonable to suggest that no individual, given free choice, would choose to live in such circumstances. This section now proceeds to outline the choice of indicators and thresholds for the seven dimensions of social exclusion identified above.

Financial situation (a measure of income poverty)
The financial, material and housing dimensions of social exclusion are traditionally linked to the notion of poverty and deprivation. Net household income is often used as a proxy of financial situation and is a key concept in almost all definitions and studies of poverty, and will continue to be in this research. The most common method of measuring income is to aggregate individual incomes to reflect resources for individuals within the household [16] (see HBAI publications for detailed explanation of such methods, DSS (2001a), and Jarvis and Jenkins (1998b) and Bardesi et al (2001) for a description of the BHPS net household income variable). The poor are defined as those people living in households with an income below a certain threshold (often considered as 'the poverty line'). The threshold is most often set at a proportion of average income, but this represents a relative rather than absolute approach to measuring poverty.

Instead of using a purely relative poverty line, the income threshold that corresponds to the notion of absolute poverty in the PSE survey will be used (see Gordon et al, 2000 for details). The PSE threshold was set at £178 for an individual living alone in 1999. For the purpose of this research this threshold is modified to take into account other households according to household size and composition inline with conventional HBAI equivalization procedures (DSS, 2001a). To retain the concept of absolute poverty over time, the PSE threshold is converted to year of survey prices using the Retail Price Index (ONS, 2001a) (see Appendix A for details). Approximately one in six working-age adults were below the absolute poverty line in Great Britain in 1996.

In developing and informing policy it is important not to let the broader perspective of social exclusion detract from the continuing importance of the distribution of financial resources in society. This is because income-related policies remain a significant tool of poverty-reduction strategies. Therefore the notion of poverty, defined primarily as a lack of income, and represented by the financial situation indicator, will be retained as a central concern of this work and remains a focal point of analysis when social exclusion is the outcome of interest. From a methodological standpoint, the financial situation indicator can be used in isolation from other indicators but also used to contribute to an understanding of the complex relationship between poverty and other forms of disadvantage.

Material possessions
One of the major criticisms of using income as a measure of poverty, and even more so as a measure of social exclusion, is that it is not a perfect indicator of command over resources (Ringen, 1988). The use of material and housing deprivation indicators offers the possibility of measuring economic disadvantage directly according to living standards, rather than simply command over resources. Deprivation is often measured according to income and access to durable

---

[16] Each individual is attributed with the equivalent net income of the household to which they belong at the time of interview. The assumption of shared household resources has been challenged, most notably with reference to children by Middleton et al (1997) and to women by Millar and Glendinning (1989), but remains the standard methodology.

household items. Being below the income poverty line and living in a household without items that are socially perceived as necessities, or that a large proportion of the population possess, is a common method of defining deprivation (Nolan and Whelan, 1996).

Household items in the BHPS questionnaire that were defined as socially perceived necessities in the comprehensive and rigorous PSE survey (Gordon et al, 2000) include a freezer, a television and a washing machine. In the 1996 wave of the BHPS approximately nine in ten (89 per cent) of all individuals (adults and children) lived in households that possessed all three items. Households without at least one of these items are defined as deprived of material possessions in this research.[17]

Housing circumstance

One of the most important physical and social needs in any society is for housing. The worst-case scenario of being without shelter is homelessness itself, something that is not picked up in household surveys such as the BHPS.[18] A measure of substandard housing is relevant to deprivation, and also to social exclusion, in a number of ways. Low quality housing, without appropriate heating and insulation in particular, can contribute to physical, economic and psychological deficiencies (Lee and Murie, 1997; Marsh et al, 1999). Overcrowded dwellings are related to excessive social demands and lack of privacy, as well as general physical health (Department of Health, 1998).

In the PSE survey (Gordon et al, 2000) the top two housing necessities were related to heating (94 per cent of respondents felt that heating to warm living areas of the home was a necessity) and to overcrowding (95 per cent of respondents felt that beds and bedding for everyone was a necessity). In the 1996 wave of the BHPS only approximately 1 per cent of all individuals (adults and children) lived in overcrowded households and 10 per cent lived in households without central heating. To be without central heating or to be living in overcrowded accommodation is the indicator of housing circumstances used in this research.[19]

---

[17] Ideally more than three items would be used to create an indicator of material disadvantage. Although the BHPS does include questions on other household items, such as a telephone, car, personal computer and video, these questions were not asked consistently over the nine waves of data used in this study. These questions are therefore not used as their inclusion would severely limit multi-dimensional and longitudinal analysis.

[18] However, Evans (1995) estimated that the non-household population is around 2 per cent of the UK population. Although these individuals had disproportionately low incomes, including them in a UK wide analysis of income poverty contributed only 0.5 per cent to the overall estimate.

[19] Ideally more than two items would be used to create an indicator of housing disadvantage. Although the BHPS does include questions on other aspects of housing quality, such as whether the accommodation has a separate kitchen and bathroom and whether it has problems with a leaky roof, damp and rot, these questions were not asked consistently over the nine waves of data used in this study. These questions are therefore not used as their inclusion would severely limit multi-dimensional and longitudinal analysis.

Neighbourhood perception

Much recent research has shown that the scale and nature of social exclusion depends partly on where you live (Oppenheim and Harker, 1996). Areas and neighbourhoods can be discriminated against for a number of reasons: the large numbers of disadvantaged people living there, its geographical location or just the nature of the locality itself. Areas with a critical mass of poorer people have less money circulating, fewer opportunities and more stigmas. Stigma, for example, can lead to place discrimination by employers, the withdrawal of local services (such as shops and public transport) and increasingly overstretched public services. Researchers and policy makers are becoming increasingly aware of the ways in which living in impoverished environments contributes to exclusionary processes (Power, 1999; Murie, 2000; Pantazis, 2000).

Given the relatively small sample of the BHPS, deriving area-level characteristics (such as local unemployment rates) is not possible. Instead proxy indicators of dissatisfaction with the local neighbourhood are used. The PSE survey investigated individual's satisfaction with their local environment and found that those dissatisfied were more likely to be income poor. A useful proxy of neighbourhood conditions is an individual's desire to move due to reasons such as unsafe areas, noise or traffic problems. In the 1996 wave of the BHPS approximately 12 per cent of working-age adults stated a desire to move house because of neighbourhood-related problems. It is the individual's wish to move house because of neighbourhood related problems that is the indicator used in this study.[20]

Social relations

The social dimension has been at the forefront of much of the most recent research into social exclusion (see Putnam 1995, for a discussion of social capital). Research for Great Britain, such as the PSE survey, has highlighted the importance of social relationships in both preventing and helping people out of exclusion. Such relationships are important not only for personal interaction and emotional support, but they can also provide information about employment opportunities, childcare and links to financial assistance (Perri 6, 1997). The PSE survey found that there are social customs, obligations and activities that substantial majorities of the population identify as among the top necessities of life (Gordon et al, 2000).

The supportive and enabling component of social cohesion is often regarded as an important part of social inclusion. Gillies (1997) suggests that communities with high levels of collectivity are characterized by high levels of trust, positive social norms and many overlapping networks for communication and exchange of information. To be excluded from such activities can lead to feelings of disempowerment and disengagement.

---

[20] Ideally a more objective indicator of neighbourhood standard would be constructed, rather than an individual's subjective view of reasons to move house. The BHPS does include questions on crime (home and car burglaries, violent and racist attacks, vandalism etc.) but these questions were not asked consistently over the nine waves of data used in this study. These questions are therefore not used as their inclusion would severely limit multi-dimensional and longitudinal analysis.

The BHPS is one of the few complex national surveys to include a range of questions on social relations. One area of particular relevance in the BHPS is a suite of questions that explore the function of social relationships and networks in providing practical and emotional support to individuals in times of need. In the 1996 wave of the BHPS approximately 4 per cent of working-age adults had no one who would listen to them, had no one to count on to offer comfort or had no one to relax with. Slightly fewer felt they had no one who really appreciates them or had someone to help in a crisis. To be without at least one of these five indicators of social relationships and networks is the indicator of lack of social relations that is used in this research.

Physical health

One major feature of the social divisions in Great Britain is the health gap between the rich and the poor (Benzeval, 1997). A number of reasons have been put forward to explain health inequalities, including people's living and working conditions, resources, social relationships and their behaviours – factors linked heavily to components of social exclusion. Although physical health can be seen as a cause of social exclusion, it is also a measurable outcome in its own right. Being in poor physical health can mean exclusion from various social systems including education, employment and housing.

The BHPS includes three questions on the respondent's subjective personal health condition. Each question measures a slightly different perspective of ill health. Berthoud (2000) used BHPS data to develop an index from these three questions to provide a measure of the underlying concept of current physical ill health. His threshold for this measure allocates approximately one-fifth of the adult population in physical ill health, which is of the same magnitude as many other binary measures of ill health derived from other surveys such as the General Household Survey (Berthoud, 2000). Berthoud's index and threshold is used in this research as the indicator of physical ill health.

Mental health

Most of the aspects of social exclusion mentioned so far impact on the individual. Consequently an outcome of this is deterioration in mental health. The BHPS includes a version of the widely used General Health Questionnaire (GHQ). The GHQ was designed by Goldberg (1972) as a screening test for detecting minor psychiatric disorders in the community. It is comprised of a 12-item set of questions that are designed to give information about the respondent's mental state. There are six positive and six negative items, and each consists of a question asking whether the respondent has experienced a partial symptom or behaviour pattern. These items include suffering from a loss of sleep, feeling constantly under strain, having problems overcoming difficulties and feeling unhappy or depressed.

In the 1996 wave of the BHPS the average GHQ score for working-age adults was two. In this research the results of analysis are reported in terms of a distinction between those scoring seven or more and all others. This provides an appropriate threshold for distinguishing between those who are likely to be classified as nonpsychotic psychiatric cases and all others (see Benzeval and Judge (2001) for discussion of the GHQ measure and other measures of mental health).

A summary of the indicators of social exclusion to be used in this study is presented in Figure 3.2. The figure provides a detailed description of each indicator, including some indication of the actual wording from the BHPS questionnaire. The definition of each indicator threshold is also detailed.

Indicator	Definition
Financial situation	*Individual lived in a household with income below the 'absolute poverty' threshold.* - Income was measured as the sum across all household members of cash income from all sources minus direct taxes deflated using the relevant McClements equivalence scale to take into account differences in household size and composition. The income threshold used was that calculated in the PSE survey to measure 'absolute poverty' (see Gordon et al, 2000 for details). This threshold was converted to current, year of survey, prices using the Retail Price Index (ONS, 2001a)
Material possessions	*Individual lived in a household disadvantaged on material possessions.* - Respondents were asked whether or not the household possessed each of the following items: a television, a freezer, and a washing machine. Respondent was disadvantaged if household lacked at least one of these items.
Housing circumstance	*Individual lived in a household with disadvantaged housing circumstances.* - Respondents were asked whether or not the household had any form of central heating (including electric storage heaters). Overcrowding was calculated according to ratio of number of household members to number of rooms, commonly defined as more than 1.5 persons per room (DETR, 2000). Respondent was disadvantaged if household had no heating or was overcrowded.
Neighbourhood perception	*Individual wanted to move house because of neighbourhood related problems.* - Respondents were asked if they could choose, would they stay in their present home or would they prefer to move somewhere else. Respondent was disadvantaged if they preferred to move house because of at least one of the following reasons: feels isolated, traffic, area unsafe, noise, unfriendly area, dislikes area.

Figure 3.2   (continued)

Social relations	*Individual lacked social support.* - Respondents were asked about their social support networks. Respondent was disadvantaged if lacking at least one of the following: someone to listen when they need to talk, someone to count on to help in a crisis, someone to be totally themselves with, someone they feel appreciates themselves as a person, someone to count on for comfort when they are very upset.
Physical health	*Individual had physical health problems or disabilities.* - Respondents were asked three questions on physical ill-health: whether they had any of a list of health problems or disabilities, how they rated their health over the last 12 months and whether they had any of five types of physical impairment, defined according to normal activities that they might not be able to do. Berthoud (2000) successfully combined answers to these three questions to create an ill-health index and threshold. According to Berthoud's measure, a respondent was defined as having 'physical health problems or disabilities' if s/he scored four or more on this index.
Mental health	*Individual had mental health problems.* - Respondents were asked whether they were suffering from a list of conditions from the General Health Questionnaire (GHQ): lack of concentration, loss of sleep, feelings of uselessness, constant strain, problems overcoming difficulties, dislike of day-to-day activities, inability to face problems, depression, loss of confidence, worthlessness, general unhappiness. Answers to these questions were scored according to standard GHQ methodology. A respondent was defined as having 'mental health problems' if s/he totalled seven or more on the 12-item GHQ score.

Figure 3.2   Definition of static BHPS indicators of poverty and social exclusion, working-age adults

One notable omission from the selected indicators is exclusion from the labour market. Labour market exclusion, especially unemployment, undoubtedly plays a major role in social exclusion, particularly for working-age adults. Daniel (1990) found that unemployment, however brief, caused both hardship and trauma. When people were asked how they viewed their experience of unemployment, they ranked it close to the worst experience they had endured. Lack of money, boredom, depression, feeling dependent, out of control and shame were all distressing experiences identified by unemployed people (also see Clasen et al, 1997; Atkinson and Hills (Eds.), 1998 and Gregg and Wadsworth, 1998).

However, as remarked by the authors of the PSE survey, there should be concerns about treating non-participation in the labour market as an indicator of social exclusion as approximately two in five adults have no paid work and over one in three of the population live in a household in which all adults are either pensioners or jobless non-pensioners (Gordon et al, 2000). Social exclusion can also be a factor for those in employment. Low paid work, working excessive hours, a hazardous work environment, de-skilled and repetitive work can be linked to poverty and processes of social exclusion (Atkinson and Hills, 1998).

For this variety of reasons, labour market exclusion is not included as an outcome indicator in this study, but is used instead as an important risk factor of poverty and social exclusion. Such a decision is vindicated by New Labour's commitment to promote employment as a means of preventing poverty and social exclusion – a promise summed up fittingly in the *Opportunity for all* report, where it is stated that 'for most people of working age, the best way to avoid poverty and social exclusion is to be in paid work' (DSS, 1999a, p. 7).

Validating the indicators

Before employing the indicators in an investigation of social exclusion it is necessary to assess their validity. This is particularly important for those indicators for which substantial coverage of information has been sacrificed for consistent and reliable information over all nine waves of the survey data, to enable multi-dimensional and longitudinal analysis to be performed – most notably, indicators of material possessions, housing circumstance and neighbourhood perception.

One of the drawbacks of sacrificing depth of information is that an indicator may lack validity. An important validation procedure therefore is to test whether the indicators are really measuring the concepts that they purport to measure. At the very minimum it should be argued that each indicator reflects the content of the concept in question ('face validity'). In this respect each indicator should identify vulnerable individuals within each specific dimension of disadvantage (for example the financial situation indicator should identify individuals with meagre financial resources). In other words, those defined as in disadvantage according to a particular indicator should have expected related behavioural patterns. One method of testing such validity is to investigate the converging relationship between each indicator of social exclusion and other measures relating to the same dimension of disadvantage ('convergent validity'). An obvious way to do this would be to investigate the relationship between each indicator and other BHPS questions that measure a similar concept (Bryman and Cramer, 1997).[21]

Table 3.3 presents the relationship between the seven selected indicators (also called core indicators) and other measures of social exclusion from the BHPS (hereon called supplementary indicators). The table presents the proportion of working-age adults in 1996 that were disadvantaged on a selection of supplementary indicators according to whether they were below or above each core indicator threshold.

---

[21] It may be difficult to assess the degree of convergence if either or both of the two measures are faulty.

Table 3.3   Internal validation of static BHPS indicators of social exclusion, working-age adults, BHPS, 1996, cell per cent (unless specified)

Domain and supplementary indicator	*Core indicator*[a]	
	Disadvantaged	Not
Financial situation		
Mean income (£ per week)[b]	**£132**	£410
Poverty gap/surplus (£ per week)[b]	**-£55**	+£223
Without savings	**82**	52
Without investments	**72**	41
Without employer or private pension	**88**	48
Difficulties with financial situation	**25**	7
Material possessions		
No car or van for private use	**41**	12
No home computer in accommodation	**75**	58
No CD player in accommodation	**40**	20
Housing circumstance		
Problems paying for housing[c]	**15**	8
Tenure – detached	**6**	25
Tenure – semi-detached	**24**	37
Tenure – terraced house	**29**	19
Neighbourhood perception		
Dislikes living in neighbourhood	**51**	5
Never attend meetings for local groups	**80**	75
Social relations		
Sees first closest friend less than once a month	**8**	4
Sees second closest friend less than once a month	**11**	6
Physical health		
Used health service in previous year	**67**	32
Long term sick or disabled	**24**	1
Had an accident in the previous year	**16**	11
Does not have private medical insurance	**85**	77
Mental health		
Has problems with anxiety and depression	**26**	4
Used psychotherapist in last year	**8**	2

Notes:
[a] Disadvantaged means below the core indicator threshold. Table should be read as follows: 82 per cent of those disadvantaged on the core financial indicator (income poverty, see Figure 3.2 for definition) were also without savings, compared with 52 per cent of those not disadvantaged on the core financial indicator. Similarly, 41 per cent of those disadvantaged on the core material indicator (household does not possess at least one of a TV, a freezer and a washing machine) were also without access to a car or van, compared with 12 per cent of those not disadvantaged on the core material indicator. Bold text indicates a statistically significant relationship (at the 5 per cent level) between core and supplementary indicators.
[b] Income inflated to 2001 prices using Retail Price Index (ONS, 2001a).
[c] Only those who rent accommodation or pay a mortgage.

It is clear from Table 3.3 that there is a strong relationship between the core indicators of social exclusion and the supplementary indicators (all the relationships are also statistically significant). For example, those below the income poverty line were significantly more likely than those above it to be disadvantaged on other indicators of financial difficulty (to be without savings, investments, personal pension etc.). Such difficulties can be accounted for in part as those below the poverty line have an average equivalized household income of just £132 per week (in 2001 prices), more than three times lower than the average for those above the poverty line.

Similar patterns occur when focusing on other dimensions of social exclusion. Over two in five of those disadvantaged on the material possessions indicator had no access to a car or van (over three times more likely than for those not disadvantaged according to the material possessions indicator) and three quarters had no home computer in their accommodation. Likewise, just under one in ten of those disadvantaged on the social support indicator saw their closest friend less than once a month (twice as many as those not defined as lacking social support).

Another useful validation procedure is to compare the proportions of individuals disadvantaged on each indicator in the BHPS with estimates from other surveys. There is a considerable amount of literature that compares different income poverty measures. Accordingly the sensitivity of the PSE 'absolute' threshold is given special attention in Table 3.4 (see bold text).

Table 3.4   Estimates of income poverty according to a number of conventional definitions, BHPS, 1996

Poverty definition	*Poverty line* (£ per week)[c]	*Per cent in poverty* (all individuals)	*Per cent in poverty* (working-age adults)
Absolute measures			
PSE 'absolute'[a]	**187**	**22**	**16**
PSE 'overall'[a]	253	41	32
Relative measures[b]			
40% mean	133	9	7
50% mean	167	16	12
60% mean	200	26	19
50% median	146	12	9
60% median	175	18	14
70% median	204	27	20
Base	10544	10544	6520

Notes:
[a] The PSE survey used a measure of income and socially perceived necessities to scientifically define the UN definition of 'absolute' and 'overall' poverty (see Chapter 2 for these definitions). An 'absolute' measure of poverty is used in this research.
[b] Relative measure averages calculated on income distribution of entire population (all adults and children).
[c] Poverty lines inflated to 2001 prices using Retail Price Index (ONS, 2001a).

As can be seen from Table 3.4 the poverty line, and hence the percentage in poverty, can vary according to the measure used. In the 1996 wave of the BHPS 22 per cent of all individuals (adults and children) were living in households below the 'absolute' poverty line. The figure for working-age adults was lower, at 16 per cent, mainly because this analysis excludes individuals known to be at particular risk of income poverty – children and adults over state retirement age (DSS, 2001b).

The PSE 'absolute poverty' estimates correspond most closely to relative measures set at 60 per cent of average (mean or median) income. The most common form of measuring relative poverty – and indeed that proposed by the European Commission – is 60 per cent of median income. This measure creates a threshold £12 a week lower (2001 prices) than the PSE absolute measure. Thus, the PSE measure of absolute income poverty defines slightly more individuals to be below the poverty line than the European Commission measure. Table 3.5 presents statistics on the remaining six core indicators of social exclusion with comparable indicators from a number of external sources.

Validating the other six core BHPS indicators using external sources is a difficult task as finding comparable information from other surveys is not straightforward. Ideally comparable information would refer to the same concept, relate to the same subset of individuals and have been collected during the same time period. Very few of the comparative indicators used in Table 3.5 fit all of these criteria and hence the table has to be interpreted with such inconsistencies taken into account. In particular, the external sources that include all adult population estimates, rather than just a subset of working-age adults, contain pensioners who are disproportionately likely to suffer from problems of poverty, deprivation and social exclusion (DSS, 1999a).

Despite these imperfections, the comparisons in Table 3.5 are encouraging. In particular, indicators of material possessions, social relations and physical health provide similar estimates to the comparable indicators from external sources. The BHPS indicators that appear most inconsistent with external sources are neighbourhood perception and mental health. The BHPS indicator seems to overemphasize the perception of unsatisfactory neighbourhoods, although the comparable indicator from the Housing in England survey does stress the importance of accommodation rather than area. The indicator of mental health in the BHPS should be reasonably robust as it uses the standard General Health Questionnaire. Yet it does appear to underestimate the proportion of working-age people with a 'neurotic disorder' as defined by the Survey of Psychiatric Mobility.

The analysis presented so far in this chapter has revealed the range of social ills prevalent in Great Britain in the mid-1990s. It is not only low income that is commonplace in British society, but also poor quality housing, dissatisfaction with neighbourhoods, a lack of social relations and so on. Such a finding will not be surprising to those who take an interest in the plight of the most disadvantaged in society – indeed the prevalence of various forms of inequality is well documented in the *Opportunity for all* reports and other much publicized academic material (see Oppenheim and Harker, 1996; Walker and Walker, 1997, Howarth et al, 1998; Gordon and Pantazis, Eds. 2000 and Gordon et al, 2000).

Table 3.5 **External validation of BHPS indicators of social exclusion, working-age adults from BHPS, population estimates from external sources, 1996**, cell per cent (unless specified)

Dimension and indicator	BHPS	External sources
Material possessions		
Household lacks a television.	1	1[a]
Household lacks a freezer.	5	9[b]
Household lacks a washing machine.	5	6[c]
Housing circumstance		
Accommodation has no central heating.	10	15[d]
Accommodation is overcrowded.	1	2[e]
Neighbourhood perception		
Individual wants to relocate due to neighbourhood related problems.	12	5[f]
Social relations		
Individual lacks social support.	9	12[g]
Physical health		
Individual has physical health problems.	15	16[h]
Mental health		
Individual has mental health problems.	10	16[i]

Notes:
[a] General Household Survey, 1996 (Office for National Statistics, 1998b). Percentage of total population living in households without a television.
[b] General Household Survey, 1996 (Office for National Statistics, 1998b). Percentage of total population living in households without a freezer.
[c] Households Below Average Income, 1996/7 (DSS, 1998). Percentage of total population living in households without a washing machine.
[d] General Household Survey, 1996 (Office for National Statistics, 1998b). Percentage of total population living in household without central heating.
[e] General Household Survey, 1996 (Office for National Statistics, 1998b). Percentage of all households that fall below the 'bedroom standard'. The bedroom standard is calculated in relation to the number of bedrooms, and the number of household members, and their relationship to each other.
[f] Housing in England, 1995 (Green and Hansbro, 1995). Percentage of all households that report 'very dissatisfied' with their accommodation.
[g] *Poverty and Social Exclusion survey*, 1999 (Gordon et al, 2000). Percentage of all adults that report 'none or not much' support when depressed or in need of advice.
[h] General Household Survey, 1996 (Office for National Statistics, 1998b). Percentage of all individuals aged 16-64 years that report 'restricted activity'.
[i] Survey of Psychiatric Mobility, 1996 (Office for National Statistics, 1998b). Percentage of all individuals aged 16-64 years that report a 'neurotic disorder'.

Despite such interest in disadvantage in British society there is relatively little empirical work that investigates the notion of social exclusion, particularly the multi-dimensional and longitudinal aspects so crucial to a thorough understanding of the concept. Previous research has failed to base investigations on a data source that allows an in-depth examination of the nature of social exclusion. Such an investigation will take place over the following chapters using the BHPS – in particular utilizing the technical qualities of the survey to focus on multi-dimensional and longitudinal models of disadvantage.

Conclusion

This chapter has detailed the construction of a set of quantitative social indicators as a tool for investigating the extent and nature of social exclusion in Great Britain, in particular its multi-dimensional and longitudinal characteristics. Various attempts to create such indicators have been made before, most notably the *Opportunity for all* indicators produced in 1999 by the Department of Social Security to monitor the government's strategy to tackle poverty and social exclusion. Although the introduction of the Government's indicators should be praised for various reasons, most notably for marking a commitment to abolishing poverty and social exclusion, they were deficient in a number of areas. Above all the indicators lacked a theoretical foundation. In particular they failed to adequately represent the notion of social exclusion in British society. They were deficient methodologically too, most notably they confused outcome and risk factors, and being from different data sources were unable to investigate the multi-dimensional and longitudinal nature of disadvantage.

Taking into account these criticisms, a range of criteria have been used to construct seven indicators of social exclusion; financial situation (that measures income poverty), material possessions, housing circumstance, neighbourhood perception, social relations, physical health and mental health. These criteria encompassed theoretical, functional and methodological features crucial to the development of a set of valid indicators appropriate for a through investigation of social exclusion (and also poverty and deprivation). On the methodological front, the need for a common dataset was paramount. The indicators have been constructed from the BHPS – a unique British data source for the investigation of social exclusion. The indicators have undergone concise methodological validation procedures that suggest they are suitable for an in-depth investigation into social exclusion.

The following chapter begins an in-depth investigation of social exclusion in Great Britain by concentrating on the multi-dimensional nature of social exclusion. The analysis makes use of the broad coverage of BHPS question topics to explore relationships between different dimensions of disadvantage at a cross-sectional level (using models of current multi-dimensional disadvantage). The application of multi-dimensional techniques helps identify the extent and nature of simultaneous disadvantage (including economic deprivation), an important precursor of social exclusion. The findings of the chapter will contribute to methodology to identify the prevalence of social exclusion in Great Britain and the socio-demographic characteristics of individuals most likely to suffer such experiences.

Chapter 4

Investigating the Multi-Dimensional
Nature of Social Exclusion
in Great Britain

The causes, nature and consequences of poverty [and social exclusion] include many aspects or dimensions ... The combination of the income and deprivation indicator approach offer the opportunity both to measure poverty [and social exclusion] more accurately and to provide a more complete picture of the life-styles of the poor (Whelan and Whelan, 1995, pp. 46, 48).[1]

Introduction

In his work on social exclusion Room (Ed. 1995, 1998, 2000) highlights the need for researchers and policy makers to concentrate on multi-dimensional disadvantage, rather than the traditional focus on financial disadvantage alone, because it is important for both policy and explanatory purposes to disentangle different elements of hardship and to identify their interrelationships. Despite such emphasis on the need for multi-dimensional analysis, there have been few attempts to operationalize a multi-dimensional notion of social exclusion for Great Britain (exceptions include Burchardt et al, 1999; Whelan et al, 2001; Barnes et al, 2002). Consequently the multi-dimensional nature of social exclusion is still to be fully understood.

The previous chapter introduced quantitative social indicators as a tool for measuring the extent and nature of social exclusion. Functional, theoretical and methodological criteria were adopted in the construction of a set of indicators for Great Britain using data from the British Household Panel Survey (BHPS). Use of the wide-ranging, longitudinal BHPS dataset has meant that the indicators can be employed to assess the benefits of adopting multi-dimensional and longitudinal models to investigate the nature of social exclusion in Great Britain – analysis fundamental to theoretical notions of social exclusion but missing from much of the previous empirical work carried out in this area. This investigation takes place over the next two chapters beginning with a focus on the complex nature of disadvantage at a cross-sectional level by utilizing models of current multi-dimensional disadvantage.

---

[1] Words in brackets added by author.

Before beginning an investigation of multi-dimensional disadvantage it is important to understand the nature of the separate indicators of social exclusion constructed in the previous chapter. This chapter begins with a brief look at the prevalence of each of the seven indicators of social exclusion and an analysis of socio-demographic risk factors associated with such disadvantage. This analysis provides the necessary background information for a thorough understanding of the multi-dimensional nature of social exclusion investigated later in this chapter.

Various empirical approaches are then used to explore the variety of difficulties individuals experienced simultaneously during the mid-1990s. This includes the magnitude of disadvantage and the pattern of disadvantage – whether those that suffer from one form of social exclusion were more likely to suffer from others and if so, the relationship between different indicators of social exclusion. As well as investigating the prevalence and nature of multi-dimensional disadvantage the chapter includes a multivariate analysis that explores individual and household level socio-demographic characteristics of multiply deprived individuals.

The prevalence and nature of current one-dimensional disadvantage in Great Britain

As discussed in the previous chapter, there have been numerous comprehensive investigations of individual elements of social exclusion (see Oppenheim and Harker, 1996; Walker and Walker, 1997, DSS, 1999a; Howarth et al, 1998, 1999; Gordon and Pantazis, Eds. 2000 and Gordon et al, 2000 for a collective analysis of various distinct dimensions of disadvantage). Such studies provide a thorough understanding of the individual components of social exclusion, which is crucial as a foundation to comprehending the more complex elements of multidimensional and longitudinal disadvantage.

Figure 4.1 shows the percentage of the working-age population who fell below the disadvantage threshold for each indicator of social exclusion in Great Britain according to the 1996 wave of the BHPS. It is clear that at a current one-dimensional level the prevalence of disadvantage was quite substantial, between nine and 16 per cent depending on the indicator in question. It is noticeable that the income poverty (financial situation) indicator captures the highest percentage of people, reinforcing the importance low income has in the study of social exclusion.[2] Later in this chapter analysis will determine the relationship between these indicators in an attempt to determine situations most likely to involve multi-dimensional disadvantage.

_____

[2] The proportion of individuals disadvantaged on each indicator is of course highly dependent on the choice of threshold (see Table 3.6 for an example of how the choice of income threshold affects the proportion of individuals in income poverty). However given that each indicator is constructed as a distinct and severe measure of aspects of social exclusion, comparisons between the indicators is justified.

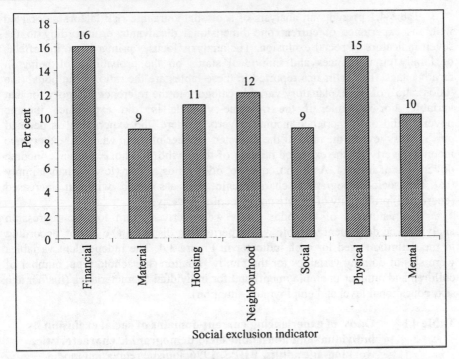

Figure 4.1   The incidence of indicators of social exclusion, working-age adults, BHPS, 1996

Also important to an understanding of multi-dimensional disadvantage is an identification of factors linked to current one-dimensional forms of disadvantage. If certain of these separate dimensions of disadvantage act as catalysts for the more complex experience of social exclusion, the identification of socio-demographic risk factors could be important for targeting welfare policies. For example, previous studies of income poverty in Great Britain have concluded that certain individual and household level socio-demographic characteristics increase the risk of experiencing low income, most notably according to sex, age, household type, number of dependent children, education level and main activity status (see for example Jarvis and Jenkins, 1996, 2000a; Gordon and Pantazis, Eds. 1997; Hills, 1998, Gordon et al, 2000). These findings have meant policy can focus on helping 'at risk' individuals to improve their own income situation wherever possible, by providing work-related education and training, and on protecting particular population subgroups that are at risk but find it difficult to help themselves, such as lone parents and disabled people. These types of risk factor are often linked to outcomes of social exclusion.[3]

---

[3] For example, the Social Exclusion Unit has chosen to focus on social exclusion risk factors such as disadvantaged neighbourhoods, rough sleeping, teenage pregnancy and school exclusion (Social Exclusion Unit, 2000b).

   Table 4.1 presents an analysis of socio-demographic risk factors associated with the experience of current one-dimensional disadvantage, according to the seven indicators of social exclusion. The analysis focuses primarily on the effects of family circumstances and individual status on the probability of being in disadvantage. The estimates reported in these tables are the ratio of the odds[4] (the 'odds ratio') of the explanatory variable category to the reference category for that variable. For example, if the outcome variable is 'did experience income poverty'/'did not experience income poverty', where 'did experience' is deemed our 'success' event, the ratio of the expected number of those who 'did experience income poverty' to the expected number of those who 'did not experience income poverty' is of interest. As a consequence, odds ratios higher (lower) than 1 imply that the socio-demographic characteristic was associated with an increased (decreased) probability of experiencing income poverty.

   The estimates of the odds ratios were derived from logistic regression analysis. The dependent variable was experiencing disadvantage or not, according to the definition used for each indicator in Figure 3.4. The independent variables were sets of dummy variables for the family situation (household type, number of children and number in employment) and for individual characteristics (his/her age, sex, educational level and employment situation).

Table 4.1   Odds[a] of experiencing current domains of social exclusion by individual and household socio-demographic characteristic, working-age adults, BHPS, 1996, logistic regression model

Socio-demographic characteristics	Social exclusion indicator						
	Fi	Ma	Ho	Ne	So	Ph	Me
Sex							
Male	ref	ref	ref	ref	ref	ref	ref
Female	1.1	0.9	1.1	1.1	**0.5**	1.0	**1.6**
Age group							
16-29 years	**1.7**	**1.8**	**1.6**	**1.5**	0.8	0.8	0.8
30-44 years	ref	ref	ref	ref	ref	ref	ref
45-59/64 years	0.9	**0.6**	**0.7**	1.0	1.1	**1.6**	1.0

---

[4] The definition of odds is similar but significantly different to that of probability. This is best explained in the form of an example. If 200 individuals out of a population of 1000 experienced income below the poverty line, the *probability* of being in poverty would be is 0.2. The *odds* in favour of being in poverty relative to not being in poverty are calculated as the ratio of these two mutually exclusive events. The odds in favour of being in poverty relative to not being in poverty, is therefore 0.2/0.8=0.25.

Table 4.1 (continued)

Household type							
Single	0.7	**5.9**	1.9	0.9	2.1	**2.1**	1.3
Couple no children	0.5	1.7	1.1	0.9	1.1	1.8	0.7
Couple, dep children only[b]	ref	ref	ref	ref	ref	ref	ref
Couple, some non-dep children[c]	0.6	0.5	0.6	0.9	1.8	1.5	0.7
Lone parent, dep children only	1.2	**2.2**	1.3	1.3	**1.6**	0.8	**1.6**
Lone parent, some non-dep children	0.8	2.1	1.6	0.9	**3.3**	1.3	0.7
Other	1.1	2.2	**2.1**	1.5	1.0	**1.9**	1.3
Number of dependent children							
None	0.9	1.8	1.1	1.1	0.5	0.7	1.3
One	ref	ref	ref	ref	ref	ref	ref
Two or moro	**2.3**	0.8	0.9	1.1	1.1	0.9	1.3
Education level							
Degree or higher	**0.5**	1.3	**0.6**	**0.7**	1.1	0.9	1.2
A-level	0.9	1.1	**0.7**	0.9	1.3	0.9	1.0
O-level	ref	ref	ref	ref	ref	ref	ref
CSE level	**1.7**	0.7	1.1	1.2	1.3	1.2	1.0
None of these	**2.0**	**1.4**	**1.4**	**1.6**	**1.6**	**1.6**	1.0
Main activity status[d]							
Employed full time	**0.7**	1.1	1.0	1.2	0.9	n/a	**0.5**
Employed part time	**3.1**	1.2	0.8	1.3	0.7	n/a	**0.6**
Uncmploycd	**3.3**	1.3	1.3	**2.6**	1.1	n/a	0.9
Care of home/family	ref	ref	ref	ref	ref	n/a	ref
Education/training	**1.6**	1.4	**0.6**	0.9	1.3	n/a	**0.3**
Other inactive	0.9	1.9	1.6	0.1	1.8	n/a	0.0
Number in household in employment							
None	**4.8**	**1.8**	1.0	1.1	**1.6**	**1.4**	1.1
One	ref	ref	ref	ref	ref	ref	ref
Two or more	**0.2**	**0.5**	**0.7**	0.9	0.8	1.0	0.3

Notes:
[a] Odds ratios higher (lower) than 1 imply that the socio-demographic characteristic is associated with an increased (decreased) odds of experiencing the event (disadvantage) compared to the reference category (ref). Bold text indicates a statistically significant (p<0.05) coefficient. For example, taking the financial situation indicator (income poverty), the odds of 16-29 year olds experiencing income poverty was 1.7 times higher (also statistically significant) than for 30-44 year olds (the reference category), holding all other socio-demographic characteristics constant.
[b] Throughout the book (dep)endent children refers to children under 16 years of age or 16 years of age and over and in full-time education. Also, 'dependent children only' means all children in the household were dependent.
[c] Throughout the book (non-dep)endent children refers to children 16 years of age and over and not in full-time education. Also, 'some non-dependent children only' means at least one child in the household was non-dependent.
[d] Main activity status is excluded from the physical health analysis as most people with poor physical health looked after the home or family, or were in the other inactive category.

As found in other studies of low income (for example, Jarvis and Jenkins, 2000b) the odds of experiencing income poverty (the financial situation indicator) increased (compared to the reference category) for; young adults, lone parents who live with dependent children (although not statistically significant), those living in a household with two or more children, individuals with low education, individuals not in full-time employment (bar the 'other inactive' category, likely to be made up primarily of sick or disabled people) and individuals living in households where no one was in employment. Indeed, working-age adults living in a household where no one was in employment had odds of income poverty almost five times higher than those living in a household with one employed person. Those least likely to be income poor were those with degree or higher-level education, those in full-time employment and those living in a household where two or more individuals were in employment.

The pattern of odds for the other domains of social exclusion suggests that different forms of disadvantage effect slightly different groups of individuals and that the magnitude of risk can vary too. The other primarily economic indicators (material possessions and housing circumstance) suggest similar socio-demographic relationships with a few exceptions. Individuals who live alone were particularly prone to lack material possessions, whilst those living in 'other' households (likely to be students and unrelated adults sharing accommodation) faced deprivation of housing circumstance. Older working-age adults were significantly less likely to suffer, perhaps as a consequence of accumulating material and housing resources during their lifetime and because their households were likely to have fewer 'needs' as a result of children leaving the parental home. Couples with some non-dependent children also appear less likely to be deprived, perhaps as a consequence of being older, but also because their children would weigh heavily in the calculation of needs in the previous analysis' calculation of equivalized household income.

Analysis of the other non-economic indicators of social exclusion suggests that whilst some socio-demographic characteristics appear linked to an increased odds in most, if not all, forms of disadvantage – most notably living alone, being a lone parent, having very low education and having no members of the household in employment – such forms of disadvantage disproportionately affect different groups of working-age adults. For example, being unemployed significantly increases the odds of having a negative neighbourhood perception; being male and having some non-dependent children significantly increases the odds of insufficient social contact; being older significantly increases the odds of poor physical health and being female and having dependent children significantly increases the odds of poor mental health. As already mentioned, many of the patterns shown in these findings are not new but provide necessary background information for an understanding of the complex notion of multi-dimensional disadvantage to be investigated later in this chapter.

Figure 4.1 and Table 4.1 have shown that measuring different aspects of disadvantage, not just low income, highlights that not only did people experience different forms of disadvantage but also that the various forms of poverty and social exclusion affected different groups of people and to varying degree. By omitting such wide-ranging dimensions of disadvantage from an investigation of social exclusion, crucial information is overlooked and attempts to understand and develop policies to eradicate such experiences likely to be severely diminished.

The prevalence and nature of current multi-dimensional disadvantage in Great Britain

Various reports have detailed the extent of poverty, deprivation and social exclusion in Great Britain in much the same way as in the previous section (Oppenheim and Harker, 1996; Walker and Walker, 1997, DSS, 1999a; Howarth et al, 1998, 1999; Gordon and Pantazis, Eds. 2000 and Gordon et al, 2000). Some have used using a wide-range of indicators to do so and acknowledged that disadvantage is a multidimensional phenomenon. For example the *Opportunity for all* report referred to social exclusion as a 'complex, multi-dimensional problem' (DSS, 1999a, p. 2). However, and a common criticism of these type of studies, the report failed to present an empirical analysis of the prevalence of multi-dimensional disadvantage and the relationship between such indicators.

The main investigation in this chapter concentrates on the prevalence and nature of current multi-dimensional disadvantage in Great Britain in the mid-1990s. Recording the prevalence of current multi-dimensional disadvantage is an important exercise as this provides evidence of the extent of the problem in British society, something lacking in many studies to date. Investigating the nature of current multi-dimensional disadvantage is crucial to understand patterns of disadvantage and to help direct resources at those most likely to experience a multitude of problems. This section begins with a descriptive inquiry into the prevalence of current multi-dimensional disadvantage in Great Britain.

The overall prevalence of current multi-dimensional disadvantage

The investigation begins with an analysis of the prevalence of current multi-dimensional disadvantage. At a descriptive level this is calculated by totalling the number of social exclusion indicators on which working-age individuals were disadvantaged in 1996 (individuals can be disadvantaged on a maximum of seven indicators). Given that each indicator represents a quite distinct and severe form of disadvantage, any degree of multi-dimensional disadvantage denotes a serious and diverse form of distress. The results are presented in Figure 4.2.

Figure 4.2 shows that just over one half of all working-age adults were disadvantaged on at least one of the seven indicators of social exclusion. Of those suffering from at least one form of social exclusion, the majority (30 per cent of all working-age adults) were disadvantaged on just one indicator. Fourteen per of all working-age individuals were disadvantaged on two indicators, one in twenty were disadvantaged on three indicators and only 2 per cent were disadvantaged on four indicators or more. In fact no individuals were excluded on all seven indicators.

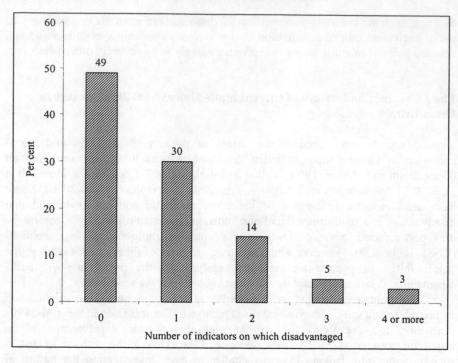

Figure 4.2   The number of indicators on which individuals were disadvantaged, working-age adults, BHPS, 1996, bar chart[a]

Note:
[a] 11 per cent missing data.[5]

The analysis suggests that although multi-dimensional disadvantage on a large number of indicators was rare, there was still a substantial proportion of the working-age population (22 per cent) who experienced disadvantage on two or more indicators. Given that each indicator is designed to represent a separate and distinct element of social exclusion at such levels that it is reasonable to suggest that no individual, given free choice, would choose to live in, the prevalence of simultaneous disadvantage amongst the working-age population should be of considerable theoretical and policy concern.

This analysis has presented a descriptive picture of multi-dimensional disadvantage amongst the working-age population and has shown it to warrant

---

[5] As multidimensional analysis relies on information from a range of questions in the BHPS, it is particularly susceptible to missing data problems. Unfortunately this is the case in much of the analysis presented in this chapter, where missing data affects approximately one in ten respondents. An analysis of missing data suggests that this does not adversely affect results, although individuals excluded from analysis because of missing data were significantly (p<0.05) more likely to be younger and to be in education or training (see Appendix B1 for further details).

further investigation. To increase understanding of the prevalence of multi-dimensional disadvantage it is necessary to explore such analysis in more detail. This begins with a focus on the relationship between disadvantage status, to ascertain whether the prevalence of a particular form of social exclusion was associated with multi-dimensional disadvantage.

Table 4.2 **Prevalence of multi-dimensional disadvantage according to disadvantage status,[a] working-age adults, BHPS, 1996,** row per cent[b]

(*'Source' indicator*)	*No. of other indicator on which disadvantaged*			
Disadvantage status	0	1	2	3 or more
All working-age adults	49	30	14	7
Financial situation				
Disadvantaged	35	38	18	9
Not disadvantaged	58	29	10	3
Material possessions				
Disadvantaged	34	40	15	12
Not disadvantaged	54	30	12	5
Housing circumstance				
Disadvantaged	37	35	19	10
Not disadvantaged	55	30	12	4
Neighbourhood perception				
Disadvantaged	43	35	15	[7]
Not disadvantaged	56	29	11	5
Social relations				
Disadvantaged	41	31	18	11
Not disadvantaged	54	29	12	4
Physical health				
Disadvantaged	42	32	19	8
Not disadvantaged	58	28	11	3
Mental health				
Disadvantaged	34	36	21	9
Not disadvantaged	55	30	11	4

Notes:
[a] Bold text represents statistically significant ($p<0.05$) relationship between disadvantage status and the number of other indicators on which disadvantaged.
[b] Table should be read as follows: of those disadvantaged on the financial situation (income poverty) indicator (the 'source' indicator in this example) 35 per cent were not disadvantaged on any other indicators, 38 per cent were disadvantaged on one other indicator, 18 per cent were disadvantaged on two other indicators and so on. Of those not disadvantaged on the financial situation (income poverty) indicator 58 per cent were not disadvantaged on any other indicators, 29 per cent were disadvantaged on one other indicator, 10 per cent were disadvantaged on two other indicators and so on. Of those disadvantaged on the material possessions indicator 34 per cent were not disadvantaged on any other indicators, 40 per cent were disadvantaged on one other indicator and so on.

The analysis presented in Table 4.2 reveals that being below the disadvantage threshold on any of the seven social exclusion indicators leads to an increased likelihood (which is statistically significant) of being in disadvantage according to at least one of the other six indicators. The link between income poverty (the financial situation indicator) and social exclusion is suggested. The table shows that just under two thirds of working-age adults living in income poor households were excluded on at least one of the other indicators of social exclusion, compared with just over two in five of those living in households not experiencing income poverty.

However the analysis by financial situation (income poverty) in Table 4.2 acts to illustrate why using only low income as an indicator of social exclusion is flawed. Although income poverty can be seen to be an important indicator of other forms of social exclusion, it is by itself not adequate to identify the most disadvantaged individuals in society. Of the income poor identified by the BHPS data, just under two thirds also experienced another form of disadvantage. In other words, the income poor were not a homogenous group – there were income poor individuals who also experienced other forms of disadvantage and those who did not. By using a multi-dimensional (and in the following chapter a longitudinal) approach in an investigation of social exclusion the most serious forms of disadvantage can be identified.

Although the likelihood of experiencing multi-dimensional disadvantage increased if already disadvantaged on one indicator, this likelihood varies depending on the 'source' indicator in question. For example, the analysis presented in Table 4.2 suggests that those disadvantaged on the primarily economic indicators of social exclusion (financial situation, material possessions and housing circumstance) were more likely, than those disadvantaged on the non-economic indicators (bar mental health), to suffer other forms of social exclusion. This finding could be important in the pursuit of risk factors of multi-dimensional disadvantage – factors that are not limited to socio-demographic characteristics but also include the social exclusion indicators themselves.

Those most likely to have experienced multi-dimensional disadvantage on at least one other indicator were those disadvantaged on the material possessions and the mental health indicators. Those disadvantaged on the material possessions indicator were also most likely to have experienced disadvantage on at least three other indicators. It appears that certain indicators were not only linked to the prevalence of multi-dimensional disadvantage, but also to the extent of multi-dimensional disadvantage.

A similar type of analysis is presented in Table 4.3, except this time it focuses on types of disadvantage from the perspective of the extent of multi-dimensional disadvantage. The table presents the likelihood of experiencing disadvantage on each indicator according to whether they were disadvantaged on one, two or three or more indicators. These estimates are presented in the form of relative disadvantage ratios.

The relative disadvantage ratio is calculated as 'the ratio of the probability of experiencing a form of disadvantage, given the number of indicators disadvantaged on', 'over the overall probability of experiencing the same form of disadvantage'.

To standardize the ratios to take into account cumulative disadvantage, the ratios are divided by the number of indicators on which individuals were disadvantaged. Therefore a relative disadvantage ratio of 1.0 means that there was no change in the likelihood of experiencing that form of disadvantage according to the number of indicators disadvantaged on, a ratio greater than 1.0 means that an individual was more likely than average to have experienced that form of disadvantage and a ratio less than 1.0 means that an individual was less likely.

Table 4.3   Likelihood of type of disadvantage by number of indicators on which disadvantaged, working-age adults, BHPS, 1996, relative disadvantage ratio

Indicator	Number of indicators disadvantaged on		
	1	2	3 or more
Financial situation	1.1	1.3	1.2
Material possessions	1.1	1.4	1.2
Housing circumstance	1.2	1.2	1.3
Neighbourhood perception	1.6	1.4	1.2
Social relations	1.3	1.1	1.3
Physical health	1.3	1.1	1.2
Mental health	1.2	1.4	1.5

Table 4.3 reveals that the likelihood of experiencing a particular form of social exclusion varies according to the number of indicators on which disadvantaged. For example, individuals disadvantaged on just one indicator were particularly likely to perceive an unsatisfactory neighbourhood. This suggests that neighbourhood-related disadvantage was the form of social exclusion most likely to occur separately from other forms. It is one of the aspects of social exclusion that is particularly difficult to remedy, moving neighbourhoods is one of the few ways, which may explain why it can be experienced in isolation from other forms of disadvantage.

Those who experienced the most severe forms of current multi-dimensional disadvantage (those disadvantaged on three or more indicators) were particularly likely to suffer from mental health problems. This suggests that a deterioration of mental health may accompany disadvantage on a number of other domains. As implied earlier, this form of disadvantage may be an outcome of the onset of other forms of social exclusion (which by definition act as risk factors, along with other features, outlined in Table 4.1, such as living alone).

The analysis presented so far in this section has revealed that multi-dimensional disadvantage was prevalent in British society in the mid-1990s and that there was a relationship between prevalence and type of indicator disadvantaged on. Clearly these findings need more investigation, for example to find out which indicators are associated with each other and to ascertain whether disadvantage on a particular indicator/s points to particular forms of disadvantage.

Thus the objective of the next section is to move from a focus on prevalence to explore in more detail the nature of current multi-dimensional disadvantage.

The overall nature of current multi-dimensional disadvantage

The investigation begins with an examination of the combination of indicators on which those suffering from multi-dimensional disadvantage were particularly likely to be disadvantaged. This commences with an analysis of the links between the seven social exclusion indicators, represented in the form of relative disadvantage ratios.

The relative disadvantage ratio used in this instance measures the link between indicators of social exclusion by presenting the likelihood of experiencing two forms of disadvantage simultaneously, taking into consideration the overall likelihood of disadvantage on each indicator. This is calculated as the ratio of the probability of experiencing one form of disadvantage (measured by the 'target' indicator) given the experience of another (the 'source' indicator), over the overall probability of experiencing the 'target' indicator. Therefore a relative disadvantage ratio of 1.0 means that there was no change in the likelihood of experiencing the 'target' indicator given experiencing the 'source' indicator, a ratio greater than 1.0 means that an individual was more likely than average to have experienced the 'target' indicator if experiencing the 'source' indicator and a ratio less than 1.0 means that an individual was less likely than average to have experienced the 'target' indicator if experiencing the 'source' indicator.

Table 4.4   Relationship[a] between indicators of social exclusion, working-age individuals, BHPS, 1996, relative disadvantage ratios

Target indicator	*Source indicator*						
	Fin	Mat	Hou	Nei	Soc	Phy	Men
Financial	-	**2.0**	**1.6**	**1.4**	**1.4**	**1.6**	**1.4**
Material	**2.0**	-	**2.2**	**1.2**	**1.4**	1.1	1.1
Housing	**1.7**	**2.3**	-	**1.3**	**1.2**	**1.2**	1.1
Neighbourhood	**1.4**	**1.2**	**1.3**	-	**1.2**	**1.2**	**1.4**
Social	**1.5**	**1.4**	**1.2**	**1.3**	-	**1.5**	**1.7**
Physical	**1.6**	1.1	**1.2**	**1.2**	**1.5**	-	**2.3**
Mental	**1.4**	1.1	1.2	**1.4**	**1.8**	**2.3**	-

Note:
[a] Bold text indicates a statistically significant (p<0.05) relationship between the source and target indicator.

The first information to be gleaned from Table 4.4 is that all of the relative disadvantage ratios are greater than one. This indicates that an individual experiencing one form of disadvantage had a greater likelihood (than average) of experiencing another form of disadvantage. This confirms earlier findings that the incidence of disadvantage was not distributed equally in society – those who experienced disadvantage in one domain were likely to have experienced it in another also.

The likelihood of experiencing multi-dimensional disadvantage varies according to the pair of 'source' and 'target' indicators in question. By comparing the magnitude of the relative disadvantage ratios various patterns emerge. For example, taking income poverty as the source indicator reveals high (and statistically significant) relative disadvantage ratios with all other target indicators. This suggests that being income poor can lead to other forms of disadvantage, particularly those that rely heavily on income resources for realization. There is no surprise then that those in income poverty were twice as likely than the average working-age adult to be disadvantaged according to the possession of household material items. Similar patterns emerge between the following indicators; income poverty and housing circumstance, housing circumstance and material possessions, physical health and income poverty, physical health and social relations, mental health and social relations, and mental health and physical health.[6]

<table>
<tr><td>

Group 1
'Household economic deprivation'

- Financial situation
- Material possessions
- Household circumstance

</td><td>

Group 2
'Personal civic exclusion'

- Neighbourhood perception
- Social relations

</td></tr>
<tr><td></td><td>

Group 3
'Personal health exclusion'

- Physical health
- Mental health

</td></tr>
</table>

Figure 4.3   **Multi-dimensional relationship between indicators of social exclusion, working-age adults, BHPS, 1996, based on factor analysis groupings[a]**

Notes:
[a] The Kaiser criterion was used to select factors that explain a greater amount of variance than would be explained by a single indicator. An orthogonal method was used to select factors independent of each other. Figure 4.3 is based on the relationship between each indicator and a number of factors (the factor loadings). The interpretation of a factor is limited to indicators that load in access of 0.3. See Appendix C for further details.

As discussed above, links between the seven indicators of social exclusion are evident. What is also clear from Table 4.4 is that these links are complex. According to Whelan and Whelan (1995) there is the need for conceptual clarity when investigating multi-dimensional disadvantage. They argue that to further an

---

[6] Again it should be noted that these findings suggests only a relationship between pairs of indicators and not information on cause and effect.

investigation of multi-dimensional disadvantage it is necessary to identify distinct patterns of disadvantage associated with particular theoretical concepts. Consequently Figure 4.3 presents an analysis of multi-dimensional disadvantage using exploratory factor analysis. Factor analysis is a technique that identifies underlying variables, or factors, which explain the pattern of association within a set of observed variables (in this case the seven social exclusion indicators). The analysis reveals associations that suggest the formation of groups of distinct concepts.

The factor analysis reveals an overlap among three groups of indicators at a cross-sectional level. Supplementing this analysis with theoretical knowledge discussed in Chapter 2, it is possible to identify three underlying factors of social exclusion. The first factor (Group 1) puts together the primarily 'economic' indicators; financial situation, material possessions and housing circumstance. This factor suggests that an underlying notion of *household economic deprivation* may be present within the indicators. This relationship is acknowledged in other work on multi-dimensional disadvantage. Nolan and Whelan (1996), in particular, suggest that poverty is made up of a number of distinct economic dimensions, including low income and housing deprivation.

The relationships between the indicators, coupled with a theoretical understanding of social exclusion (discussed in Chapter 2), propose two more groups. These groups cover notions of '*personal civic exclusion*' (Group 2), which draws on the relational and communal aspects of exclusion, and includes indicators of social relations and neighbourhood perception, and, '*personal health exclusion*' (Group 3), which includes the indicators of mental health and physical health.[7]

The prevalence and nature of three integral elements of current multi-dimensional disadvantage

The notions of current *household economic deprivation*, current *personal civic exclusion* and current *personal health exclusion* will now be explored in more detail, with particular emphasis on the relationship between each notion and income poverty (often regarded as a cause of various forms of disadvantage). As with earlier analysis, the investigation begins with a focus on the prevalence on each element of social exclusion before shifting attention to identifying the characteristics of individuals most likely to have experienced each form of current multi-dimensional disadvantage.

Current household economic deprivation

Poverty of resources has been the focus of many previous studies of disadvantage. Nolan and Whelan (1996) have been influential in attempts to develop the notion of disadvantage due to lack of resources away from a traditional focus on income

---

[7] Factor analysis confirms that these relationships were found for the majority of waves of available BHPS data (1991-1999) and hence can be attributed to working-age adults in Great Britain in the 1990s (see Appendix C for further details).

poverty. They have moved away from sole concentration on income to also include investigations of non-monetary items, such as material possessions and housing circumstances. According to their conceptualization, the poor were those who have both low levels of income and who suffer deprivation of 'necessary' household items. A similar approach will be used to investigate *household economic deprivation* in this section, using indicators of financial situation, material possessions and housing circumstance. The investigation begins with a focus on the non-monetary indicators of *household economic deprivation*.

Table 4.5   Non-monetary indicators of current *household economic deprivation*, working-age adults, BHPS, 1996, total per cent

Housing circumstance	*Material possessions*	
	Disadvantaged	Not disadvantaged
Disadvantaged	2	9
Not disadvantaged	7	83

Table 4.5 presents the prevalence of disadvantage amongst the working-age population according to material possessions and housing circumstance. The prevalence of disadvantage according to the separate indicators of economic deprivation was illustrated in Table 4.1 (this analysis can be confirmed by adding the appropriate row or column cells in Table 4.5). Table 4.5 shows that, in fact, just over one in six (17 per cent) of working-age adults experienced at least one form of *household economic deprivation* in 1996.[8] What Table 4.5 also provides is the prevalence of simultaneous disadvantage on both indicators. In fact very few, only 2 per cent, of the working-age population were disadvantaged on both the material possessions and housing circumstance indicators (this represents just under one in four of all those lacking material possessions and just under one in five of all those with poor quality housing).

Table 4.6   The prevalence of current *household economic deprivation* including financial situation (income poverty status)**, working-age adults, BHPS, 1996, column per cent** (total per cent in brackets)

Material possessions	*Housing circumstance*	*Financial situation*	
		In poverty	Not in poverty
Disadvantaged			
	Disadvantaged	5 (1)	2 (1)
	Not disadvantaged	13 (2)	6 (5)
Not disadvantaged			
	Disadvantaged	13 (2)	8 (6)
	Not disadvantaged	70 (11)	85 (71)
Base			

---

[8] This percentage is of course not the same as adding the percentage of those disadvantaged on each indicator because some individuals were disadvantaged on both indicators.

According to Nolan and Whelan (1996), it is not sufficient to measure economic deprivation with either non-monetary indicators or income alone, but to adopt a definition that uses both. Consequently Table 4.6 presents the prevalence of non-monetary indicators of economic deprivation by income-poverty status. By adding and comparing the appropriate rows it is clear that income poverty increases the risk of experiencing disadvantage according to both material possessions and housing circumstance (this is also statistically significant) – just under one in five of the income poor suffered from a lack of material possessions and a similar proportion suffered from poor quality housing.

The most extreme form of *household economic deprivation* is measured according to disadvantage on all three indicators. According to the analysis presented in Table 4.6 very few working-age individuals experienced all three forms of economic deprivation simultaneously. Only 1 in 20 income-poor individuals suffered from disadvantage according to both the non-monetary deprivation indicators, just 1 per cent of the whole working-age sample.

The next stage of the investigation is to determine the individuals most at risk of current *household economic deprivation*. Given that only very few working-age adults were disadvantaged on all three indicators it is not possible to investigate the characteristics of these individuals, given the cell size conventions employed in this book.[9] Instead a more lenient definition of current *household economic deprivation* will be employed. Therefore the investigation of the economically deprived will focus on the characteristics of individuals who were income poor *and* disadvantaged on either the material possessions indicator or the housing circumstance indicator. This amounts to almost one-third (31 per cent) of the income poor and one in twenty (5 per cent) of all working-age adults.

Table 4.7 presents logistic regression analysis according to two models. The first model considers the relationship between various socio-demographic characteristics and the likelihood of experiencing *household economic deprivation*. The second model adds to this analysis the individual's disadvantage status on the remaining four indicators of social exclusion, to determine whether they have any additional affect on *household economic deprivation* (and indeed whether they affect the socio-demographic estimates of the first model).

The first model suggests that young adults, lone parents with dependent children, individuals living in households with two or more dependent children, individuals with no academic qualifications, the unemployed and individuals living in households where no one works, were significantly more likely than the respective reference categories to have experienced *household economic deprivation*. Adding the disadvantage status of the other social exclusion indicators reveals that they add nothing significant to the socio-demographic model and make no noticeable difference to the original socio-demographic effects.

---

[9] Even though the logistic regression technique is based on linear models, which does not require such large sample sizes to produce robust results, there are still too few cases for analysis of these multiply disadvantaged individuals.

Table 4.7 **Odds of experiencing current *household economic deprivation*[a] by individual and household socio-demographic characteristic, working-age adults, BHPS, 1996, logistic regression model[b]**

Socio-demographic characteristics	Socio-demographic model	Socio-demographic and indicator model
Sex		
Male	ref	ref
Female	1.1	1.2
Age group		
16-29 years	**2.1**	**1.9**
30-44 years	ref	ref
45-59/64 years	0.8	0.9
Household type		
Single	2.0	2.0
Couple no children	0.6	0.7
Couple, dep children only	ref	ref
Couple, some non-dep children	0.4	0.4
Lone parent, dep children only	**1.7**	**1.7**
Lone parent, some non-dep children	2.2	2.2
Other	1.8	1.4
Number of children		
None	1.3	1.1
One	ref	ref
Two or more	**1.8**	**1.8**
Education level		
Degree or higher	0.7	**0.5**
A-level	1.2	1.2
O-level	ref	ref
CSE level	1.2	1.2
None of these	**1.9**	**1.9**
Main activity status		
Employed full time	0.7	0.7
Employed part time	1.5	1.5
Unemployed	**2.2**	**2.3**
Care of home/family	ref	ref
Education/training	1.2	**1.9**
Other inactive	0.1	0.1
No. in household in employment		
None	**2.4**	**2.3**
One	ref	ref
Two or more	**0.1**	**0.1**

Table 4.7   (continued)

Neighbourhood perception		
Not disadvantaged	ref	ref
Disadvantaged	Not in model	1.1
Social relations		
Not disadvantaged	ref	ref
Disadvantaged	Not in model	1.0
Physical health		
Not disadvantaged	ref	ref
Disadvantaged	Not in model	1.1
Mental health		
Not disadvantaged	ref	ref
Disadvantaged	Not in model	0.9

Notes:

[a] *Household economic deprivation* is defined as individuals who were income poor *and* who were disadvantaged on either the material possessions indicator or the housing circumstance indicator.

[b] Odds ratios higher (lower) than 1 imply that the socio-demographic characteristic is associated with an increased (decreased) odds of experiencing the event (*household economic deprivation*) compared to the reference category (ref). Bold text indicates a statistically significant (p<0.05) coefficient.

Comparing the analysis in Table 4.7 to the analysis of the component models of *household economic deprivation* (financial situation, material possessions and housing circumstance) detailed in Table 4.1, reveals similar estimates. It is apparent however, that for those who experienced current one-dimensional economic deprivation certain characteristics were linked to multi-dimensional economic disadvantage – most notable being a lone parent with dependent children, having no academic qualifications and being unemployed.

Current personal civic exclusion

This section moves away from a focus on a purely economic notion of deprivation to consider the notion of *personal civic exclusion*. According to Room (Ed. 1995, 1998, 2000) the analysis of relational aspects of disadvantage are crucial to an investigation of social exclusion. Although the correlation analysis in Table 4.4 did not produce a definitive relationship between the indicators of neighbourhood perception and social relations, the factor analysis loadings (see Appendix C) did suggest the grouping of these indicators. In any case it is reasonable to suggest that both contribute to a notion of *personal civic exclusion*. In particular an individual's social relationships were likely to contribute much to their perception of their neighbourhood and their feeling of inclusion, and vice-versa (see the work of Mumford (2001) for evidence of this in British society).

Table 4.8 **The prevalence of current** *personal civic exclusion*, **working-age adults, BHPS, 1996, total per cent**

Social relations	Neighbourhood perception	
	Disadvantaged	Not disadvantaged
Disadvantaged	2	8
Not disadvantaged	10	81

Table 4.8 considers the prevalence of *personal civic exclusion* according to the relationship between indicators of neighbourhood perception and social relations. Just under one in five (19 per cent) of working-age adults experienced at least one form of *personal civic exclusion* in 1996. As with an analysis of *household economic deprivation*, very few individuals (only 2 per cent) experienced disadvantage according to both the neighbourhood perception and social relation indicators. Before investigating the characteristics of the individuals who suffer from this simultaneous exclusion, the relationship between indicators of civic exclusion and income poverty, possibly a crucial factor in the acquisition of civic resources, is explored.

Table 4.9 **The prevalence of current** *personal civic exclusion* **by income poverty status, working-age adults, BHPS, 1996, column per cent** (total per cent in brackets)

Neighbourhood perception	Social relations	Financial situation	
		In poverty	Not in poverty
Disadvantaged			
	Disadvantaged	3 (1)	1 (1)
	Not disadvantaged	13 (2)	9 (8)
Not disadvantaged			
	Disadvantaged	11 (2)	7 (6)
	Not disadvantaged	74 (11)	82 (70)

In Table 4.4 income poverty was seen to have a positive and statistically significant relationship with all of the other indicators of social exclusion.[10] This is confirmed in Table 4.9 for civic exclusion. Those in income poverty were more likely, than those not, to have experienced disadvantage according to indicators of neighbourhood perception and social relations. In terms of multi-dimensional disadvantage, the income poor were three times more likely to have experienced simultaneous disadvantage on both indicators, although the prevalence of such disadvantage was still very low.

---

[10] However, this relationship is not evident when other socio-demographic characteristics are taken into consideration, see Table 4.10 below.

Table 4.10 considers the relationship between socio-demographic characteristics and the odds of experiencing *personal civic exclusion* (defined as simultaneous disadvantage on both the neighbourhood perception and social relations indicators). As with Table 4.7, the analysis uses two models, the second of which includes the individual's disadvantage status on the remaining five indicators of social exclusion.

Table 4.10   Odds of experiencing current *personal civic exclusion*[a] by individual and household socio-demographic characteristic, working-age adults, BHPS, 1996, logistic regression model[b]

Socio-demographic characteristics	Socio-demographic model	Socio-demographic and indicator model
Sex		
Male	ref	ref
Female	**0.4**	**0.4**
Age group		
16-29 years	1.1	1.2
30-44 years	ref	ref
45-59/64 years	1.1	1.2
Household type		
Single	3.9	3.3
Couple no children	2.0	1.9
Couple, dep children only	ref	ref
Couple, some non-dep children	3.6	3.6
Lone parent, dep children only	1.5	1.3
Lone parent, some non-dep children	**6.7**	**5.5**
Other	3.6	3.2
Number of children		
None	0.3	0.3
One	ref	ref
Two or more	1.2	1.1
Education level		
Degree or higher	0.7	0.8
A-level	0.6	0.6
O-level	ref	ref
CSE level	1.8	1.8
None of these	1.5	1.2
Main activity status		
Employed full time	0.7	1.0
Employed part time	0.0	0.0
Unemployed	2.1	**2.4**
Care of home/family	ref	ref
Education/training	1.1	1.6
Other inactive	0.0	0.0

Table 4.10   (continued)

Number in household in employment		
None	1.3	1.1
One	ref	ref
Two or more	0.9	0.9
Financial situation		
Not disadvantaged	ref	ref
Disadvantaged	Not in model	1.3
Material possessions		
Not disadvantaged	ref	ref
Disadvantaged	Not in model	1.2
Housing circumstance		
Not disadvantaged	ref	ref
Disadvantaged	Not in model	**1.7**
Physical health		
Not disadvantaged	ref	ref
Disadvantaged	Not in model	**2.4**
Mental health		
Not disadvantaged	ref	ref
Disadvantaged	Not in model	1.4

Notes:
[a] *Personal civic exclusion* is defined as individuals who experience disadvantage on the neighbourhood perception indicator *and* the social relations indicator.
[b] Odds ratios higher (lower) than 1 imply that the socio-demographic characteristic is associated with an increased (decreased) odds of experiencing the event (*personal civic exclusion*) compared to the reference category (ref). Bold text indicates a statistically significant ($p<0.05$) coefficient.

The logistic regression analysis in Table 4.10 reveals that, for the socio-demographic model, lone-parents with dependent children have odds of civic exclusion almost seven times as high as the reference category (couple with dependent children only). The analysis shows that females were significantly less likely than males to have experienced civic exclusion. This could be driven by the fact that females were less likely to lack social relations (illustrated in Table 4.1). However as lone parents disproportionately tend to be female, civic exclusion can be found amongst this distinct subset of females.

The introduction of the other five indicators of social exclusion into the regression model shows that housing circumstance and physical health play a role in the civic exclusion experience. Disadvantage on either of these indicators suggests that civic exclusion was more likely to occur. There are a number of reasons to suggest why this may be so. Having poor quality housing was likely to adversely affect neighbourhood perception, particularly if poor quality housing was widespread in the area, and may also reduce confidence in harbouring social events. Likewise, physical exclusion can limit an individual's ability to socialize outside the household. The capacity to attend social activities outside the household was limited even further if the neighbourhood fails to provide adequate access to local services and amenities, something that was likely to result in a negative perception of the neighbourhood and local surroundings. Also, the model suggests that income poverty was not significantly associated with *personal civic exclusion* when other economic and socio-demographic factors are taken into account (this finding has been replicated in a number of other studies, for example Perri 6, 1997 and Gallie and Paugam, Eds. 2000).

Current personal health exclusion

There has been a large amount of research on the relationship between ill health and inequality, much of which has demonstrated that social and economic circumstances are strongly related to morbidity and mortality (Link and Phelan, 1995; Webb, 1995; Davey Smith et al, 1997; Lynch and Kaplan, 1997). Consequently, in this research ill health (both physical and mental) is used primarily as an outcome indicator that contributes to a notion of social exclusion. To be in physical ill health and/or to be in mental ill health suggests an individual who was in the process of being shut out, fully or partially, from the systems that determine the social integration of a person in society. For example, being in poor physical health can mean exclusion from various social systems including education, employment and housing. An investigation of *personal health exclusion* begins with an examination of the prevalence of current *personal health exclusion* in Great Britain in the mid-1990s.

Table 4.11   The prevalence of current *personal health exclusion*, working-age adults, BHPS, 1996, total per cent

Mental health	Physical health	
	Disadvantaged	Not disadvantaged
Disadvantaged	3	7
Not disadvantaged	11	79

Over one in five (21 per cent) working-age adults experienced a form of *personal health exclusion* in 1996. According to the correlation analysis presented in Table 4.1 the relationship between physical and mental health disadvantage was the strongest amongst the seven social exclusion indicators. Almost one-third of all those with poor mental health were also experiencing poor physical health and just over one-fifth of all those in physical ill health also had poor mental health (derived from Table 4.11). This suggests that although the two indicators are measuring very different notions of health, both quite strictly defined in this study, there is noticeable association between the two conditions.

Despite the relatively high correlation between the two health indicators, there were actually very few working-age individuals experiencing simultaneous disadvantage. Only 3 per cent of the working-age population experienced health disadvantage on both the physical and mental health indicators. The characteristics of these individuals will be examined in later analysis. Before that, the investigation concentrates on the relationship between health and income poverty.

Table 4.12 **The prevalence of indicators of current** *personal health exclusion* **by income poverty status, working-age adults, BHPS, 1996, column per cent** (total per cent in brackets)

Physical health	Mental health	Financial situation	
		In poverty	Not in poverty
Disadvantaged			
	Disadvantaged	7 (1)	3 (2)
	Not disadvantaged	16 (3)	10 (9)
Not disadvantaged			
	Disadvantaged	8 (1)	7 (6)
	Not disadvantaged	69 (11)	80 (67)

Table 4.12 presents the prevalence of indicators of *personal health exclusion* by income poverty status. On average, working-age individuals who experienced income poverty were around one and a half times as likely as those not in poverty to have experienced either form of health problem. The difference between the poor and non poor intensifies when the combined health exclusion measure is used – the income poor were over twice as likely as the non income poor to have experienced disadvantage on both health indicators simultaneously. An indicator of income poverty is used in the second model of the logistic regression analysis below to assess whether the relationship with *personal health exclusion* holds when other variables are taken into account.

Table 4.13 **Odds of experiencing current** *personal health exclusion*[a] **by individual and household socio-demographic characteristic, working-age adults, BHPS, 1996, regression model odds**[b]

Socio-demographic characteristics[c]	Socio-demographic model	Socio-demographic and indicator model
Sex		
Male	ref	ref
Female	**1.3**	**1.4**
Age group		
16-29 years	0.7	**0.6**
30-44 years	ref	ref
45-59/64 years	1.3	1.3

Table 4.13   (continued)

Household type		
Single	1.4	1.2
Couple no children	0.8	0.8
Couple, dep children only	ref	ref
Couple, some non-dep children	0.6	0.6
Lone parent, dep children only	1.4	1.0
Lone parent, some non-dep children	0.7	0.6
Other	0.8	0.8
Number of children		
None	1.3	1.4
One	ref	ref
Two or more	1.1	0.9
Education level		
Degree or higher	1.2	1.4
A-level	1.0	1.2
O-level	ref	ref
CSE level	1.7	1.7
None of these	**2.4**	**2.0**
Financial situation		
Not disadvantaged	ref	ref
Disadvantaged	Not in model	**2.1**
Material possessions		
Not disadvantaged	ref	ref
Disadvantaged	Not in model	0.7
Housing circumstance		
Not disadvantaged	ref	ref
Disadvantaged	Not in model	1.3
Neighbourhood perception		
Not disadvantaged	ref	ref
Disadvantaged	Not in model	1.4
Social relations		
Not disadvantaged	ref	ref
Disadvantaged	Not in model	**2.6**

Notes:
[a] *Personal health exclusion* is defined as individuals who experience disadvantage on the physical health indicator *and* the mental health indicator.
[b] Odds ratios higher (lower) than 1 imply that the socio-demographic characteristic is associated with an increased (decreased) odds of experiencing the event (*personal health exclusion*) compared to the reference category (ref). Bold text indicates a statistically significant (p<0.05) coefficient.
[c] Main activity status is excluded from the analysis as most people with poor physical health looked after the home or family, or were in the other inactive category.

The socio-demographic model suggests that certain socio-demographic characteristics show a significant increase in the odds of experiencing *personal health exclusion* over the reference category. Being female and having no academic education qualifications increases the odds by a factor of 1.3 and 2.4 respectively. In the one-dimensional disadvantage models (see Table 4.1) being female was associated with an increased odds of mental ill health, although perhaps a consequence of females being more likely to acknowledge such problems, whilst having no academic qualifications was linked to an increased odds of physical ill health, perhaps a result of these individuals having labour-intensive manual jobs.

Introducing the other five social exclusion indicators maintains the effects of these two socio-demographic characteristics, whilst establishing the fact that young adults were less likely to become ill. Being in income poverty significantly increases the likelihood of experiencing *personal health exclusion*, confirming the interest in the association between low income and health. The social relations indicator suggests that those who lack social companionship were more likely to have experienced *personal health exclusion* also. This may be a consequence of those with physical health being unable to travel to meet friends and family, whilst those without social contact being likely to harbour feelings of isolation and distress.

Identifying comprehensive forms of current multi-dimensional disadvantage

The final section in this chapter focuses on identifying individuals who experienced the most wide-ranging forms of current multi-dimensional disadvantage. Previous analysis in this chapter has revealed that no individuals experienced disadvantage on all seven social exclusion indicators (in fact only 7 per cent did so on three indicators or more). This however does not mean that multi-dimensional disadvantage was not a problem in British society in the 1990s. As the indicators selected for this study are each strict measures of distinct aspects of social exclusion, to be excluded on any more than one indicator signifies quite extreme forms of simultaneous distress.

There are a number of methods that could be used to identify the most extreme forms of simultaneous distress in British society in the 1990s. For example, individuals who were disadvantaged on the most number of indicators could be singled out as experiencing the most severe multi-dimensional disadvantage. However, previous analysis in this chapter, particularly the identification of distinct integral elements of social exclusion – *household economic deprivation, personal civic exclusion* and *personal health exclusion* – suggests a measure that identifies individuals who experienced at least one form of disadvantage on all three of these notions. Table 4.14 examines the association between these three elements by presenting bivariate and three-way relationships.

Table 4.14   The prevalence of comprehensive current multi-dimensional disadvantage, working-age adults, BHPS, 1996, total per cent

Personal civic exclusion[a]	Personal health exclusion[b]	Household economic deprivation[c]	
		Disadvantaged	Not disadvantaged
Disadvantaged			
	Disadvantaged	3	4
	Not disadvantaged	5	8
Not disadvantaged			
	Disadvantaged	5	11
	Not disadvantaged	16	49

Notes:
[a] *Household economic deprivation* is defined as individuals who experience disadvantage on the financial situation indicator or the material possessions indicator or the housing circumstance indicator.
[b] *Personal civic exclusion* is defined as individuals who experience disadvantage on the neighbourhood perception indicator or the social relations indicator.
[c] *Personal health exclusion* is defined as individuals who experience disadvantage on the physical health indicator or the mental health indicator.

Table 4.14 partitions the entire working-age population into eight sections according to the relationship between the three integral elements of social exclusion, ranging from those who were not disadvantaged on any of the three elements to those who were disadvantaged on all three. As revealed in Figure 4.1 almost half of the working-age population (49 per cent) were not disadvantaged on any of the seven social exclusion indicators (and therefore, of course, not disadvantaged on any of the three integral elements of social exclusion).

Fourteen per cent of the sample was disadvantaged on two of the elements of social exclusion. Assuming that each of the seven indicators adequately portray the associated notion of social exclusion, this suggests a considerable amount of multi-dimensional and wide-ranging disadvantage. The most extreme form of wide-ranging multi-dimensional disadvantage presented reveals that 3 per cent of working-age individuals experienced disadvantage on at least one indicator in all three of the integral elements of social exclusion. The characteristics of these individuals, and those who experienced each two-way combination, are investigated in Table 4.15.

Table 4.15 Odds[a] of experiencing current comprehensive multi-dimensional disadvantage by individual and household socio-demographic characteristic, working-age adults, BHPS, 1996, logistic regression model

| Socio-demographic characteristic | Multi-dimensional disadvantage models[b] | | | |
	HED and PCE	HED and PHE	PCE and PHE	HED and PCE and PHE
Sex				
Male	ref	ref	ref	ref
Female	**0.7**	1.2	1.0	0.8
Age group				
16-29 years	**1.5**	1.1	1.1	1.5
30-44 years	ref	ref	ref	ref
45-59/64 years	0.7	1.1	1.1	0.8
Household type				
Single	**3.6**	1.5	2.0	3.1
Couple no children	1.6	0.6	1.2	0.9
Couple, dep children only	ref	ref	ref	ref
Couple, some non-dep children	1.2	0.4	1.2	0.4
Lone parent, dep children only	**1.9**	1.4	**2.3**	**3.2**
Lone parent, some non-dep children	**2.9**	0.4	1.4	1.2
Other	**3.9**	0.9	**3.0**	2.1
Number of children				
None	0.5	1.4	0.8	1.1
One	ref	ref	ref	ref
Two or more	1.1	1.3	1.0	1.5
Education level				
Degree or higher	**0.6**	0.8	0.9	**0.3**
A-level	0.9	1.1	1.1	1.0
O-level	ref	ref	ref	ref
CSE level	1.1	1.3	1.0	1.4
None of these	**2.0**	**1.9**	**1.8**	**2.2**
Main activity status				
Employed full time	0.9	**0.4**	**0.4**	**0.3**
Employed part time	1.1	0.8	**0.5**	0.6
Unemployed	**1.8**	0.9	0.9	0.5
Care of home/family	ref	ref	ref	Ref
Education/training	1.0	**0.3**	**0.4**	0.5
Other inactive	0.1	0.0	2.4	0.0
No. in household in employment				
None	**1.7**	**1.9**	1.2	1.4
One	ref	ref	ref	Ref
Two or more	**0.4**	**0.5**	1.0	0.7

Table 4.15   (continued)

Financial situation				
Not disadvantaged	---	---	ref	---
Disadvantaged	---	---	1.0	---
Material possessions				
Not disadvantaged	---	---	ref	---
Disadvantaged	---	---	0.9	---
Housing circumstance				
Not disadvantaged	---	---	ref	---
Disadvantaged	---	---	1.2	---
Neighbourhood perception				
Not disadvantaged	---	ref	---	---
Disadvantaged	---	1.2	---	---
Social relations				
Not disadvantaged	---	ref	---	---
Disadvantaged	---	**1.6**	---	---
Physical health				
Not disadvantaged	ref	---	---	---
Disadvantaged	1.2	---	---	---
Mental health				
Not disadvantaged	ref	---	---	---
Disadvantaged	**1.4**	---	---	---

Notes:
[a] Odds ratios higher (lower) than 1 imply that the socio-demographic characteristic is associated with an increased (decreased) odds of experiencing the event compared to the reference category (ref). Bold text indicates a statistically significant ($p<0.05$) coefficient.
[b] *Household economic deprivation* (HED) is defined as individuals who experience disadvantage on the financial situation indicator or the material possessions indicator or the housing circumstance indicator. *Personal civic exclusion* (PCE) is defined as individuals who experience disadvantage on the neighbourhood perception indicator or the social relations indicator. *Personal health exclusion* (PHE) is defined as individuals who experience disadvantage on the physical health indicator or the mental health indicator.

Earlier, Table 4.1 revealed that certain socio-demographic characteristics were associated with the experience of current one-dimensional aspects of social exclusion. Tables 4.7, 4.10 and 4.13 explored the relationship between socio-demographic characteristics (and social exclusion indicators) and the most severe form of multi-dimensional disadvantage within each of the three integral elements of social exclusion – *household economic deprivation*, *personal civic exclusion* and *personal health exclusion* respectively. Table 4.15 investigates whether these associations hold when multi-dimensional disadvantage on more than one of these three elements of social exclusion exists. The analysis in Table 4.15 is split into four sections detailing the three two-way combinations of disadvantage and the comprehensive three-way measure of multi-dimensional disadvantage.

The analysis begins with individuals disadvantaged simultaneously on at least one indicator of *household economic deprivation* and on at least one indicator of *personal civic exclusion*. Table 4.7 showed that young adults, lone parents with dependent children, the unemployed, individuals in education or training and individuals living in households where no one works (in particular) were significantly associated with an increased odds (compared with the reference group) of experiencing *household economic deprivation*. Likewise, according to Table 4.10, males, lone parents with dependent children (in particular), the unemployed, individuals living in poor housing and individuals with poor physical health were significantly associated with an increased odds of experiencing *personal civic exclusion*. As Table 4.15 shows, much of these associations remain when focusing on those who experienced both forms of disadvantage, particularly being male, a lone parent with dependent children, having no academic education, unemployed and having no workers in the household. Other individuals were significantly associated with an increased odds of simultaneous disadvantage, such as being young, those living alone, lone parents with some non-dependent children, those living in 'other' households (likely to be students and others sharing with non-related adults) and those with mental health problems. The analysis suggests, quite understandably, that those living alone were particularly likely to have experienced forms of *household economic deprivation* and *personal civic exclusion* simultaneously. Factors significantly associated with the avoidance of this pattern of multi-dimensional disadvantage are being female, having a high education level and living in a household with two or more workers.

The second analysis column of Table 4.15 considers the characteristics of individuals who experienced both a form of *household economic deprivation* and *personal health exclusion*. According to Table 4.13 individual characteristics linked to the experience of both physical and mental ill health are being female, having no academic education, suffering from income poverty and lacking social relations. Certain of the characteristics associated with these individual measures of disadvantage – having no academic qualifications, living in a household where no one works and lacking social relations – are linked to simultaneous disadvantage on both these elements of social exclusion. Factors significantly associated with the avoidance of this pattern of multi-dimensional disadvantage are being in full-time employment or education or training and living in a household with two or more workers.

The third part of this analysis concentrates on those individuals who did not experience any form of *household economic deprivation* but instead were disadvantaged on at least one aspect of both *personal civic exclusion* and *personal health exclusion*. These individuals tend to be lone parents with some non-dependent children, those living in 'other' households (likely to be students and others sharing with non-related adults) and those with no academic qualifications. Factors significantly associated with the avoidance of this pattern of multi-dimensional disadvantage are being employed, either full- or part-time, and being in education or training.

The final column in Table 4.15 identifies individuals who suffer the most wide-ranging forms of current multi-dimensional disadvantage in British society – disadvantage on at least one aspect of all three integral elements of social exclusion. The analysis suggests just two groups of individuals particularly likely to suffer such experiences – lone parents with dependent children and those with no academic qualifications. The analysis also suggests two factors significantly associated with the avoidance of such wide-ranging multi-dimensional disadvantage, being employed full-time and having degree-level or higher education. It is noticeable that both of these factors are seen to be at the forefront of much of New Labour's policies aimed at the prevention of social exclusion.

Conclusion

Even though most analysts would now concede that disadvantage should be conceptualized using a multitude of outcome measures, it is still striking that it is generally operationalized through relative income measures alone (Layte et al, 2000). Room (Ed. 1995, 1998, 2000) has emphasized the need for empirical studies of social exclusion to shift from a focus on one-dimension of disadvantage (most commonly financial hardship) to a focus on a number of dimensions, including aspects of relational and neighbourhood-related disadvantage. This chapter has implemented this theory in an investigation of the prevalence and nature of current multi-dimensional disadvantage in Great Britain using data from the 1996 wave of the BHPS. The analysis has shown that such an approach is useful in attempts to understand the heterogeneity of disadvantage and to identify individuals at most risk.

The chapter began with an analysis of models of current one-dimensional disadvantage. In this analysis, a measure of income poverty was adopted – the most common measure of disadvantage in studies to date. The analysis suggested approximately one in six working-age adults lived below the poverty line in Great Britain in the mid-1990s and that a variety of characteristics disproportionately increased the odds of being income poor – including being young, living in a lone parent household, having two or more dependent children, having very low or no education, being out of work and living in a household where no one works. When different dimensions of social exclusion are the focus of investigation these findings alter. This suggests that a diverse range of disadvantage was prevalent in British society to varying extent, which affected particular subgroups of the working-age population in different ways.

The chapter has gone on to show the usefulness of adopting a multi-dimensional approach to measuring disadvantage. Although individuals were unlikely to be disadvantaged on a large number of indicators of social exclusion, there were substantial instances of individuals experiencing multi-dimensional disadvantage (made even more serious by the fact that the seven indicators reflect quite distinct and severe forms of current disadvantage). An analysis of the relationship between the indicators revealed three distinctive and integral elements of disadvantage – *household economic deprivation*, *personal civic exclusion* and *personal health exclusion*. Again different proportions and characteristics of individuals are linked to disadvantage according to these different dimensions and when measures of simultaneous disadvantage on these were constructed the findings altered again (albeit only slightly).

In general experiences of *household economic deprivation* were linked most heavily to being out of work and living in households where no one worked, employment being the most obvious way of attaining and accumulating economic resources. The groups of individuals most likely to have faced such disadvantage were lone parents, households with children and those living alone, each of which may find obstacles to work (for example childcare) and/or have no other potential workers to rely on and/or have to provide for other non-working household members (for example children).

To understand the other, non-economic related elements of social exclusion a different perspective has to be taken. The experience of *personal civic exclusion* was most heavily linked to being unemployed, with lone parents with dependent children and the physically ill most prone (probably linked to an inability to meet others, due to the responsibilities of having children and a lack of mobility). The experience of *personal health exclusion* was associated with being income poor (probably a reflection of the inability to work and consequently the reliance on health-related benefits) and having a low education (perhaps linked to the likelihood of previous or current physically demanding manual employment). Many of these associations continued when the experience of disadvantage according to two of these three integral elements of social exclusion was examined.

The measure of the most wide-ranging multi-dimensional disadvantage, that is disadvantage on at least one indicator in all three of the integral elements of social exclusion, revealed only a very small subset of afflicted individuals – approximately 3 per cent of the whole working-age population. Education level was a good predictor of wide-ranging disadvantage – those with a degree or higher education were disproportionately likely to avoid such experiences, the opposite being the case for those with no academic education at all. Having a full-time job also suggests the avoidance of such widespread forms of disadvantage. The sub-group of the working-age population most prone to such experiences were lone parents with dependent children. The fact that this analysis has discovered some individuals, albeit a minority, who experienced multi-dimensional disadvantage suggests that welfare policies were inefficient in certain areas. The methodology employed to identify such individuals means that these areas can be identified, as can the factors that increase the likelihood of escaping such situations.

Alongside recommendations for a shift from one-dimensional to multi-dimensional measures of social exclusion, the theoretical discussion in Chapter 2 outlined the need for a consideration of the longitudinal nature of disadvantage. For many communities, households and individuals, resources are accumulated and eroded over time, thus cross-sectional measures may fail to distinguish between those with similar current levels of a resource but different histories. Such analysis is crucial in attempts to identify and understand the true nature of social exclusion. The following chapter makes use of the panel element of the BHPS to investigate in detail the longitudinal nature of social exclusion that implies multi-dimensional and longitudinal disadvantage. In particular, models of persistent one-dimensional disadvantage are used to explore longitudinal patterns of disadvantage over nine waves of BHPS data and to compare current and persistent forms of disadvantage.

Chapter 5

Investigating the Longitudinal Nature of Social Exclusion in Great Britain

> ... time seldom features in debates about poverty ... without taking time into account it is impossible to fully appreciate the nature and experience of poverty or truly understand the level of suffering involved. Equally, it is impossible to develop policies that successfully tackle the multiple causes of the problem or offer lasting solutions (Walker and Ashworth, 1994, p. 1).

Introduction

The experience of poverty, and social exclusion, is largely determined by the structure of disadvantage, its distribution within society and over time. As Room (Ed. 1995, 1998, 2000) points out, recent advances in the study of social exclusion have seen a shift from static to dynamic analysis. Important insights into the nature of social exclusion can result from making time explicit in the conceptualization, definition and measurement of the concept (Walker, 1995).

The previous chapter emphasized the advantages of using a number of aspects of economic, personal and social life to be able to adequately measure and understand social exclusion, making use of models of current multi-dimensional disadvantage. This chapter utilizes the panel element of the BHPS to investigate the longitudinal nature of social exclusion in Great Britain, paying particular attention to the prevalence and nature of the most persistent forms of disadvantage in British society during the 1990s.

The chapter begins with an examination of trends in point-in-time indicators of social exclusion over the range of available BHPS data, using the survey as a series of cross-sections covering the years 1991 to 1999. This analysis provides a useful insight into the occurrence and magnitude of each dimension of social exclusion over time and how trends have affected particular 'at risk' population sub-groups (identified in models of current one-dimensional disadvantage in Chapter 4).

Analysis of aggregate changes in social exclusion indicators cannot provide information on the timing and duration of such experiences, crucial to an understanding of the longitudinal nature of social exclusion. Consequently empirical investigations move on to fully utilize the panel element of the BHPS. A sample of working-age adults present in all nine waves of the BHPS is selected and validated. Analysis of the panel sample begins with a focus on models of persistent one-dimensional disadvantage. Descriptive statistics are presented on the overall duration of disadvantage over the nine observations, the number of spells of disadvantage and the average duration by the total number of spells. Longitudinal patterns of disadvantage are developed for each of the separate social exclusion indicators using techniques only previously applied in studies of income poverty. Models of persistent one-dimensional disadvantage also provide background information to construct and fully explore models of longitudinal multi-dimensional used to identify social exclusion in the following chapter.

Aggregate levels of current one-dimensional disadvantage in Great Britain during the 1990s

In Chapter 3 the 1996 wave of the BHPS was used to construct and validate the seven indicators of social exclusion. The indicators provided a snap shot of the extent of disadvantage in Great Britain in the mid-1990s, according to models of current one-dimensional disadvantage. As the BHPS is a continuous survey, with questions replicated throughout, the indicators can be constructed in every wave to illustrate trends in the incidence of indicators of social exclusion in Great Britain during the decade. This provides important background information that can be used to interpret the behaviour of indicators of longitudinal disadvantage, set up later in this chapter. The incidence of each social exclusion indicator in Great Britain between 1991 and 1999 is presented in Figure 5.1.

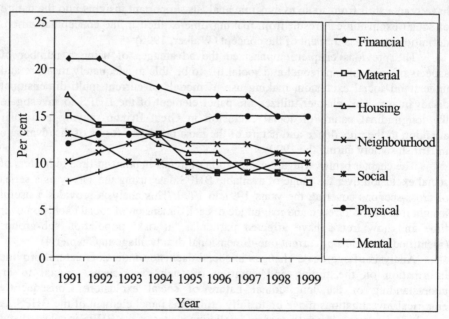

Figure 5.1   Trends in aggregate levels of current one-dimensional disadvantage in Great Britain in the 1990s, working-age adults, BHPS, 1991-1999

Figure 5.1 presents a graphical representation of trends in the seven social exclusion indicators for Great Britain in the 1990s. As the indicators were constructed as absolute measures, Figure 5.1 displays actual changes in living conditions and experiences. The three economic indicators (financial situation, material possessions and housing circumstance) showed a marked decline over the decade, clearly reflecting the prosperous condition of the British economy of the 1990s. Each of the three indicators showed a decline of at least five percentage points over the period.

Three of the indicators (neighbourhood perception, social relations and mental health) showed some variation but generally remained fairly constant. In the latter stages of the decade the neighbourhood perception and social relations indicators remained stable after an initial shift in incidence in the early 1990s (upwards for neighbourhood perception and downwards for social relations). The incidence of mental health increased in the early 1990s but after a period of stability decreased to the same degree at the end of the decade. The last of the seven indicators – physical health – was the only indicator to increase during the decade. In 1991, 12 per cent of working-age adults had physical health problems and this had risen to 15 per cent by the end of the decade.

Cross-sectional surveys, or panel data set up as a series of cross-sections, are often used in an analysis of aggregate change at the level of population sub-groups (for example, see Dirven and Berghman, 1991). Whereas Figure 5.1 presented trends in the aggregate levels of indicators of social exclusion, an analysis by population sub-group can reveal whether these trends hold according to individual characteristics or whether there was mobility between disadvantage statuses. Table 5.1 illustrates such analyses for each of the seven social exclusion indicators taking various risk groups, gleaned from the analysis of models of current one-dimensional disadvantage in Table 4.1, as examples of population sub-groups.

Table 5.1   **Trends in indicators of current one-dimensional disadvantage by selected socio-demographic risk groups, working-age adults, BHPS, 1991-1999, cell per cent**

High risk group by indicator excluded on	Wave								
	91	92	93	94	95	96	97	98	99
Financial situation									
All	21	21	20	19	17	17	17	15	15
Lone parent all dep ch	57	55	55	52	51	48	54	47	42
Two or more dep ch	32	36	33	33	27	27	27	24	24
Unemployed	63	64	60	57	56	56	61	63	65
No one in hhold works	72	68	67	64	64	63	63	63	59

Table 5.1   (continued)

Material possessions									
All	15	14	14	13	10	9	10	9	8
Lives alone	52	50	50	48	42	38	39	37	35
No academic educ	17	14	14	16	11	10	11	9	9
Unemployed	28	22	26	20	14	17	19	24	19
No one in hhold works	38	36	36	30	25	23	21	20	18
Housing circumstance									
All	17	14	14	12	11	11	9	9	9
Lives alone	24	21	23	21	20	19	16	16	13
No academic educ	21	18	17	15	15	13	13	12	11
Unemployed	28	23	23	21	18	17	12	14	17
No one in hhold works	29	23	19	20	18	16	13	14	12
Neighbrhd perception									
All	10	11	12	13	12	12	12	11	11
Aged 16-29 years	12	14	14	15	14	15	14	14	15
Lone parent all dep ch	18	18	18	15	19	15	18	15	18
No academic educ	11	13	14	15	16	15	16	14	13
Unemployed	18	17	18	19	19	25	[15]	17	18
Social relations									
All	13	12	10	10	9	9	9	10	10
Lives alone	22	20	15	14	13	14	10	12	14
Couple non-dep ch	9	10	10	9	9	9	9	9	9
No academic educ	16	15	13	13	12	13	12	12	12
No one in hhold works	22	19	16	14	16	17	13	12	14
Physical health									
All	12	13	13	13	14	15	15	15	15
Aged 45-59/64 years	21	21	23	23	23	25	25	24	22
Lives alone	19	20	17	16	17	20	19	22	21
No academic educ	20	22	23	22	25	27	29	28	28
No one in hhold works	26	28	28	28	31	34	36	36	38
Mental health									
All	8	9	10	10	10	10	10	11	10
Female	9	11	12	12	13	13	13	13	13
Lives alone	12	14	12	11	15	15	13	16	14
Lone parent all dep ch	14	16	16	15	18	18	18	18	16
Two or more dep ch	7	9	10	10	10	12	11	12	10

Although only selected socio-demographic groups have been used in Table 5.1, albeit groups with a particularly high risk of current one-dimensional disadvantage, it is clear to see how a breakdown by population group can aid interpretation of aggregate trends. For instance, trends for all three economic indicators experienced an aggregate decline. These appear consistent when taking socio-demographic characteristic into account, with a few exceptions. For example during the latter years of the 1990s, when income poverty rates were fairly stable, the rates for the unemployed increased. This was the case for none of the other selected risk groups (although the rates for lone parents did increase between 1996 and 1997). The unemployed also failed to follow the aggregate trend for the material possessions indicator, although by the end of the decade they had experienced a significant decline in incidence.

The other indicators tend to show less aggregate change over the decade, although there are still some noticeable differences in trends between the risk groups. For example, for those with no academic qualifications and those who lived in a household where no one works, the incidence of ill health increased quite substantially during the 1990s, much more so than other high-risk groups such as those aged 45 to retirement age and those living alone.

The above analysis, based on repeated cross-sections of the BHPS, has provided an insight into the aggregate change of social exclusion indicators at a national level and broken down by social sub-groups. An investigation of the longitudinal nature of social exclusion requires analysis of mobility patterns at the individual level to determine the patterns and prevalence of disadvantage. Individual patterns will be influenced in part by aggregate changes at national and sub-group levels. For example, if national income poverty rates decrease, and this is constant amongst population sub-groups, the chances of exiting or avoiding income poverty will increase at an individual level.

To perform a longitudinal analysis on the social exclusion indicators the panel element of the BHPS needs to be utilized. The next section details the selection and validation of a longitudinal sample of working-age adults, on whom such analysis will be performed in the remainder of this, and the following, chapter.

Selecting and validating the longitudinal sample

To enable longitudinal analysis to be performed, a longitudinal sample of working-age individuals was selected. Individuals rather than households were selected in the longitudinal sample because, although household level information can be assembled as an associated characteristic of an individual and analysed in its own right at a cross-sectional level, it is not possible to look at wave-to-wave transitions affecting whole households. This is because a household can change, and therefore not explicitly exist, from one wave to the next. A household that contains individuals who separate, have children, or die, for example, is not the same entity before and after such an event.

By choosing to analyse nine waves of the BHPS data it is possible to present a broad picture of social change in Great Britain during the 1990s. For an individual to be selected in the longitudinal sample they must have been present, and of working age, in all nine waves of the survey. To minimize missing data it is important that each member of the longitudinal sample completed a full individual interview and lived in a household where a full household interview was completed also, in every wave of the survey. This ensures a continuous flow of multi-dimensional and longitudinal data. Analysis becomes complicated and of less value if gaps appear in the longitudinal array of data (when imputation of missing data and techniques to account for such modifications is often required, something beyond the scope of this research). Table 5.2 presents statistics on the construction of the working-age longitudinal sample.

Table 5.2   Longitudinal sample construction, working-age adults with full
             individual and household interviews, BHPS, 1991-1999,
             frequency unless specified

Sample	Wave of survey (time t)								
	1991	1992	1993	1994	1995	1996	1997	1998	1999
Sample at t-1	--	7041	5778	4987	4510	4050	3803	3569	3341
Attrition rate[a]	--	18%	14%	10%	10%	6%	6%	6%	7%
Sample at t[b]	7041	5778	4987	4510	4050	3803	3569	3341	3106

Notes:
[a] Attrition rate is calculated as ((longitudinal sample at time t-1 - longitudinal sample at time t)/(longitudinal sample at time t-1))*100.
[b] 1997, 1998 and 1999 waves exclude BHPS-Scotland, BHPS-Northern Ireland and ECHP sub-samples (introduced in 1997 wave).

In the first wave (1991) of the BHPS there were 7,041 adults of working-age who completed full individual interviews and were living in households where a full household interview was completed. By the second wave (1992) 1,263, almost one in six, of these adults had dropped out of the sample. It is commonplace in panel surveys for attrition rates to decrease after a few waves – non-respondents are particularly likely to drop out in the early waves of the survey (Leisering and Walker, Eds. 1998) – and this is the case with the longitudinal sample selected here. By the 1994 wave the attrition rate for working-age adults had dropped to 10 per cent and steadied to a rate of around 6 per cent from the 1996 wave onwards. There were 3,106 working-age individuals present in all nine waves of the survey. It is these individuals that make up the panel sample on which longitudinal analysis in this chapter will concentrate.

Having selected the 3,106 working-age adults who make up the longitudinal sample, it is necessary to establish how representative these individuals are of the population at large – all working-age individuals in 1991 who were still of working age in 1999. Such analysis provides an estimate of any differential sample attrition that may have occurred during the course of the panel. Panel attrition can seriously distort the representativeness of the sample if it is highly selective amongst particular population sub-groups.

As there is a dearth of other longitudinal data for Great Britain, it is not possible to make any worthwhile external validity checks. Instead an internal assessment of differential sample attrition is made from the BHPS data. To estimate panel attrition the 1991 socio-demographic characteristics of the longitudinal sample are compared with the 1991 socio-demographic characteristics of all working-age adults who could still be of working age in 1999. The second group of individuals includes those who were once members of the BHPS sample but who fail to make the longitudinal sample, for reasons including non-response and attrition. The issue therefore becomes whether those who fail to answer a full interview, or come from a household where some members fail to do so, or who drop out of the survey, differ systematically from those who remain in the longitudinal sample. Differences between these two samples can lead to a bias in estimates, due to the resultant change in the sample composition over time.

Table 5.3 shows that there are some, albeit minor, differences between the two samples. The longitudinal sample appears slightly less likely to include those who were younger, lived in lone parent with dependent children households, lived in rented accommodation, had no qualifications or were inactive. These findings are consistent with other BHPS analysis (Taylor, 1994) that suggests that individuals who are highly mobile and less attached to their household are difficult to track throughout the life of the panel survey. However, despite only negligible differences, it is important to bear in mind the characteristics that are over-represented in the longitudinal sample when interpreting analysis presented later in the book. This is particularly important as the socio-demographic characteristics of those less likely to be in the panel sample suggest that they were individuals at high risk of experiencing social exclusion.

Table 5.3 **Estimate of panel attrition amongst longitudinal sample of working-age adults, BHPS, 1991-1999**

Socio-demographic characteristics in 1991	*Potential panel members*[a] Column % per category	*Actual panel Members*[b] Column % per category	Frequency
Sex			
Male	51	50	1557
Female	49	50	1549
Age group			
16-29 years	37	33	1032
30-44 years	43	46	1414
45 years-retirement age	20	21	660
Family type			
Single	8	8	233
Couple, no children	21	23	722
Couple, dep children	46	47	1473
Couple, non-dep children	13	12	377
Lone parent, dep children	6	4	128
Lone parent, non-dep children	3	3	86
Other	4	3	87
Tenure			
Owner occupier	73	77	2398
Private renter	10	8	249
Public renter	17	15	549

Table 5.3   (continued)

Highest education qualification			
Degree or higher	15	17	537
A-level or equivalent	19	19	581
O-level/GCSE or equivalent	31	31	953
CSE/GCSE equivalent	8	8	248
None	28	25	786
Main activity status			
Employed full-time	68	71	2169
Employed part-time	6	7	204
Unemployed	6	4	135
Inactive	17	15	470
Education/training	3	3	80
Other	<1	<1	13
Base	6206	3106	3106

Notes:
[a] Potential panel members are all males between 16 and 56 years and females between 16 and 51 years in 1991 (e.g. to be a male of working age in 1991 through to 1999, must be between 16 and 56 years in 1991, to be present in survey and under state retirement age in 1999).
[b] Actual panel members are individuals of working age in every wave from 1991 to 1999.

Table 5.3 illustrates another disadvantage with the BHPS, as with virtually all panel surveys, that of small sub-sample cell size. The 3,106 longitudinal working-age sample members are broken down by socio-demographic characteristic presenting the proportion and frequency in each sub-group. Given that the research will focus on both the multi-dimensional and dynamic nature of social exclusion, the break down of the longitudinal sample is likely to be fairly severe. It is clear that because of low sample size the data will not be able to provide focussed studies into specific sectors of the population or specific issues within these populations.

Investigating longitudinal one-dimensional disadvantage

Investigations into the longitudinal nature of social exclusion in Great Britain are relatively underdeveloped in current empirical studies. Previous studies have used panel data to investigate certain individual elements of social exclusion in Great Britain, most notably low income (Jarvis and Jenkins, 1996, 1998a, 2000a; Jenkins and Rigg, 2001) and poor health (Benzeval and Judge, 2000; Berthoud, 2000). Fewer attempts have been made to explore other aspects of social exclusion over time [1] and fewer still that concentrate on the longitudinal nature of multi-dimensional disadvantage in Great Britain.

The main focus of this chapter is to contribute to attempts to operationalize social exclusion by using the panel element of the BHPS to investigate the nature of the seven indicators of social exclusion constructed in Chapter 3 from a longitudinal perspective. This will be achieved by employing models of persistent one-dimensional disadvantage. The BHPS data will be used to explore the longitudinal nature of individual elements of social exclusion, including the total amount of time spent in disadvantage over the nine waves of panel data, the length of each disadvantage spell and the extent and pattern of disadvantage spell repetition. Particular emphasis is given to identifying the prevalence of long-term persistent disadvantage. Multivariate techniques will also be applied to identify the characteristics of working-age individuals that experienced these most enduring forms of disadvantage according to each of the seven dimension of social exclusion.

Before beginning this section it is important to note the complications that can occur in the construction of measures of longitudinal disadvantage. These complications stem from the fact that the observation period truncates spells of disadvantage. In other words, some spells may be in progress at the start of the observation period and others may still be in progress at the end of the period. This means that lengths of completed spells cannot be observed directly and therefore statistics tend to understate the duration of disadvantage (presented in Table 5.4) because some of the spells have begun before the beginning of the observation period (left-hand censorship), while others have continued after the end of the observation period (right-hand censorship). In particular the analysis is likely to underestimate long-run spells of disadvantage. [2]

Problems also occur when estimating the number of spells of disadvantage individuals have had, as the longitudinal prevalence of disadvantage is dependent to some degree on the length of the observation period. The longer the observation period the greater likelihood of recording short spells of disadvantage. This has resulted in some researchers choosing an observation period that coincides with a certain 'life stage' such as childhood, youth or old age (Leisering and Walker, 1998). To date the BHPS has only produced nine waves of data so it is not possible to construct an observation window to correspond with the life stage of interest in this research – working age. Also, although there are statistical procedures in use to deal with these problems of panel censoring, these tend to focus on estimating single spells, something not of primary interest in this research. Therefore the estimates should be taken for what they are – estimates of the longitudinal nature of disadvantage over a nine year period in the 1990s (an approach adopted by

---

[1] Although not an indicator of social exclusion in this research, there has been much longitudinal research on the labour market, including the relationship between the labour market and living standards. Much of this analysis has been possible through the use of retrospective surveys, such as the Labour Force Survey, but some has been performed on household panel surveys (Taylor, 2000).

[2] For a discussion of the problems in using panel data to estimate spells of disadvantage see Walker (1994) and Ashworth et al (2000).

Jenkins and Rigg, 2001, in their descriptive analysis of poverty dynamics in Great Britain, also using BHPS data).

The duration of one-dimensional disadvantage

Qualitative work on income poverty (Kempson et al, 1994) has found that individuals experience different types of hardship. Studies such as this, applicable to other dimensions of social exclusion, have shown that the cross-sectional low-income population is heterogeneous, comprised of those who experience low income for varying lengths of time. Different durations of disadvantage may index entirely different social experiences. For example, short spells of income poverty are inherently less destructive than long ones. During short spells of income poverty, individuals may be able to maintain their living standards by drawing on savings or building up debts in periods of low income. As income increases they may pay off debts or build up reserves of savings rather than change their immediate standards of living. As Walker (1995) explains, when shifting attention from a cross-sectional to a longitudinal analysis of disadvantage one is forced to recognize the different characteristics of disadvantage over time. For some it is the duration of hardship that generates such experiences whilst for others it is whether they experience disadvantage recurrently or for persistent periods. This section focuses on the duration of one-dimensional disadvantage.

There are a number of ways to define the longitudinal prevalence of disadvantage, but two methods stand out as the most frequently used – both of which have been used primarily in the study of low income. Hill and Jenkins (2001) measure the prevalence of longitudinal income poverty by computing a longitudinal average of an individual's incomes observed over consecutive interviews and comparing this with a poverty line. The second, rather more simplistic approach takes account of the plain count of the number of times individuals are below the poverty line during the observation period (each annual interview counts as one observation). According to an analysis of low income using BHPS data by Jenkins and Rigg (2001), results from the two methods do not differ substantially. The second approach will be used in the following analysis.

Table 5.4 is split into two halves, providing the frequency of the number of observations adults of working age experienced disadvantage during the nine waves of BHPS data,[3] according to each of the seven indicators of social exclusion. The top half of the table presents statistics on all individuals, including those who were not disadvantaged on a particular indicator at all during the decade. These findings show that for each indicator a substantial proportion of working-age adults,

---

[3] Because observations in the BHPS data are taken at annual intervals, referring to a time around the survey interview, the analysis does not take into account any additional movements into and out of disadvantage occurring between consecutive observations. It is also useful to point out that other studies have found that prevalence and duration of disadvantage is sensitive to the choice of disadvantage threshold. This is especially so if the threshold is located in a relatively crowded section of the disadvantage range (see Jarvis and Jenkins, 2000a, for further discussion).

varying between approximately one fifth and one third, were disadvantaged for at least one of the nine observations. As these numbers are higher than the proportions experiencing disadvantage at any one time (see Chapter 4, Figure 4.1 for examples), the analysis suggests that disadvantage can affect many individuals over the period, for varying lengths of time and often at numerous instances. The analysis also implies that for each of the indicators there was quite considerable movement across the disadvantage thresholds over the nine observations.[4]

Table 5.4   Longitudinal prevalence of one-dimensional disadvantage, working-age adults panel sample, BHPS, 1991-1999, row per cent

Dimension of disadvantage	Number of observations in disadvantage					
	0	1	2-3	4-6	7-8	9
All individuals						
Financial situation	59	13	12	9	5	1
Material possessions	75	7	10	5	2	2
Housing circumstance	75	9	6	5	3	4
Neighbourhood perception	64	16	12	6	2	<1
Social relations	73	6	12	6	2	1
Physical health	67	11	10	5	3	3
Mental health	61	19	14	6	1	<1
Individuals disadvantaged at least once						
Financial situation	--	33	30	22	12	4
Material possessions	--	29	38	19	7	7
Housing circumstance	--	34	23	19	10	15
Neighbourhood perception	--	43	34	18	4	1
Social relations	--	23	45	23	8	2
Physical health	--	33	32	17	9	9
Mental health	--	48	36	14	2	<1

---

[4] The distance an individual moves across a threshold may have an important affect on their standard of living. This is particularly the case for the financial situation (income poverty) indicator as it is derived from a continuous variable (household income) where small movements in the income distribution were likely to reflect small changes in living conditions. For example, a movement across the income poverty line and an increase in needs-adjusted income of £10 per week is likely to indicate a smaller change in financial circumstance than a movement across the income poverty line and an increase in needs-adjusted income of £100 per week. When investigating changes in income poverty status it is commonplace to only record a change when a move over the poverty line is accompanied by a significant change in income (see Jarvis and Jenkins, 1996). Here the magnitude of change is not taken into account when recording the prevalence of disadvantage over time. Instead the measures simply record whether or not an individual is disadvantaged. Jenkins and Rigg (2001) use a similar approach in their work on the dynamics of poverty in Great Britain.

It is clear from the top half of Table 5.4 that longitudinal prevalence varies according to the dimension of social exclusion under investigation. Of the seven indicators of social exclusion it was the financial situation (income poverty) indicator that individuals were most likely to have experienced during the decade, with over two in five working-age adults experiencing income poverty at least once. The other two economic indicators (material possessions and housing circumstances) were far less likely to be experienced over the decade – three quarters of working-age adults did not encounter these over the nine observations suggesting perhaps that they were caused by lengthy periods of low income.

The bottom half of Table 5.4 presents information on the duration of disadvantage for those who experienced disadvantage on each particular indicator of social exclusion at least once during the 1990s. This analysis suggests that two of these forms of disadvantage, neighbourhood perception and mental health, were more likely to occur for relatively short periods – only one, two or three observations during the decade. Also notable is that those who experienced poor quality housing had more chance of doing so for long periods – seven, eight or nine observations – probably as improvements in circumstance may require quite major transformations, which may only occur after a considerable time-span of disadvantage, whether continuous or intermittent. The upshot of this analysis is that many more people were affected by elements of social exclusion over several observations than suffered at just one observation and that only a minority of individuals experienced disadvantage at a considerable number of observations.

The number of spells of one-dimensional disadvantage

One of the problems with the analysis presented in Table 5.4 is that duration is accumulated over the observation period rather than viewed in terms of the length of individual spells. This means that, for example, someone who has four spells each lasting one observation, is put in the same category as a person who has two spells of two consecutive observations and a person who has one spell of four consecutive observations and so on. It may be that having different numbers of spells (and for different durations) denotes quite dissimilar experiences of disadvantage. Table 5.5 presents statistics on the distribution of individual's total number of spells for each of the seven social exclusion indicators.

Table 5.5 shows that by focussing on the number of spells, rather than the number of observations, a different picture of disadvantage over the 1990s emerges. Experiencing no spells of disadvantage over the period is the same as experiencing no observations, but here is where the similarity between the two tables ends. As a spell of disadvantage can contain a number of observations, the percentage of individuals who experienced few spells is high. The majority of individuals who experienced a particular form of disadvantage during the 1990s did so for just one spell. This is likely to be influenced by the length of the observation period and the duration of spells (see Table 5.6 below) but suggests that repeated spells were fairly uncommon during the decade.

Table 5.5 Total number of spells[a] of one-dimensional disadvantage, working-age adults panel sample, BHPS, 1991-1999, row per cent

Dimension of disadvantage	Total number of spells of disadvantage					
	0	1	2	3	4	5
All individuals						
Financial situation	59	26	12	3	<1	0
Material possessions	75	20	5	1	0	0
Housing circumstance	75	22	3	1	0	0
Neighbourhood perception	64	22	11	3	*	0
Social relations	73	22	5	*	0	0
Physical health	67	21	10	3	*	0
Mental health	61	25	11	3	*	0
Individuals disadvantaged at least once						
Financial situation	--	63	29	7	1	0
Material possessions	--	78	19	4	0	0
Housing circumstance	--	85	12	4	0	0
Neighbourhood perception	--	61	31	8	*	0
Social relations	--	81	19	*	0	0
Physical health	--	63	29	9	*	0
Mental health	--	64	28	8	*	0

Note:
[a] Analysis includes completed and non-completed spells.

Indeed, very few individuals had more than two spells of each form of disadvantage during the 1990s. Only for the dimensions of financial situation (income poverty), neighbourhood perception, physical health and mental health did individuals experience up to four spells of disadvantage. Although the proportion of individuals who experienced three or four spells was low, this suggests that for some people such experiences were broken up by spells of non-disadvantage. The mental health indicator has already been mentioned as a condition more likely to be experienced for a short total duration over the decade (see Table 5.4). This suggests that any repeated spells were likely to be of short duration also.

The propensity for some spells of disadvantage to occur only once is highlighted in the bottom half of Table 5.5. Of individuals who experienced at least one spell of disadvantage on a particular indicator, approximately four in five did so only once on the material possessions, housing circumstance and social relations indicators. Table 5.4 stressed the total duration of disadvantage on the housing circumstance to be particularly high, which suggests that this form of disadvantage was likely to be continuous, rather than intermittent, also.

Average duration by number of spells of one-dimensional disadvantage

As well as the number of spells of disadvantage another factor crucial to an understanding of longitudinal disadvantage is the length of these spells. Table 5.5 showed that the majority of individuals who experienced a particular form of disadvantage during the 1990s did so for just one spell, but it is the length of these spells that determine the intensity of the disadvantage experience. Long spells of disadvantage may be perceived as worse than short ones, although this is often difficult to ascertain (McLaughlin, Millar and Cooke, 1989). Table 5.6 presents the average duration according to the total number of spells of disadvantage that individuals record for each of the seven social exclusion indicators.

Table 5.6   Average duration according to total number of spells of one-dimensional disadvantage, working-age adults panel sample, BHPS, 1991-1999, mean (standard deviation)

Dimension of disadvantage	Total number of spells of disadvantage					
	0	1	2	3	4	5
Financial situation	0.0	2.7	2.1	1.6	1.2	0.0
	(0.0)	(2.5)	(1.0)	(1.7)	(1.3)	(0.0)
Material possessions	0.0	3.0	1.9	1.6	0.0	0.0
	(0.0)	(2.0)	(1.5)	(1.3)	(0.0)	(0.0)
Housing circumstance	0.0	3.7	2.3	1.7	0.0	0.0
	(0.0)	(3.1)	(1.0)	(0.6)	(0.0)	(0.0)
Neighbourhood perception	0.0	1.8	1.7	1.5	*	0.0
	(0.0)	(1.7)	(0.9)	(0.4)		(0.0)
Social relations	0.0	2.7	2.4	*	0.0	0.0
	(0.0)	(2.0)	(0.8)		(0.0)	(0.0)
Physical health	0.0	3.2	1.8	1.5	*	0.0
	(0.0)	(3.1)	(1.0)	(0.5)		(0.0)
Mental health	0.0	1.5	1.5	1.3	*	0.0
	(0.0)	(1.1)	(0.7)	(0.4)		(0.0)

Table 5.6 shows that there are some differences between the average durations according to spell number and indicator of social exclusion. Across all indicators the average duration of spells decrease as the total number of spells increases. This is partly because the length of the observation period affects the likelihood of experiencing a spell of longer duration than a previous spell.

The table does confirm some of the conclusions drawn from previous analysis presented above. It is still clear that longer spells of disadvantage were associated with housing circumstances and physical health. This suggests that these forms of disadvantage were particularly likely to be continuous and lengthy once set in. Conversely shorter spells of disadvantage were associated with neighbourhood perception and mental health.

The analysis from Table 5.6 suggests that, although there are differences between the seven indicators of social exclusion, in general there were relatively short spells of disadvantage for the majority of those who were touched by disadvantage during the decade, but relatively long spells for a significant minority. However, as is clear from the picture of longitudinal disadvantage presented so far, a variety of information on the nature of disadvantage is necessary to fully understand its main features. The following section attempts to combine the information explored so far to construct a suitable measure of longitudinal disadvantage that can be used to differentiate experiences of disadvantage over time. This measure can then be used to explore the most enduring forms of disadvantage in society and help to identify the individuals most at risk of such experiences.

Measuring longitudinal one-dimensional disadvantage

The previous section has shown that a variety of information is required to understand fully the nature of longitudinal disadvantage. Using this knowledge this section attempts to create a longitudinal measure of one-dimensional disadvantage that categorizes individuals according to different kinds of disadvantage experience. Various attempts have been made to construct longitudinal indicators to recognize the different patterning of income poverty over time (see Ashworth, Hill and Walker, 1991; Walker and Ashworth, 1994; Jarvis and Jenkins, 1995 and Jenkins and Rigg, 2001). However, to date there has been little empirical work that constructs longitudinal measures for non-monetary indicators of social exclusion.

In the early 1990s Ashworth, Hill and Walker (1991) argued for the importance of combing information on the frequency, duration and spacing of spells of low income to identify different experiences of longitudinal income poverty. More recently, Jenkins and Rigg (2001) used nine waves of BHPS data to classify individuals into five categories to summarize their experience of income poverty over time. It is the Jenkins and Rigg approach that is modified here to categorize individuals according to longitudinal patterns of disadvantage for each of the seven social exclusion indicators. These categories take into account the investigations of the previous section that looked at the frequency, duration and spacing of spells of disadvantage.   The categories are constructed as follows:

- 'None', no disadvantage in any of the nine observations.
- 'Occasional', disadvantage in any one of the nine observations.
- 'Recurrent', disadvantage in between two and six observations of the nine, separated by at least two observations of non-disadvantage.
- 'Short-term persistent', disadvantage between two and six observations of the nine separated by no more than one observation of non-disadvantage.
- 'Long-term persistent', disadvantage in seven or more of the nine observations.

By defining the categories in the same way for each of the seven indicators it is possible to compare patterns of longitudinal disadvantage across different domains of social exclusion. These results are presented in Table 5.7.

Table 5.7   Longitudinal patterns of one-dimensional disadvantage, working-age adults, BHPS, 1991-1999, column per cent

Longitudinal pattern	Dimension of disadvantage						
	Fin	Mat	Hou	Nei	Soc	Phy	Men
All individuals							
None	59	75	75	64	73	67	61
Occasional	13	7	9	16	6	11	19
Recurrent	9	4	2	9	4	8	10
Short-term persistent	13	11	9	10	14	8	10
Long-term persistent	6	4	6	2	3	6	1
Individuals disadvantaged at least once							
None	--	--	--	--	--	--	--
Occasional	32	27	35	43	22	33	47
Recurrent	22	15	8	24	15	24	25
Short-term persistent	32	42	35	27	52	24	25
Long-term persistent	15	15	23	6	11	18	3

Given that the results presented in Table 5.7 are quite complex to calculate and that longitudinal analyses such as these are rarely produced in studies of disadvantage, it is useful to perform a consistency check on the findings. There are very limited examples, if any, of longitudinal patterns of non-monetary disadvantage in the existing literature. Therefore the financial situation (income poverty) indicator will be used and comparisons made between this study and Jenkins and Riggs (2001) study. The results do match up to the findings from the Jenkins and Rigg study, taking into account the slight differences in the definition of recurrent poverty and short-term persistent poverty. For example, Jenkins and Rigg found 53 per cent of all individuals to be never poor over the nine-wave period (59 per cent in Table 5.7), 13 per cent to be occasionally poor (13 per cent in Table 5.7) and 8 per cent to be long-term persistently poor (6 per cent in Table 5.7). Differences in estimates can be accounted for as the Jenkins and Rigg analysis was performed on all adults and children, rather than working-age adults only. One would expect more individuals to be poor in the Jenkins and Rigg study, as their analysis would include children and adults over state-retirement age – sub-groups of the population more likely to be income poor.

Given that the financial situation indicator appears consistent with the Jenkins and Rigg study, it seems reasonable to assume that the categories for other domains of disadvantage satisfactorily summarize much of the information on the nature of longitudinal disadvantage presented earlier in this chapter. Previous analysis on the total amount of time spent in disadvantage and the number and duration of disadvantage spells suggested that there were distinct differences in the longitudinal nature of disadvantage according to particular dimensions of social exclusion. For example longer spells of disadvantage were associated with housing circumstances and physical health, although physical ill health appeared to occur more frequently. Consequently, the five-category classification of longitudinal disadvantage presented in Table 5.7 shows that both the housing circumstance and physical health domains show relatively high levels of long-term persistent disadvantage. The physical health domain also records relatively high levels of recurrent disadvantage (that is, repeated spells of short-term disadvantage).

Some of the most notable statistics to be derived from Table 5.7 are the disproportionately high likelihood of occasional and recurrent existence of disadvantage according to neighbourhood perception and mental health, and of long-term persistent disadvantage according to the housing circumstance indicator. It is particularly important to note that the behaviour of indicators of social exclusion do not necessarily take the same form as that of income poverty, on which most studies of longitudinal disadvantage have focussed to date.

The chapter now goes on to focus on long-term persistent disadvantage. Long-term persistent disadvantage is a core component of the notion of social exclusion. According to Room (Ed. 1995, 1998, 2000) it is individuals who experience disadvantage for long periods of time who are at most risk of social exclusion. This analysis begins with a comparison of the prevalence of current and long-term persistent one-dimensional disadvantage. Current disadvantage is recorded from the 1999 wave of the BHPS and persistent disadvantage takes the definition outlined above – that is, disadvantage in seven or more of the nine available waves. Multivariate analysis [5] is then used to examine the socio-demographic characteristics of individuals who experienced forms of long-term persistent one-dimensional disadvantage.

The prevalence of persistent longitudinal disadvantage

Figure 5.2 compares the average proportion of working-age adults disadvantaged for any one observation during the decade (in other words, the average proportion of individuals below the threshold across all nine observations) with the proportion that had suffered long-term persistent disadvantage, for each of the seven social exclusion indicators. The results are shown in a bar chart, where the two bars for each domain show the prevalence of (average) current disadvantage and long-term persistent disadvantage respectively.

---

[5] In this logistic regression analysis the binary dependent variable is constructed as follows: the 'success' event is long-term persistent disadvantage, the 'non-success' event is all other forms of disadvantage and non-disadvantage combined. This analysis therefore compares the socio-demographic characteristics of the long-term persistent disadvantaged with all other working-age adults. If comparisons between the socio-demographic characteristics of individuals in each of the five categories of longitudinal disadvantage were of interest, multinomial logistic regression would be the required analytical technique. This is not done here, as the focus is on long-term persistent disadvantage only.

The gap between the two bars measures the relationship between the likelihood of current and long-term persistent disadvantage during the 1990s. A small gap between the bars implies a high likelihood that an individual disadvantaged in a particular wave was long-term persistently disadvantaged throughout the decade. Conversely, a large gap between the bars implies that very few of the current disadvantaged experienced long-term persistent disadvantage during the 1990s.

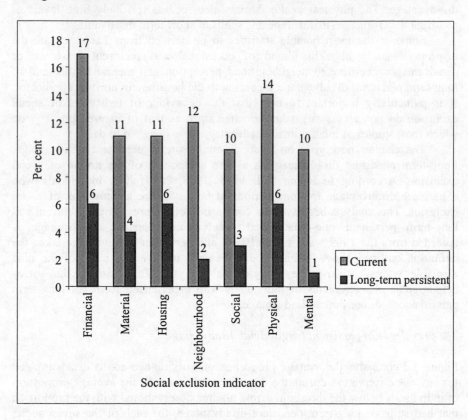

Figure 5.2   Prevalence of (average) current disadvantage[a] and long-term persistent disadvantage[b] in Great Britain in the 1990s, working-age adults, BHPS, 1991-1999

Notes:
[a] Current disadvantage means the being below the respective indicator threshold, averaged over all waves from 1991 to 1999.
[b] Long-term persistent disadvantage means being below the respective indicator threshold for at least seven of the nine observations taken annually between 1991 and 1999.

Figure 5.2 highlights how a different picture of the prevalence of disadvantage is presented when a longitudinal perspective is taken. As would be expected the proportion of working-age adults in long-term persistent disadvantage is lower than the proportion in current disadvantage for all seven social exclusion indicators. However the magnitude of the gap between the two measures (bars) varies according to the social exclusion indicator in question. It is the housing circumstance indicator where the magnitude of the relationship is highest, as on average 11 per cent of individuals experienced current disadvantage and over half of this figure (6 per cent of all working-age adults) experienced long-term persistent disadvantage during the 1990s. The physical health indicator shows the next strongest relationship, followed by the material possessions indicator.

The strong relationship between current and long-term persistent housing circumstance disadvantage is likely to have arisen because of the possibility that quite substantial sums of income were required to purchase items or repairs that move individuals out of housing disadvantage. To move out of housing circumstance disadvantage the household needed to afford new central heating or create more space, presumably by moving to a bigger house or having a household member leave the household. To afford such changes may have meant that income was accumulated over time, resulting in long periods of disadvantage being experienced in the process. This theory applies to the material possessions indicator as well, whilst certain forms of physical ill health may have been likely to last for enduring periods of time depending on the gravity of the illness.

The gap between current and long-term persistent disadvantage for the other indicators of social exclusion is much smaller. Very few of those experiencing disadvantage on the neighbourhood perception, social relations and mental health indicators were likely to have done so persistently during the 1990s. This suggests that these forms of disadvantage were likely to be irregular or sporadic. The findings reconfirm the occasional and recurrent patterns of longitudinal disadvantage for these indicators identified in Table 5.7.

Socio-demographic characteristics of individuals who experienced persistent one-dimensional longitudinal disadvantage

The final section in the investigation of longitudinal one-dimensional disadvantage examines the socio-demographic characteristics of individuals most likely to have experienced long-term persistent disadvantage (that is disadvantage for seven of the nine waves of the panel survey). It was these individuals that were likely to have the highest risk of social exclusion. A multivariate (logistic regression) analysis that demonstrates the odds of experiencing long-term persistent disadvantage is presented in Table 5.8.

Table 5.8   **Odds[a] of experiencing persistent one-dimensional disadvantage[b] by individual and household socio-demographic characteristic, BHPS, 1991-1999** logistic regression model

Socio-demographic characteristics (1999)	*Indicator of one-dimensional persistent disadvantage*						
	Fi	Ma	Ho	Ne	So	Ph	Me
Sex							
Male	ref	ref	ref	ref	ref	ref	ref
Female	0.7	**0.5**	0.8	0.8	**0.3**	1.3	**2.5**
Age group							
16-29 years	1.6	1.1	0.7	**2.2**	0.9	1.0	0.2
30-44 years	ref	ref	ref	ref	ref	ref	ref
45-59/64 years	**0.5**	**0.5**	**0.5**	1.3	1.3	**1.8**	1.3
Household type							
Single	4.9	8.3	2.0	1.0	3.4	1.5	**4.5**
Couple no children	2.2	2.0	1.0	1.2	0.8	1.8	**0.1**
Couple, dep children only	ref	ref	ref	ref	ref	ref	ref
Couple, some non-dep	3.3	0.1	1.6	1.3	2.3	3.6	**1.8**
Lone parent, dep children only	6.3	2.0	1.8	1.1	1.8	0.4	0.1
Lone parent, some non-dep	**14.0**	3.4	**4.1**	0.6	6.5	2.2	**6.4**
Other	0.7	6.1	2.7	2.5	0.1	0.4	0.1
Number of children							
None	0.1	6.0	1.3	1.2	0.8	0.7	**0.1**
One	ref	ref	ref	ref	ref	ref	ref
Two or more	**3.2**	3.1	1.1	1.7	1.3	0.8	0.9
Education level							
Degree or higher	**0.2**	2.3	**0.5**	**0.5**	0.9	**0.4**	1.9
A-level	0.7	0.8	1.0	1.1	1.2	0.6	1.5
O-level	ref	ref	ref	ref	ref	Ref	ref
CSE level	1.7	0.5	1.8	1.1	1.1	1.5	1.2
None of these	**4.7**	**2.5**	**1.9**	**1.9**	1.2	**1.9**	1.8
Main activity status[c]							
Employed full time	**0.3**	0.8	0.8	1.2	0.9	N/A	**0.2**
Employed part time	1.7	1.1	1.3	0.6	1.0	N/A	0.2
Unemployed	**7.7**	1.3	1.1	0.5	1.2	N/A	0.9
Care of home/family	ref	ref	ref	ref	ref	N/A	ref
Education/training	1.1	4.2	2.4	2.7	0.1	N/A	0.1
Other inactive	4.7	3.2	1.0	5.4	1.7	N/A	4.9

Table 5.8   (continued)

No. in hhold in employment							
None	**4.7**	1.1	0.7	1.3	**3.0**	**3.1**	2.1
One	ref	ref	ref	Ref	ref	Ref	ref
Two or more	**0.2**	**0.4**	**0.5**	0.7	1.1	**0.2**	1.2

Notes:

[a] Odds ratios higher (lower) than 1 imply that the socio-demographic characteristic is associated with an increased (decreased) odds of experiencing the event (*household economic deprivation*) compared to the reference category (ref). Bold text indicates a statistically significant (p<0.05) coefficient.

[b] Persistent one-dimensional disadvantage is defined as experiencing disadvantage on a particular indicator for at least five of the seven observations. Long-term persistent disadvantage for neighbourhood perception indicator defined as disadvantage for 6 observations or more as too few cases for 7 observations or more definition. Long-term persistent disadvantage for social relations indicator defined as disadvantage for 6 observations or more as too few cases for 7 observations or more definition.

[c] Main activity status is excluded from the physical health analysis as most people with poor physical health looked after the home or family, or were in the other inactive category.

In Chapter 4 (Table 4.1) various socio-demographic characteristics were linked with an increased risk of current one-dimensional disadvantage, according to each of the seven social exclusion indicators. These patterns remain fairly constant when the outcome category is long-term persistent one-dimensional disadvantage, although various characteristics appear to have an increased association with the experience of longitudinal disadvantage.

Taking the primarily economic indicators first, lone parents with at least one non-dependent child were particularly likely to have experienced long-term persistent financial disadvantage (income poverty) – with odds 14 times that of the reference category, a couple with dependent children only. As the socio-demographic characteristics of the individual are taken in 1999, these lone parents were likely to have had dependent children for a substantial proportion of the decade. These households were also likely to have experienced long-term persistent disadvantage of housing circumstance. Unemployed people were another group with high odds of experiencing long-term persistent income poverty, almost eight times higher than the reference group. Unemployed people also increased their odds of experiencing long-term persistent income poverty compared to a measure taken at a point in time (see Chapter 4, Table 4.1).

According to Table 5.8 the experience of negative long-term neighbourhood perception is linked to a number of socio-demographic characteristics, most notably being a young adult and having no academic qualification. These characteristics show up at a cross-sectional level also (see Chapter 4, Table 4.1). There are some risk factors that appear to reduce their effect on experiencing disadvantage when a longitudinal measure is adopted. Being unemployed increases the odds of having a negative neighbourhood perception by more than a factor of two at a cross-sectional level (see Chapter 4, Table 4.1), but unemployment is not associated with increased odds when looking at long-term persistent disadvantage. One of the reasons why such findings are possible is that current socio-demographic status is not a perfect indicator of socio-demographic status during the decade (as has also been found with indicators of social exclusion). For example, the current unemployed were likely to be a fairly heterogeneous group comprised of individuals with varied labour market status histories, ranging from the persistently unemployed to the occasional unemployed. Unfortunately, the small sample sizes involved in longitudinal analysis mean that longitudinal measures of socio-demographic characteristics cannot be taken into account.

Factors linked to long-term persistent disadvantage of social relations point to single people, lone parents and those where no one in the household works. These factors are also associated with long-term persistent mental health problems, which suggest the longitudinal nature of these two indicators of social exclusion may be linked (the longitudinal relationship between the indicators is explored in Chapter 6). The chances of being long-term persistently physically ill appear reduced if an individual had a degree or higher education, something not picked up at a cross-sectional level of analysis (see Chapter 4, Table 4.1).

Conclusion

This chapter has introduced a longitudinal approach to the investigation of social exclusion in Great Britain. According to Room (Ed. 1995, 1998, 2000), the longitudinal aspect of disadvantage is crucial to an understanding of social exclusion as it distinguishes individuals who experienced short or intermittent spells of disadvantage from individuals who suffer such events persistently. It was this latter group who are at most risk of social exclusion. If described from purely a static viewpoint therefore, the true nature of social exclusion can be confused or totally neglected.

A longitudinal approach to the investigation of social exclusion has been made possible through the use of the British Household Panel Survey, which measures the experiences of individuals, and their households, over time. This has allowed the experience of disadvantage during the 1990s to be categorized according to the duration and sequence of disadvantage spells. For each of the seven domains of social exclusion, five categories of longitudinal disadvantage pattern were formed: none, occasional, recurrent, short-term persistent and long-term persistent. Individuals were particularly likely to have experienced disadvantage at least once during the decade on the financial situation (income poverty) and mental health indicators. Long-term persistent disadvantage was particularly likely on the housing circumstance indicator, possibly as the ability to make housing improvements requires a prolonged period of income saving.

The final section of this chapter concentrated on measuring long-term persistent one-dimensional disadvantage. Predictably, the prevalence of enduring disadvantage amongst the working-age population was lower than for disadvantage measured at a point in time. However the relationship between current and long-term persistent disadvantage varied according to the domain of social exclusion in question. It was the currently disadvantaged of material possessions and housing circumstance that were most likely to have been long-term persistently disadvantaged, suggesting again the relationship between income accumulation and resource acquisition mentioned above.

From an empirical viewpoint, adopting a longitudinal method does not generate an entirely new profile of disadvantaged individuals compared to an approach that measures disadvantage at a point in time. Although some socio-demographic and economic factors pervade certain groups of long-term and persistently disadvantaged individuals, most notably education and labour market status, certain characteristics, such as age and household type, were particularly associated with certain domains of social exclusion. This analysis is therefore particularly useful for modifying the relative risks attributed to the different groups according to the area of social exclusion under investigation.

The following chapter brings together the methodological approaches used in this and the previous chapter. A multi-dimensional and longitudinal measure of disadvantage is employed to identify the rate of social exclusion in Great Britain. This approach is then taken forward (in Chapter 7) to a European Union level of analysis to compare the prevalence of social exclusion in the UK with other Member States.

Chapter 6

Identifying Social Exclusion in Great Britain During the 1990s

Being socially excluded carries the implication of suffering such a degree of multi-dimensional disadvantage, of such duration, and reinforced by such material and cultural degradation of the local neighbourhoods, that relational links with the wider society are ruptured to a degree that is in some considerable degree irreversible (Room, 2000, p. 171).

Introduction

The previous two chapters have explored in detail, but separately, the multi-dimensional and longitudinal nature of social exclusion in Great Britain. Chapter 3 investigated the relationship between the seven social exclusion indicators at a cross-sectional level and revealed patterns of disadvantage that suggested notions of *household economic deprivation*, *personal civic exclusion* and *personal health exclusion*. A small proportion of working-age adults were seen to have suffered from multiple disadvantages in each of these three areas. Chapter 5 investigated longitudinal patterns of disadvantage for each indicator separately and categorized individuals according to their longitudinal experience of disadvantage, ranging from none to long-term persistent. For each of the seven social exclusion indicators only a small proportion of working-age adults experienced long-term persistent disadvantage during the 1990s.

This chapter combines the techniques utilized in the previous two chapters to investigate the nature of social exclusion using models of longitudinal multi-dimensional disadvantage. As already mentioned, there have been limited studies that have examined social exclusion from either a multi-dimensional or longitudinal perspective, and, therefore, even fewer that have combined both methods. The chapter moves on to formulate a working definition of social exclusion for Great Britain to identify individuals who experienced long-term persistent disadvantage simultaneously on a number of domains. The chapter concludes by examining the prevalence of such experiences and the socio-demographic characteristics of affected individuals.

Investigating longitudinal multi-dimensional disadvantage

The investigation begins by exploring a variety of approaches to investigate the nature of longitudinal, multi-dimensional disadvantage. The chosen method is then used to investigate the longitudinal and multi-dimensional nature of disadvantage based on models that consider the relationship between the seven indicators of social exclusion over time.

Methods to investigate longitudinal multi-dimensional disadvantage

Longitudinal, multi-dimensional disadvantage can be measured in a number of ways. Probably the most comprehensive means of combining both multi-dimensional and longitudinal information in an investigation of social exclusion is to identify individuals who were consistently disadvantaged on a particular combination of social exclusion indicators for a substantial duration of time. However, given the cell size constraints of the BHPS data, coupled with the fact that very few individuals encountered simultaneous disadvantage at a cross-sectional level, such analysis is not possible here.

There are a variety of alternative methods that can be used to investigate longitudinal, multi-dimensional disadvantage, but two seem most obvious. These methods are illustrated graphically in Figure 6.1.

The first method is used to identify individuals who experienced disadvantage on a pre-determined number of indicators (for example, more than three) at any one observation for a number of observations during the decade. This method concentrates on categorizing individuals according to the number of observations of multi-dimensional disadvantage. The example of this method given in the top half of Figure 6.1 would thus conclude that an individual with this array of observations would be defined as having experienced six observations of multi-dimensional disadvantage (observations 1, 2, 3, 5, 6 and 7).

The second method, illustrated in the lower half of Figure 6.1, identifies individuals who experienced disadvantage for a number of observations on a number of different indicators. These individuals would have experienced enduring periods of disadvantage (for example for six or more of the nine observations) on a number of social exclusion domains. The example of this method given in Figure 6.1 would determine that the individual experienced enduring disadvantage on three indicators during the decade (financial situation, housing circumstance and mental health). Thus the first method focuses more on repeated experiences of multiple disadvantage and the second method more on a number of forms of long-term disadvantage.

This section begins with a descriptive analysis of multi-dimensional, longitudinal disadvantage in Great Britain in the 1990s in order to establish which of these two approaches is most appropriate to an investigation of social exclusion. This commences with information on the cumulative number of disadvantage 'events' – where an event is defined as an observation of disadvantage. Figure 6.2

illustrates the percentage of events individuals experienced across all of the seven social exclusion indicators combined during the 1990s.[1]

Method 1. A number of observations of multi-dimensional disadvantage.

Indicators:

	1	2	3	4	5	6	7	8	9
Financial	X	X	X		X	X	X		
Material	X		X		X	X	X		
Housing	X	X				X	X	X	X
Nbrhood	X								
Social		X							
Physical		X	X						
Mental		X	X	X	X	X	X		
	1	2	3	4	5	6	7	8	9

Observation (wave of survey)

Method 2. Periods of disadvantage on a number of social exclusion domains.

Indicators:

	1	2	3	4	5	6	7	8	9
Financial	X	X	X		X	X	X		
Material	X		X		X		X		
Housing	X	X				X	X	X	X
Nbrhood	X								
Social		X							
Physical		X	X						
Mental		X	X	X	X	X	X		
	1	2	3	4	5	6	7	8	9

Observation (wave of survey)

Notes:
X signifies disadvantage event.
In method 1, shaded column signifies an observation of multi-dimensional disadvantage.
In method 2, shaded row signifies a period of enduring disadvantage.

Figure 6.1   Methods of investigating longitudinal, multi-dimensional disadvantage for individuals in the BHPS: examples

---

[1] Because longitudinal and multi-dimensional analysis required individuals with consistent information on seven indicators of social exclusion over nine observations, missing data was a notable problem. In fact approximately one quarter of the longitudinal sample selected for this analysis had missing data. Individuals excluded from longitudinal investigations because of missing data were more likely to have been male, younger or older rather than middle aged, lived alone, lived without dependent children, had no educational qualifications, were out of the labour market and lived in a household where no one works. Again it is these characteristics than were associated with individuals at most risk of social exclusion. Although the magnitude of difference between missing and non-missing data status was less than at a cross-sectional level, theses differences should be kept in mind when interpreting the analysis presented in this chapter. See Appendix B1 for further details.

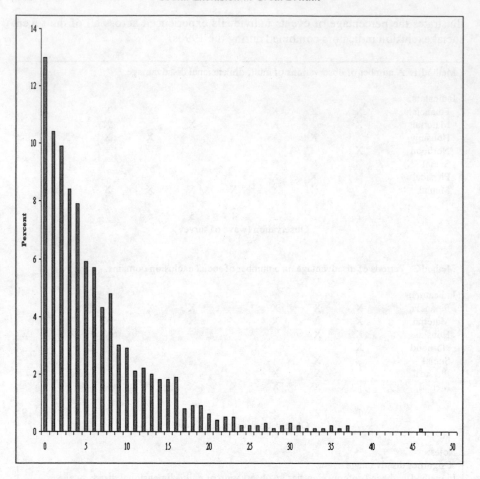

Figure 6.2   Total number of times individuals were disadvantaged during the 1990s,[a] working-age adults, BHPS, 1991-1999

Notes:
[a] Theoretically, the total number of times an individual could have been disadvantaged during the 1990s ranges from a minimum 0 – did not experience any disadvantage events in every observation – to a maximum 63 – experienced disadvantage on all indicators (7) in every observation (9).

Figure 6.2 illustrates how elements of social exclusion touched the working-age population during the 1990s. Over five in six (87 per cent) working-age adults experienced some form of disadvantage throughout the entire decade. This implies that, when taking the decade as a whole, the experience of disadvantage was widespread. There were very few individuals (13 per cent) who avoided experiencing at least one of these events during the decade, whether it was low income, poor housing, a lack of social relations, ill health or another of the seven social exclusion indicators.

What Figure 6.1 also makes clear is that certain individuals, albeit a minority, experienced a large number of disadvantage events during the 1990s – some up to and in excess of 30 events (of which some could have been continuous). It is these individuals who would have experienced both multi-dimensional and longitudinal forms of disadvantage and were most likely to be at risk of social exclusion. The following analysis categories these individuals according to the two methods outlined above (in Figure 6.1).

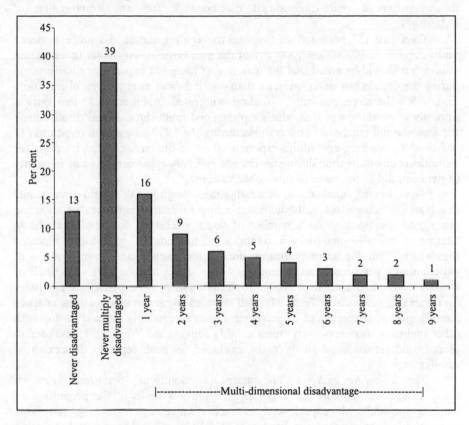

Figure 6.3   Total number of times individuals experienced multi-dimensional disadvantage during the 1990s,[a] working-age adults, BHPS, 1991-1999

Note:
[a] 'Never multiply disadvantaged' individuals did experience disadvantage during the decade but never on more than one indicator at any given observation.

The first method categorizes individuals according to the number of observations of multi-dimensional disadvantage. By definition, an individual who experienced more than seven disadvantage events during the decade must have experienced at least one observation of multi-dimensional disadvantage (defined as more than one disadvantage event at any one observation) as it is only possible to have experienced seven events at any one observation. Chapter 4 revealed that at any one observation, multi-dimensional disadvantage was relatively uncommon, particularly on a large number of indicators. This suggests that there were only a minority of individuals who experienced a number of observations of multi-dimensional disadvantage during the 1990s. Figure 6.3 presents the percentage of individuals according to the number of observations during the decade in which they experienced multi-dimensional disadvantage (on any combination of indicators).

Over half (52 per cent) of the working-age population did not experience multi-dimensional disadvantage at any of the nine observations under investigation, although it should be noted that the majority of these did experience disadvantage during the decade but never on more than one indicator at any given observation. Figure 6.3 therefore confirms a finding suggested in Figure 6.2, that only a minority of working-age individuals experienced multi-dimensional disadvantage for a substantial number of observations during the 1990s. Less than one-third (32 per cent) of working-age adults experienced multi-dimensional disadvantage for more than one observation during the decade and only approximately one in twenty (5 per cent) did so for seven or more observations.

The second method of investigating longitudinal, multi-dimensional disadvantage categorizes individuals according to their experiences of enduring periods of disadvantage on a number of social exclusion domains. Analysis in Chapter 5 revealed that only a minority of individuals experienced repeated disadvantage on the same indicator during the decade and even fewer still experienced persistent disadvantage. The interpretation of longitudinal disadvantage gave special attention to individuals who experienced persistent disadvantage, particularly those who had done so for seven observations or more (see Chapter 5). Experiences of persistent disadvantage were defined in line with other studies of income poverty (most notably Jenkins and Rigg, 2001) and used to identify individuals most likely to be excluded on each separate dimension of disadvantage.

The following analysis concentrates on identifying persistent forms of disadvantage, either short- or long-term. Figure 6.4 looks at the proportion of working-age adults who experienced persistent disadvantage (both long- and short-term), and long-term persistent disadvantage only, on a number of social exclusion indicators in Great Britain during the 1990s.

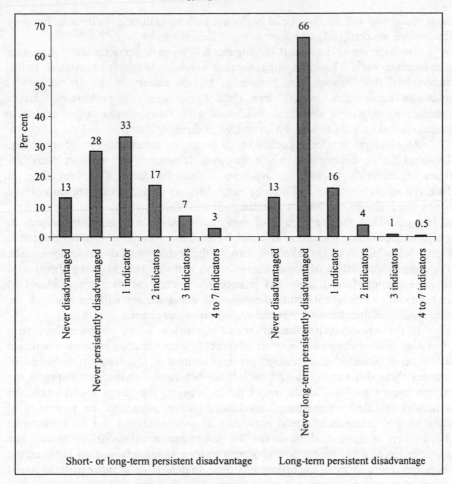

Figure 6.4   The number of indicators on which individuals experienced persistent disadvantage[a] in Great Britain in the 1990s, working-age adults, BHPS, 1991-1999

Note:
[a] Short-term persistent disadvantage is disadvantage between two and six waves of the nine separated by no more than one wave of non-disadvantage. Long-term persistent disadvantage is disadvantage in seven or more of the nine waves on a particular indicator. 'Never long-term persistent disadvantaged' individuals did experience disadvantage during the decade but never for seven or more observations on any one indicator. 'Never persistently disadvantaged' individuals did experience disadvantage during the decade but never persistently, either short- or long-term.

The left-hand bar chart in Figure 6.4 considers individuals who experienced persistent disadvantage during the 1990s, whether short- or long-term. Just over one quarter (27 per cent) of working-age individuals experienced persistent disadvantage on at least two social exclusion indicators during the decade, but very few, only 3 per cent, did so on four or more indicators.

The right-hand bar chart in Figure 6.4 focuses on long-term persistent disadvantage only. The chart suggests that although long-term persistent multi-dimensional disadvantage was present in British society in the 1990s, it was relatively uncommon. Indeed, less than 1 per cent of working-age adults experienced long-term persistent disadvantage on four or more social exclusion indicators and only 5 per cent did so on two or three indicators.

An assumption often associated with persistent disadvantage is that because disadvantage is experienced wave-on-wave, 'resources' – whether they are financial, material, housing or whatever – can be diminished over time. If disadvantage is continuous it can be very difficult to accumulate resources and hence disadvantage can have a spiralling effect (Walker, 1995). This is less likely to happen where there are gaps of non-disadvantage, and therefore periods in which to accumulate resources, as could be the case with the analysis presented in Figure 6.3, which does not take into account the regularity of disadvantage events. The longitudinal affect of disadvantage plays a major role in many theories of social exclusion (see Chapter 2). Hence the second of the two methods of investigating longitudinal, multi-dimensional disadvantage will be used in the empirical operationalization of social exclusion in this chapter.

If the operationalization of social exclusion is to consider long-term persistent disadvantage on a number of indicators the question remains whether it should also consider disadvantage on a combination of related dimensions or whether these dimensions should be left for separate analysis. In Chapter 4 the cross-sectional analysis of the relationship between the seven social exclusion indicators revealed some strong correlations, which suggested the formation of three integral elements of social exclusion. It was concluded that these elements should form a theoretical basis for the investigation of social exclusion. The investigation in this chapter now proceeds to look at the relationship between the seven indicators of social exclusion over time, to determine whether patterns found at a cross-sectional level remain when longitudinal data are used.

Table 6.1   Longitudinal relationship between indicators of social exclusion, working-age adults, BHPS, 1991-1999, correlation matrix[a]

	Fin	Mat	Hou	Nei	Soc	Phy	Men
Financial	----						
Material	0.150	----					
Housing	0.215	0.233	----				
N'brhood	0.117	0.056	0.108	----			
Social	0.156	0.070	0.059	0.144	----		
Physical	0.189	0.035	0.055	0.078	0.133	----	
Mental	0.118	0.030	0.018	0.145	0.185	0.332	----

Notes:
[a] Bold text indicates significant relationship (p<0.05).

Table 6.1 presents the longitudinal relationship between indicators of social exclusion in the form of a correlation matrix. The matrix presents correlations based on the number of observations spent in disadvantage for each pair of social exclusion indicators.

The correlation coefficients in Table 6.1 are all greater than zero. This implies that as the duration of disadvantage on one indicator increased so did the duration of disadvantage on the other indicator (and vice-versa). The magnitude of the correlation coefficient displays the strength of this relationship. The strongest correlation between indicators over time, as at a cross-sectional level, was for physical and mental health (0.332). The economic indicators also noticeably correlate with each other, particularly material possessions and housing circumstance, and, financial situation and housing circumstance. However, it is important to note that even the strongest relationship involves only modest levels of correlation.

As in Chapter 3, factor analysis was performed to determine whether the multi-dimensional patterns identified at a cross-sectional level remain when focussing on disadvantage over time. The longitudinal factor analysis produced similar results to the cross-sectional analysis (see Appendix C for details), identifying three factors related to:

- *Household economic deprivation* (made up of the financial situation, material possessions and housing circumstance indicators);
- *Personal civic exclusion* (made up of the neighbourhood perception and social relations indicators), and;
- *Personal health exclusion* (made up of the physical health and mental health indicators).

This analysis confirms that individuals who experienced disadvantage over time were likely to experience other forms of disadvantage according to patterns present at a cross-sectional level – that is, patterns connected to notions of *household economic deprivation*, *personal civic exclusion* and *personal health exclusion*. The following sections explore in more detail the prevalence of each of these integral forms of social exclusion, paying particular attention to individuals who experienced long-term, persistent periods of disadvantage on a number of indicators.

Given that simultaneous, long-term disadvantage on a number of indicators is relatively uncommon (see Figure 6.4) undertaking analysis in this area is problematic, particularly given the sample size constraints of the BHPS. This has meant that less stringent definitions of longitudinal disadvantage have been used in some analysis, most notably 'sporadic' disadvantage (combining 'occasional' and 'recurrent' disadvantage) and 'persistent' disadvantage (combining 'short-term persistent' and 'long-term persistent' disadvantage). Where these definitional amendments have had to be made, they are clearly noted in the following investigations.

Longitudinal household economic deprivation

In Chapter 4, relationships between static indicators of *household economic deprivation* revealed the heterogeneity of the income-poor population, some of who were also disadvantaged on the material possession and/or the housing circumstance indicators and some of who were not. Other cross-sectional studies of poverty have suggested a dynamic link between income and material living standards that can explain such findings (for example see Nolan and Whelan, 1996). For example, members of the income-poor population who are found to have a high standard of living may be in the process, or 'at risk', of economic disadvantage. This process could be triggered by the loss of work and immediate drop in income, followed by the erosion of existing resources if new employment is not found quickly.

Without the use of longitudinal information it is difficult to be able to test such assertions.[2] Likewise, without longitudinal information it is difficult to identify individuals who experienced the most severe forms of economic deprivation – that is, low income and disadvantage on other economic indicators for long periods. The aim of this section is to identify individuals who experienced the most severe and enduring forms of *household economic deprivation*. Table 6.2 considers the longitudinal relationship between indicators of financial situation (income poverty) and the other two indicators of *household economic deprivation*.

Table 6.2   **Relationship between longitudinal indicators[a] of *household economic deprivation*, working-age adults, BHPS, 1991-1999, column per cent (total per cent) per section**

| Material possessions | Financial situation disadvantage | | |
Disadvantage	None	Sporadic	Persistent
None	79 (47)	69 (15)	65 (12)
Sporadic	8 (5)	13 (3)	16 (3)
Persistent	12 (7)	18 (4)	19 (4)
Housing circumstance	*Financial situation disadvantage*		
Disadvantage	None	Sporadic	Persistent
None	82 (50)	66 (14)	59 (11)
Sporadic	8 (5)	12 (3)	16 (3)
Persistent	10 (6)	21 (5)	25 (5)

Notes:
[a] Sporadic disadvantage combines the occasional and recurrent definitions. Persistent disadvantage combines the short-term and long-term persistent definitions (see Chapter 5 for more details).

---

[2] Although longitudinal data does allow for an investigation of the accumulation and erosion of resources over time this analysis is complex, involving the precise timing of events, and beyond the scope of this research.

As suggested in Table 6.1 there is evidence of a longitudinal relationship between financial situation (income poverty) and the other two, non-monetary, indicators of *household economic deprivation*. This was particularly strong for housing circumstance disadvantage, as suggested in Table 6.1, as rates of persistent disadvantage doubled for those who faced sporadic rather than no income poverty, and increased even more for the persistently income poor. This suggests that a long period of low income may restrict the capability of the household to accumulate resources to allow the repair and replacement of household items and fabric that would record a move out of such measured disadvantage.

Despite the evidence of a longitudinal relationship between income poverty and the other non-monetary indicators of *household economic deprivation*, there appears to be little evidence of extreme forms of multiple disadvantages during the 1990s. Only 4 per cent of working-age adults experienced persistent income poverty and persistent material possession disadvantage, slightly more individuals (5 per cent) experienced persistent income poverty and persistent household circumstance disadvantage. This small subset of the working-age population can be seen to have faced quite severe multiple forms of household economic disadvantage for enduring periods during the 1990s.

The following analysis presents information on the odds of experiencing persistent *household economic deprivation* according to an individual's socio-demographic characteristics. This analysis can help to identify particular problem groups in terms of characteristics associated with an increased risk of such extreme disadvantage. To identify the most extreme form of *household economic deprivation* the following definition is used: individuals who were long-term persistently[3] income poor *and* who were long-term persistently disadvantaged on either the material possessions indicator or the housing circumstance indicator.

Table 6.3   Odds[a] of experiencing long-term persistent *household economic deprivation*[b] by individual and household socio-demographic characteristic, working-age adults, BHPS, 1991-1999, logistic regression model

Socio-demographic characteristics (1999)	*Odds*
Sex	
Male	ref
Female	0.9
Age group	
16-29 years	0.5
30-44 years	ref
45-59/64 years	0.7

[3] In this analysis long-term persistently disadvantaged identifies individuals who experienced six or more observations of disadvantage during the 1990s, rather than seven or more as defined in Chapter 5, so to allow enough cases for valid analysis.

Table 6.3　　(continued)

Household type	
Single	3.3
Couple no children	0.3
Couple, dependent children only	ref
Couple, some non dependent children	2.0
Lone parent, dependent children only	1.0
Lone parent, some non dependent children	5.5
Other	0.1
Number of children	
None	0.3
One	ref
Two or more	1.9
Education level	
Degree or higher	**0.1**
A-level	0.5
O-level	ref
CSE level	0.8
None of these	1.5
Main activity status	
Employed full time	0.5
Employed part time	1.0
Unemployed	0.1
Care of home/family	ref
Education/training	0.6
Other inactive	1.8
Number in household in employment	
None	2.1
One	ref
Two or more	**0.3**

Notes:

[a] Odds ratios higher (lower) than 1 implies that the socio-demographic characteristic is associated with increased (decreased) odds of experiencing the event (persistent *household economic deprivation*) compared to the reference category (ref). Bold text indicates a statistically significant ($p<0.05$) coefficient.

[b] *Household economic deprivation* is defined as individuals who were long-term persistently (six observations or more) income poor *and* who were persistently disadvantaged (six observations or more) on either the material possessions indicator or the housing circumstance indicator during the 1990s.

The first point to note from Table 6.3 is that very few of the findings were statistically significant. This is likely to be a consequence of the low numbers of economically deprived individuals in the BHPS dataset, but also the relative similarity in odds across many of the socio-demographic categories. Individuals who were most at risk of long-term persistent *household economic deprivation* (although not statistically significant) were those who lived alone and lone parents (who were likely to have spent the majority of the survey period living with dependent children). These types of household suffer from having only one potential worker in the household meaning the accumulation of resources was unlikely. For lone parents in particular, many were likely to have worked for only a few hours a week, meaning their earnings potential was reduced and hence they were reliant on low-level social assistance payments. Other research, using ECHP data, has found that single-person households are also less likely to receive formal or informal financial assistance through family networks (Barnes et al, 2002).

Those most likely to avoid persistent *household economic deprivation* were individuals with a degree or higher educational qualifications and those who lived in a household where two or more members worked. Individuals with a degree were likely to be in secure, permanent, well-paid employment and hence had the opportunity to accumulate economic resources. Similarly households where two or more members worked would have had the potential to accumulate economic resources quickly (although this would of course have been dependent on the type of work they did).

Longitudinal personal civic disadvantage

To have experienced persistent *personal civic exclusion* during the 1990s would have meant consistently having had negative perceptions about the neighbourhood in which one lives, coupled with a lack of social relations for many observations. Such experiences would be likely to negate an individual's ability to enjoy a satisfactory lifestyle and increase the possibility of facing exclusion and isolation. Consequently the investigation of longitudinal multi-dimensional disadvantage moves away from a focus on purely economic notions of disadvantage to consider the prevalence of persistent *personal civic exclusion* amongst working-age adults.

Table 6.4 **Relationship between longitudinal indicators[a] of *personal civic exclusion*, working-age adults, BHPS, 1991-1999**, total per cent

Social relations longitudinal pattern	Neighbourhood perception longitudinal pattern		
	None	Sporadic	Persistent
None	50	16	8
Sporadic	6	3	2
Persistent	9	5	3

Notes:
[a] Sporadic disadvantage combines the occasional and recurrent definitions. Persistent disadvantage combines the short-term and long-term persistent definitions (see Chapter 5 for more details).

Table 6.4 considers the relationship between longitudinal indicators of *personal civic exclusion* for working-age adults in the 1990s. The analysis does not consider the likely effect of one indicator on the other as, unlike with *household economic deprivation*, it is not clear which indicator would be likely to influence the other, if at all. Instead the table presents the percentage of all working-age adults who fall into particular categories based on the combination and duration spent disadvantaged on each indicator.

Table 6.4 reveals that half of the working-age population were not disadvantaged on either the neighbourhood perception or the social relations indicator for any of the nine survey observations. Of individuals disadvantaged on either of the indicators at least once during the decade, the majority were so on only one of the indicators. As was shown in Chapter 5 individuals were more likely to have experienced disadvantage on the neighbourhood perception indicator during the decade.

The cross-sectional analysis of the relationship between neighbourhood perception and social relations revealed that very few working-age adults were simultaneously disadvantaged on both indicators at a point in time (see Chapter 4, Table 4.8). Taking a longitudinal perspective confirms that this relationship remains over time. However, as with household economic disadvantage, there was a small proportion of the population (3 per cent) who persistently experienced disadvantage on both indicators.

The socio-demographic characteristics of individuals who experienced persistent *personal civic exclusion* are explored in Table 6.5. To identify the most extreme form of *personal civic exclusion* the following definition is used: individuals who were long-term persistently [4] disadvantaged on both the neighbourhood perception indicator and the social relations indicator.

Table 6.5 Odds[a] of experiencing long-term persistent *personal civic exclusion*[b] by individual and household socio-demographic characteristic, working-age adults, BHPS, 1991-1999, logistic regression model

Socio-demographic characteristics (1999)	Odds
Sex	
Male	ref
Female	**0.5**
Age group	
16-29 years	**2.5**
30-44 years	ref
45-59/64 years	1.0

---

[4] In this analysis long-term persistently disadvantaged identifies individuals who experienced six or more observations of disadvantage during the 1990s, rather than seven or more as defined in Chapter 5, so to allow enough cases for valid analysis.

Table 6.5   (continued)

Household type	
Single	3.9
Couple no children	3.2
Couple, dependent children only	ref
Couple, some non-dependent children	4.3
Lone parent, dependent children only	1.2
Lone parent, some non-dependent children	**5.1**
Other	0.1
Number of children	
None	0.3
One	ref
Two or more	1.4
Education level	
Degree or higher	1.2
A-level	1.1
O-level	ref
CSE level	1.4
None of these	**3.1**
Main activity status	
Employed full time	1.7
Employed part time	3.7
Unemployed	**6.2**
Care of home/family	ref
Education/training	**6.8**
Other inactive	0.1
Number in household in employment	
None	1.3
One	Ref
Two or more	**0.3**

Notes:

[a] Persistent *personal civic exclusion* is defined as individuals who were persistently (6 or more observations) disadvantaged on the neighbourhood perception indicator *and* who were persistently (6 or more observations) disadvantaged on the social relations indicator.

[b] Odds ratios higher (lower) than 1 implies that the socio-demographic characteristic is associated with increased (decreased) odds of experiencing the event (*household economic deprivation*) compared to the reference category (ref). Bold text indicates a statistically significant (p<0.05) coefficient.

At a cross-sectional level the individual characteristics linked to increased odds of experiencing *personal civic exclusion* were being a lone parent, unemployed, living in poor housing and having ill health. It was argued that these factors can act to restrict an individual's inclusion in civic acts of society whether because of childcare, low income, lack of self esteem, dissatisfaction with housing (whether to live in or to entertain others), and the physical inability to meet others.

The longitudinal analysis links these factors to persistent personal civic also, along with other individual and household characteristics.

Other factors that appear significantly linked to persistent *personal civic exclusion* are labour market status and education. Any labour market-related activity (whether working or not) was associated with increased odds of experiencing persistent *personal civic exclusion* compared with those who cared for the home or family. The odds were especially high for those in education or training. Many of those in education or training were likely to have been individuals returning to education and/or taking training as a route back into employment (because of panel sample selection rules, they were at least in their mid-twenties in 1999). Conversely, living in a household where two or more members were in work significantly reduced the likelihood of experiencing persistent *personal civic exclusion*, perhaps a consequence of being able to afford to live in an agreeable neighbourhood and to socialize in and out of the work place.

The longitudinal analysis suggests that working-age females were significantly less likely than males to have experienced persistent *personal civic exclusion* during the 1990s. Although income poverty and economic deprivation disproportionately affect women (see Rowlingson et al, 1999 for further evidence of this) it appears the same cannot be said regarding *personal civic exclusion*, and in particular it is not true in respect of a lack of social relations (see also analysis of one-dimensional persistent disadvantage in Chapter 5, Table 5.9).

Longitudinal personal health deprivation

To suffer persistent *personal health exclusion* during the 1990s meant experiencing physical or mental ill health, or a combination of both, for most part of the decade. Such experiences are not generally associated with adults of working age. However, cross-sectional analysis of the BHPS data has shown that a significant proportion of working-age adults did experience ill health at a point in time. This section will go on to show that there were a small group of individuals who faced such experiences persistently – experiences that could have restricted efforts to participate in society and have contributed to feelings of exclusion.

Table 6.6 considers the relationship between longitudinal indicators of *personal health exclusion* for working-age adults in the 1990s. The analysis considers the likely effect of physical health disadvantage on mental health disadvantage (column per cent in table) given the suggested link between these two indicators in Table 6.1. Table 6.6 is constructed to suggest that a spell of physical ill health may have led to mental ill health, rather than vice-versa. The table also presents the percentage of all working-age adults who fall into particular categories based on the combination and duration spent disadvantaged on each indicator (total per cent in table).

Table 6.6 **Relationship between longitudinal indicators[a] of *personal health exclusion*, working-age adults, BHPS, 1991-1999**, column per cent (total per cent)

Mental health longitudinal pattern	Physical health longitudinal pattern		
	None	Sporadic	Persistent
None	68 (46)	47 (9)	43 (6) .
Sporadic	25 (17)	37 (7)	29 (4)
Persistent	7 (5)	16 (3)	29 (4)

Notes:
[a] Sporadic disadvantage combines the occasional and recurrent definitions. Persistent disadvantage combines the short-term and long-term persistent definitions (see Chapter 5 for more details).

The relationship between physical and mental ill health suggested above is confirmed at a longitudinal level in Table 6.6. Occurrences of physical ill health appear to increase the likelihood of time spent suffering from mental ill health. Almost three in ten (29 per cent) of those who experienced persistent physical health disadvantage during the decade also encountered persistent periods of mental ill heath. This was four times higher than those who experienced no physical health disadvantage at all.

Table 6.6 shows that only just under one half (46 per cent) of working-age adults did not record any forms of ill health, either physical or mental, during the nine-observation period. Of those that did experience ill health, the majority did so according to the mental health indicator (see also Chapter 5, Table 5.7). Earlier analysis has shown that spells of mental ill health tend to be widespread and short, with most people experiencing only occasional or recurrent periods (see Chapter 5, Table 5.4 and Table 5.7). Fewer than three in ten working-age adults experienced sporadic periods of mental ill health. Of these only three in five did not experience forms of physical ill health during the decade as well.

Table 6.7 **Odds[a] of experiencing long-term persistent *personal health exclusion*[b] by individual and household socio-demographic characteristic, working-age adults, BHPS, 1991-1999, regression model odds[b]**

Socio-demographic characteristics (1999)	Odds
Sex	
Male	ref
Female	1.5
Age group	
16-29 years	0.4
30-44 years	ref
45-59/64 years	**3.6**

Table 6.7   (continued)

Household type	
Single	**3.0**
Couple no children	1.8
Couple, dependent children only	ref
Couple, some non-dependent children	4.4
Lone parent, dependent children only	0.3
Lone parent, some non-dependent children	2.0
Other	3.3
Number of children	
None	0.3
One	ref
Two or more	1.5
Education level	
Degree or higher	0.8
A-level	1.2
O-level	Ref
CSE level	0.1
None of these	1.6
Main activity status	
Employed full time	**0.1**
Employed part time	0.5
Unemployed	0.8
Care of home/family	Ref
Education/training	0.1
Other inactive	0.1
Number in household in employment	
None	**2.4**
One	ref
Two or more	0.4

Notes:

[a] Persistent *personal health exclusion* is defined as individuals who were persistently (6 or more observations) disadvantaged on the physical health indicator *and* who were persistently (6 or more observations) disadvantaged on the mental health indicator.

[b] Odds ratios higher (lower) than 1 implies that the socio-demographic characteristic is associated with increased (decreased) odds of experiencing the event (*household economic deprivation*) compared to the reference category (ref). Bold text indicates a statistically significant (p<0.05) coefficient.

There are other occurrences of individuals experiencing both forms of ill health. Overall this happened for approximately one in five of the sample (18 per cent). It is also clear to see that there was a small, but noticeable, proportion of individuals who experienced persistent forms of both types of ill health. Four per cent of all working-age adults were persistently disadvantaged on both the physical health and mental health indicators during the 1990s. The socio-demographic characteristics of these individuals are examined in Table 6.7. To identify the most extreme form of *personal health exclusion* the following definition is used: individuals who were long-term persistently[5] disadvantaged on both the physical health and mental heath indicators.

In Chapter 5 analysis of models of persistent one-dimensional disadvantage showed that poor health was associated with individuals living alone, lone parents, low education and living in a household where no one works (see Chapter 5, Table 5.9). These characteristics were again associated with the experience of persistent *personal health exclusion*. For example, a working-age adult who lived alone had odds of experiencing *personal health exclusion* three times that of a working-age adult living in a couple with dependent children only household.

The socio-demographic characteristic most linked to increased odds of *personal health exclusion* was being aged over 45 years of age. It is unsurprising that older working-age adults were associated with long-term health problems given that poor health, both physical and mental, correlates with age (Benzeval and Judge, 2000). The validity of this effect is upheld by the fact that the age information used in the logistic regression analysis is appropriate for all observations of the survey data. As mentioned above, this cannot be said of other socio-demographic information used in these analyses as individual circumstances, such as main activity and household type, can change over the decade (see Chapter 5 for further discussion on the problems of using static indicators of socio-demographic characteristics).

Avoiding *personal health exclusion* during the 1990s was associated with a main activity that did not involve caring for the home or family. In previous analyses of physical health disadvantage, main activity status was excluded from a socio-demographic breakdown because of the obvious connection between ill health and inability to work. This may in part explain the findings presented in Table 6.7. This point should not be lost in interpretation though, as although mental health problems may not necessarily result in an individual being unable to work, the most serious cases probably do. It is likely that suffering from physical and mental health problems that result in the inability to work increase feelings of exclusion.

Identifying social exclusion

The analysis presented so far in this chapter has shown that working-age individuals in Great Britain in the 1990s suffered from disadvantage in a multitude of forms and that this disadvantage persisted for a varied length of time. The final investigation in this chapter attempts to identify those individuals that suffered from numerous and wide-ranging problems for an extensive period of time. These are the individuals identified by Room as suffering from 'such a degree of multi-

---

[5] In this analysis long-term persistently disadvantaged identifies individuals who experienced six or more observations of disadvantage during the 1990s, rather than seven or more as defined in Chapter 5, so to allow enough cases for valid analysis.

dimensional disadvantage, of such duration, that exclusion from mainstream society is often the result' (Room, 2000, page 171).

To identify social exclusion the two conditions that Room identifies in the above statement need to be satisfied: multi-dimensional and enduring disadvantage. The importance of duration has been examined extensively in this and other studies (see Chapter 5). Particular emphasis has been given to the effects of long-term, persistent disadvantage and how it can severely limit the potential for an individual or household to accumulate resources and how it can result in previously accumulated resources being quickly eroded. Long-term persistent disadvantage causes the most severe experiences and it is this form of disadvantage that is used to operationalize social exclusion in the remainder of this chapter.

The other condition, and more difficult to define, requires evidence of multi-dimensional disadvantage. The multi-dimensional nature of disadvantage has been investigated in detail so far (see in particular the previous sections in this chapter and Chapter 4). One of the main findings from this investigation was that there appears to be three integral elements of social exclusion: *household economic deprivation*, *personal civic exclusion* and *personal health exclusion*. Multi-dimensional disadvantage was seen to occur within these elements to identify the most disadvantaged individuals – for example, an individual who was living in a household with low income and poor quality housing was determined to be more disadvantaged than someone with just one of these conditions.

The definition of multi-dimensional disadvantage used in the operationalization of social exclusion employed in the remainder of this section is slightly different. It implies that the multi-dimensional nature of social exclusion cuts across these integral elements. In other words, social exclusion is about multiple forms of disadvantage that occur in all three of the integral elements rather than those that are restricted to just one element. This means that social exclusion affects an individual (and their household) in a number of different ways, not purely for economic or civic or health reasons. For example, an individual who suffered from persistent forms of income poverty and housing circumstance disadvantage is judged to have been severely economically deprived but not necessarily socially excluded. Instead it is the individual who suffered from persistent forms of *household economic deprivation*, *personal civic exclusion* and *personal health exclusion* who is at most risk of experiencing social exclusion.

The next stage of analysis is to ascertain to what extent persistent disadvantage cuts across these three elements and, where it does, to investigate the prevalence and nature of the most socially excluded working-age individuals in British society. Theoretically the most extreme definition of social exclusion would imply continuous disadvantage on all seven social exclusion indicators for all nine observations of the survey data. Unsurprisingly there were no individuals who suffered such fate. It already has been established that very few individuals experienced persistent or multi-dimensional disadvantage. This means that analysis that identifies social exclusion is going to be restricted by the low number of individuals facing such predicaments in the BHPS dataset. Where these limitations have an affect on the analysis they are detailed in the text accordingly.

The prevalence of social exclusion

The BHPS data is used to define social exclusion according to duration and multi-dimensionality. Social exclusion is therefore measured as persistent wide-ranging multi-dimensional disadvantage – that is, disadvantage on at least one indicator in all three integral elements (*household economic deprivation, personal civic exclusion* and *personal health exclusion*) for at least six of the available nine observations of BHPS data. Table 6.8 looks at the relationship between indicators of persistent disadvantage defined in this way, where each indicator identifies at least one of the components of the three integral elements of social exclusion.

Table 6.8   The prevalence of wide-ranging multi-dimensional disadvantage, working-age adults, BHPS, 1991-1999, column per cent (total per cent in brackets)

Persistent personal civic exclusion[a]	*Persistent personal health exclusion*[b]	*Persistent household economic deprivation*[c]	
		Disadvantaged	Not disadvantaged
Disadvantaged			
	Disadvantaged	**1 (1)**	2 (2)
	Not disadvantaged	2 (2)	2 (2)
Not disadvantaged			
	Disadvantaged	2 (2)	2 (2)
	Not disadvantaged	95 (2)	94 (87)

Notes:
[a] *Household economic deprivation* is defined as individuals who experience disadvantage on the financial situation indicator or the material possessions indicator or the housing circumstance indicator.
[b] *Personal civic exclusion* is defined as individuals who experience disadvantage on the neighbourhood perception indicator or the social relations indicator.
[c] *Personal health exclusion* is defined as individuals who experience disadvantage on the physical health indicator or the mental health indicator.

From Table 6.8 the prevalence of social exclusion in Great Britain in the 1990s can be obtained – it is the three-way combination of disadvantage on *household economic deprivation, personal civic exclusion* and *personal health exclusion* (highlighted in bold text). The findings suggest that persistent wide-ranging multi-dimensional disadvantage was extremely rare amongst the working-age population in Great Britain during the 1990s. There were very few working-age adults (approximately 1 per cent) who experienced persistent disadvantage on all three elements of social exclusion and few who did so on two elements.

The table reinforces findings from the factor analysis presented in Chapter 4. This suggested that similar types of disadvantage group together (according to the integral elements: *household economic deprivation, personal civic exclusion* and *personal health exclusion*) and that individuals were unlikely to have experienced disadvantage in more than one of these. Hence Room's notion of 'catastrophe'[6] was unlikely to be experienced at a wide-ranging level, but more so within the bounds of each integral element of social exclusion.

Identifying individuals most at risk of social exclusion

Despite the extremely low likelihood of working-age adults experiencing social exclusion during the 1990s, there was a very small minority who did experience persistent disadvantage on all three integral elements. These individuals would have spent the *majority* of the 1990s suffering from at least one form of *household economic deprivation* (such as income below the poverty line or housing that has no central heating or is overcrowded) *and* at least one form of *personal civic exclusion* (such as wanting to move house because their neighbourhood is unsafe or lacking social support networks they can rely on in times of need) *and* at least one form of *personal health exclusion* (such as physical health problems or mental health disorders). There can be no doubt that these individuals were suffering quite extreme forms of disadvantage, that many would regard as unacceptable in a British society approaching the twenty-first century.

The final table in this chapter identifies the family circumstances and individual status associated with individuals most likely to have experienced social exclusion in Great Britain in the 1990s.

Table 6.9   Odds[a] of experiencing social exclusion[b] by individual and household socio-demographic characteristic, working-age adults, BHPS, 1991-1999, logistic regression model

Socio-demographic characteristics (1999)	Odds
Sex	
Male	ref
Female	0.9
Age group	
16-29 years	1.6
30-44 years	ref
45-59/64 years	**0.7**
Household type	
Single	**3.1**
Couple no children	0.1
Couple, dependent children only	ref
Couple, some non-dependent children	1.7
Lone parent, dependent children only	0.4
Lone parent, some non-dependent children	**5 0**
Other	0.0

---

[6] According to Room, 'catastrophe' occurs when people experience discontinuity in relationships with the rest of society in terms of multi-dimensional and enduring disadvantage.

Table 6.9   (continued)

Number of children	
None	0.1
One	ref
Two or more	**1.8**
Education level	
Degree or higher	0.7
A-level	0.9
O-level	ref
CSE level	1.2
None of these	**2.7**
Main activity status	
Employed full time	**0.4**
Employed part time	**0.4**
Unemployed	0.2
Care of home/family	ref
Education/training	0.1
Other inactive	0.7
Number in household in employment	
None	**3.5**
One	ref
Two or more	0.7

Notes:
[a] Social exclusion is defined as 6 observations or more suffering from: at least one form of *household economic deprivation, and* at least one form of *personal civic exclusion, and* at least one form of *personal health exclusion.*
[b] Bold text indicates an odds ratio derived from a statistically significant (p<0.05) coefficient.

The socio-demographic characteristics linked with social exclusion have been repeatedly associated with forms of current and longitudinal one-dimensional disadvantage and current multi-dimensional disadvantage. It is these characteristics that were associated with the most enduring and wide-ranging forms of disadvantage in British society during the 1990s and suggest a number of risk groups on which poverty, deprivation and social exclusion policy should be targeted.

The cross-sectional analysis of current wide-ranging multi-dimensional disadvantage revealed that being a lone parent and having no academic education were characteristics associated with increased odds of such experiences. These findings remain true when looking at persistent wide-ranging multi-dimensional disadvantage (social exclusion), along with living alone, living in a household with two or more children and living in a household where no one works.

Identifying sub-groups of the population at particular risk of social exclusion can point policy makers towards needy groups. Conversely, identifying the socio-demographic characteristics of those who appear to avoid social exclusion can help to identify factors linked to preventing such experiences. Table 6.9 suggests that older working-age adults and those in work, either full- or part-time, were particularly unlikely to experience social exclusion. These findings suggest that the government is justified in trying to avert problems of social exclusion by promoting employment-related policies (such as the New Deal programmes) and policies aimed at young adults and lone parents.

However, making sweeping generalizations about individuals based on their socio-demographic characteristics can sometimes be unhelpful. For example, although previous analysis has shown that in general older working-age adults and those in employment were particularly less likely to suffer economic problems, this is not to say that older working-age adults and those in employment avoid all aspects of social exclusion. Older people in particular were likely to experience forms of physical ill health and working-age adults can face the problems associated with low paid, irregular and unsatisfactory work. Nevertheless the analysis presented in this chapter does suggest that these groups were at less risk of facing an array of social exclusion related problems and for considerable periods of time.

Conclusion

This chapter has built on the exploratory work of Chapters 4 and 5 to combine longitudinal and multi-dimensional techniques in an investigation of social exclusion in Great Britain in the 1990s. There have been very few attempts to employ a multi-dimensional *and* longitudinal approach to measuring social exclusion in previous studies. In doing so the chapter provides a working definition of social exclusion that encapsulates the most wide-ranging and enduring forms of disadvantage in British society.

The investigation of the nature of social exclusion in previous chapters revealed that there were very few working-age adults in Great Britain who were disadvantaged on a number of social exclusion indicators, nor who experienced disadvantage for an extensive duration of time. The cross-sectional analysis of multi-dimensional disadvantage revealed the three integral elements of social exclusion – *household economic deprivation, personal civic exclusion* and *personal health exclusion*. These relationships remained when longitudinal information was taken into account. This supports the finding of other studies (Burchardt et al, 1999; Whelan et al, 2001) that suggest that social exclusion should not be considered as a single entity but instead according to different dimensions (or elements as discussed here).[7]

The number of individuals who suffered on each of the three elements of social exclusion was minimal, less than one in twenty of the working-age population. To gauge the comprehensive nature of social exclusion only individuals who were long-term disadvantaged in all three elements were identified.

---

[7] The following chapter considers the benefits of using a composite measure to investigate social exclusion in Europe.

Again the number of excluded individuals was very low. This suggests that very few working-age adults experienced wide-ranging and enduring disadvantage (social exclusion) in Great Britain in the 1990s and that Room's notion of 'catastrophe' affects only a very small minority of the working-age population living in private households.

As only very few working-age individuals were encompassed by the chosen definition of social exclusion, an examination of the socio-demographic risk factors of these individuals was limited. However, the analysis did suggest that certain socio-demographic characteristics were linked to increased odds of social exclusion, most notably living in a lone parent household, living alone, living in a household with two or more children and living in a household where no one works.

The following chapter applies and adapts the methodological advances of this investigation to compare the findings for Great Britain with other European Member states using the European Community Household Panel survey. In particular the analysis explores the prevalence and risk of social exclusion in Great Britain with other countries and contributes to the cross-country study of social exclusion across Europe.

Chapter 7

Social Exclusion in Europe: Comparing the UK to Other European Union Member States

... the analysis of social exclusion may assist analysis of many basic dimensions of European social life in its complex, dynamic and comparative aspects. ... [However] not all of the data that are relevant to the analysis and monitoring of social exclusion, at a EU level, are yet being sufficiently exploited (Berghman, 1995, p. 25).

Introduction

This study has so far concentrated on the nature of social exclusion in Great Britain, yet social exclusion and the role of the welfare state in alleviating these are currently at the centre of the public discourse in all countries across the EU. Empirical investigations of social exclusion across Europe are few and far between, confirming the need, both from a research and policy perspective, for comparable information on social exclusion across different European countries. This type of analysis performed cross-nationally is central to compare the prevalence and nature of social exclusion in Great Britain across the European Union and, from a policy perspective in particular, within different types of welfare state.

This chapter uses data from the European Community Household Panel (ECHP) survey to investigate social exclusion in Europe. The ECHP is a dataset that provides a new opportunity to examine the extent and nature of social exclusion in Europe. It collects information on a range of social and economic factors, following the same people over time and has the unique advantage of being genuinely comparative across countries.

The chapter begins with a brief review of previous studies of the most disadvantaged individuals in Europe. The majority of the chapter concentrates on an empirical investigation of social exclusion in Europe using data from the first three waves of the ECHP survey. The ECHP data is first used to create comparable indicators of social exclusion across the EU-12. The indicators are constructed using a similar methodology to that used in Chapter 3 – where social exclusion indicators were constructed for Great Britain using BHPS data – although a relative rather than absolute approach is taken to ensure comparability between countries.

Investigations consider the relationship between dimensions of social exclusion across the EU-12. Given that only three waves of the ECHP are available, analysis of the longitudinal nature of social exclusion is somewhat limited. However a definition of social exclusion is adopted that incorporates persistent disadvantage – that is disadvantage in all three waves – with disadvantage on a number of indicators. The chapter concludes with an analysis of the prevalence of social exclusion across the EU-12 and of the socio-demographic characteristics associated with increased odds of such experiences.

Investigating social exclusion in Europe: the story so far

As already mentioned, to date investigations into social exclusion across Europe have been limited. However, the growth of poverty has been the concern of European policy makers since European-level poverty work began to get off the ground in the mid-1970s (see Room, Ed. 1995, for a summary of the first three European anti-poverty programmes). It was not until the third poverty programme that considerable progress was made on the use of different poverty concepts and measures, and the ranking of countries according to these (Ramprakash, 1994). However these studies were among the first comparative studies to draw on microdata in Europe and consequently the research suffered from some serious limitations. One of the main limitations was that the information drawn from each country was still not truly comparable. Not only did some of the national household surveys suffer from small sample size, but also the survey methodology varied between countries. This meant that attempts to harmonize the information in the surveys proved difficult.

Probably the most resourced comparative data on living standards has been the Luxembourg Income Study (LIS). The LIS was set up in 1983, gathering together datasets on household income from more than 25 countries, for one of more years. However, work using this source has tended to focus mainly on comparisons of poverty and income inequality rather than multi-dimensional disadvantage (Forssen, 1998; Bradbury and Markus, 2001). More recently, cross-national studies have appeared which are based on national panel surveys. For example the Panel Comparability Project (PACO) has created an international database integrating microdata from various national household panel surveys over a number of years in an attempt to harmonize living standards concepts ex post (Schaber et al, 1993).

In 1994 Eurostat provided a breakthrough in attempts to provide comparable European poverty and deprivation statistics, with the introduction of the European Community Household Panel (ECHP) survey. The survey provided for the first time truly comparable microdata on living standards in participating countries of the European Union (for more information on the ECHP see below). Initially the ECHP microdata was only available to researchers inside the European

Commission and those employed on European Commission funded projects.[1] Therefore, to date only a few studies have examined income poverty rates across European countries using comparable data and methodologies, let alone information on multi-dimensional disadvantage and social exclusion.

Much of the work on disadvantage using the ECHP has been conducted by Eurostat researchers and has indeed focussed on income poverty across Europe (European Commission, 1990, 1994). Eurostat has also performed a modest amount of descriptive analysis on non-monetary deprivation across the EU-12 countries (European Commission, 1999, 2000). They concluded that approximately two in five of persons living in income poverty in the European Union faced multiple disadvantages in at least two of the following domains: arrears with repayments, inability to afford household necessity items (such as diet and new clothes) and problems with accommodation (such as lack of space and damp).

Given the limitations of adequate data, at present there are few studies that attempt to operationalize social exclusion at a European level. Instead studies have tended to focus on either the multi-dimensional or longitudinal nature of disadvantage, and usually only from an economic perspective. Some studies have looked at various dimensions of social exclusion in Europe from a national context only – for example see studies of Greece, (Tsakloglou and Panopoulou, 1998); the Netherlands (Muffels et al, 1992); Sweden (Hallerod, 1995); Ireland (Nolan and Whelan, 1996); Great Britain (see references from Chapter 2) and France (Paugam, 1995) – and some with a cross-country perspective – for example see studies by Paugam (1996), Bradshaw (1999), Goodin et al (1999), Gallie and Paugam, (Eds. 2000); Hauser et al, (2000); Mejer and Linden, (2000); Whelan et al, (2001); Barnes et al, (2002) and Apospori and Millar (Eds., 2002). Generally however there is a lack of truly comparable work on social exclusion in Europe. Part of the reason for this scarcity is the lack of truly comparable longitudinal information on multi-dimensional disadvantage at a European level. The introduction of the ECHP survey into the academic research environment provides an opportunity for such research.

The European Community Household Panel survey

This section explains the main features of the ECHP survey. It also details the selection and validation of the sample used to investigate social exclusion across Europe in this chapter.

---

[1] For more details of direct access to ECHP data go to the Eurostat website http://europa.eu.int/comm/eurostat/.

Describing the survey

There are three unique qualities of the ECHP survey that make it ideal for an investigation into social exclusion in the EU Firstly, it is comparable between participating countries of the EU Secondly, it is a panel survey and therefore allows longitudinal analysis to be performed, and thirdly it is a multi-dimensional survey that covers a wide range of demographic, economic and social topics.

Comparable
The ECHP is the first survey that collects truly comparable dynamic information on a wide range of demographic, social and economic indicators across Europe. To allow accurate comparisons between countries, the survey is based on a harmonized questionnaire. This means that a core questionnaire, designed centrally at Eurostat in close consultation with member states, is administered in each of the countries included in the survey. The use of a common instrument ensures not only common concepts and contents for the surveys, but also a common approach to their operationalization and implementation.[2]

The first wave of the survey was conducted in 1994 in 12 European countries and two extra countries joined the survey in the following two waves. The only EU country not to be included in the ECHP by the third wave of the survey was Sweden.[3] The countries included in the first three waves of the ECHP are Belgium, Denmark, France, Germany, Greece, Ireland, Italy, Luxembourg, the Netherlands, Portugal, Spain and the UK. It is these countries that will be used in an investigation of social exclusion in Europe in this chapter.

Longitudinal
The second quality of the ECHP is that it is a panel survey. This design is similar to that employed in the BHPS and allows the same individuals to be followed over time by annually re-interviewing original sample members (those in households selected for inclusion in the first wave of the survey) on a yearly basis. As demonstrated in Chapter 5, longitudinal information is crucial in the operationalization of social exclusion. Although only the first three waves of ECHP data are available to this research, they provide a useful insight into the longitudinal nature of social exclusion in Europe.

Achieved sample sizes in each country of the ECHP can vary quite considerably. This can result from non-contact, non-response, failure to follow-up sample cases for other reasons and households ceasing to exist. These shortfalls are compensated to some extent by the inclusion of new (split-off) households coming into the sample as a result of the movement of sample persons. The cross-sectional

---

[2] The ECHP does allow for flexibility for adaptation to specific national circumstances that can vary considerably between the Member States.
[3] Other European countries not included in the survey due to their non-membership of the EU include Norway, Switzerland, Iceland, and eastern European countries.

household response rates for wave 2 of the ECHP were relatively high; the average for all the countries was approximately 90 per cent (Clémenceau and Verma 1996).[4]

Multi-dimensional

The third important characteristic of the ECHP survey is that it covers a wide range of demographic, economic and social topics. The survey itself is administered in two stages. The first stage involves a household interview, covering topics related to the household as whole and answered by a reference person. This is followed by the personal interview, which is administered to all individuals in the household 16 years of age and older.

Many of the topics in the ECHP are relevant to the investigation of social exclusion. The household interview covers information on: household composition, demographic information, housing, income, and the possession of non-monetary household items. The individual interview covers topics such as the labour market, individual income, health, social relations, social responsibilities and the degree of satisfaction with various aspects of work and life.

Selecting and validating the sample

For each country a sample of adults of working-age, and who completed a full individual interview, was taken for cross-sectional (1996) and longitudinal (1994-1996) analysis. The three-wave cross-sectional and panel sample statistics are presented in Table 7.1.[5]

---

[4] As with all surveys, non-response bias can occur when households and individuals that failed to respond to the survey are systematically different from those who do respond. This can result in biased estimates when the survey results are used to make generalizations regarding the whole population. The normal method of compensating for survey non-response is to use weights that adjust the responding survey units for those that fail to respond. The ECHP applied this method in formulating non-response rates, which were combined with weights to account for design effect and to correct the distribution of households and individuals on variables such as age, sex, main activity status and other relevant characteristics. Appropriate weights are used in all analysis presented in this chapter.

[5] As stated in all contracts on the use of ECHP data, there are statistical requirements to be followed in any 'publication' of results, including this research. Cell size thresholds will be distinguished for ECHP cross-sectional and longitudinal results in this chapter as follows: Cross-sectional, 1) Below 20 observations (unweighted sample), results may not be published (represented instead as an asterisk); 2) From 20 to 49 observations (unweighted sample), results may be published but are to be individually identified, shown in brackets [ ]. Longitudinal, 1) Below 10 observations (unweighted sample), results may not be published (represented instead as an asterisk); 2) From 10 to 29 observations (unweighted sample), results may be published but are to be individually identified, shown in brackets [ ].

Table 7.1   Number of working-age adults in the cross-sectional and panel samples,[6] ECHP, 1994-1996, frequency[7]

Country	Cross-sectional sample			Panel sample
	1994	1995	1996	1994-1996
Belgium	4510	5035	4797	4197
Denmark	3657	4324	3927	3358
France	9861	10496	10275	9044
Germany	6825	6955	6803	6301
Greece	8107	9040	8374	7188
Ireland	5809	6988	6115	5309
Italy	13361	14430	14076	12387
Luxembourg	1546	1631	1579	1462
Netherlands	6908	7412	7570	6305
Portugal	8015	8732	8709	7365
Spain	11342	12432	11760	9991
UK	**5078**	**6400**	**5320**	**4826**
EU-12	85019	93875	89305	77733

As with all panel surveys the ECHP suffers from attrition. According to Eurostat analysis of the first three waves of the survey, more than 75 per cent of all persons participating in the ECHP were interviewed in all waves (European Commission, 2000). According to Table 7.1 the number of individuals included in the 3-wave panel sample constructed for analysis in this chapter indicates lower attrition rates. This is mainly because the sample excludes individuals often under-represented in panel surveys, such as adults of retirement age and older (Taylor, 1994).[8]

Constructing and validating a set of social exclusion indicators

In this section, a set of indicators of social exclusion is constructed using data from the ECHP survey. The indicators are constructed using many of the key criteria for selecting and constructing indicators for Great Britain using the BHPS data (see Chapter 2, Table 2.3). Chapter 3, above, outlined the dimensions of social

---

[6] In all tables presented in this chapter analysis is performed on working-age adults – defined as adults (male or female) aged 16 to 64 years – who completed a full individual interview and lived in a household where a full household interview was completed also.

[7] All tables presented in this chapter represent own analysis of ECHP data unless indicated otherwise. Results published in this chapter may be slightly different than other published results of ECHP data due to the use of different concepts, definitions and samples.

[8] Missing data can also occur for other reasons, such as when respondents fail to respond to particular questions or there are errors in data coding. For ECHP missing data analysis see Appendix B2.

exclusion to be identified from the BHPS data. These dimensions are used for constructing indicators using the ECHP.

The dimensions are:

- Financial situation (income poverty).
- Material possessions.
- Housing circumstances.
- Neighbourhood perceptions.
- Social relations.
- Physical health.
- Mental health.

The following section details the construction and validation of these indicators.

Defining indicators for cross-country analysis

One of the major barriers to performing a comparative analysis of social exclusion is obtaining a measure of social exclusion that is relevant to each and every country under investigation. The most conventional and valid way to measure social exclusion across countries is therefore to use a relative approach (Hallerod, 1998). The relative approach is more suited to cross-country analysis than the absolute approach (used to investigate social exclusion in Great Britain in Chapters 3 to 6) as it ensures that social exclusion is measured against a standard that has social relevance in each country involved in the analysis.

Using a standard that has social relevance in each country means choosing indicators that are valuable for the study of social exclusion in every country in the study. Given that standards and practices vary across countries, constructing each indicator from a range of information and weighting this information according to certain country specifics best achieve this. This approach is possible with the ECHP data as the survey was designed with the aim of measuring social exclusion across the EU and hence the questionnaire contains in-depth coverage of the dimensions of disadvantage outlined above.

The most popular method of combining information on a number of aspects of disadvantage with a relative approach is to use a Proportional Disadvantage Index (PDI). The PDI approach (based on the work of Mack and Lansley, 1985; Hallerod, 1995) combines information on individual and population levels of the possession of resources (or participation), at a country level in this case, to create a direct measure of disadvantage. The PDI approach selects a number of items to form an indicator to represent a particular domain of disadvantage. The score on the PDI is the outcome of the number of items a person (or their household) possesses (or participates in) and the specific weight assigned to each item according to possession (participation) of the item in the population as a whole.[9]

---

[9] Depending on whether information in the ECHP was available for the whole population or just a subset of the population (e.g. adults), appropriate weights were applied in the construction of the indicators. See Table 7.2 for details of these weights.

The construction of a PDI can be illustrated using the material possessions indicator as an example. The index assigns to each population member whose household is disadvantaged on each of a list of disadvantage items (a car or van, a colour TV, a video recorder, a microwave oven, a dishwasher and a telephone) a weight equal to the proportion of the population living in dwellings not disadvantaged on the corresponding item. As a result, if a particular item is very common (or very rare), an individual whose household is without this item is given a high (low) weight. Then, the weights of each population member are added together and divided by the sum of the average 'materially privileged' score in the entire population (that is, the sum of the proportions of the population not lacking the particular item).[10]

The PDI approach was used in the construction of all bar the financial situation indicator.[11] Thresholds were attributed to each indicator based on a percentage of the average disadvantage score. Deciding on an appropriate threshold is more or less an arbitrary decision and one of the main criticisms of using the relative approach to measuring disadvantage. Thresholds were chosen that identify a distinct minority of individuals in each country, maintaining the aim of identifying a notion of 'exclusion', and which withstood a number of validation procedures including sensitivity testing.[12] The definition of each indicator is outlined in detail in Table 7.2.

Table 7.2   Definition of indicators of social exclusion, working-age adults, ECHP

Indicator	Definition
Financial situation	*Individual lives in a household below relative income poverty line.*
	- The income poverty threshold used in this research is 60 per cent of the median equivalized net disposable weekly household income for all household members. Household income was deflated using the modified OECD equivalence scale (which assigns a weight of 1.0 to the first adult in the household, 0.5 to each subsequent adult and 0.3 to each children aged under 14 years), to take into account differences in household size and composition. The median was calculated on the cross-sectional weighted distribution of all individuals (adults and children).

---

[10] For an algebraic summary of this calculation, adapted from Tsakloglou and Papadopoulos (2002), see Appendix F.

[11] The financial situation indicator is based on the distribution of household income and adopts a purely relative approach.

[12] This meant that the percentage of the average PDI score used to define the disadvantage threshold was not necessarily the same for all indicators.

Table 7.2   (continued)

Material possessions	*Individual lives in a household below relative durable item disadvantage threshold.* - Respondents were asked whether or not the household possesses a list of durable items: a car or van, a colour TV, a video recorder, a microwave oven, a dishwasher and a telephone. If a household does not possess a particular item respondents were asked whether this is because they do not want it or cannot afford it. A PDI was constructed according to the proportion of the population (adults and children) who live in households with an enforced lack of each item. Individuals were disadvantaged on this index if their score was below 60 per cent of the median weighted score of all individuals.
Housing circumstance	*Individual lives in a household below relative amenity disadvantage threshold.* - Respondents were asked whether or not the household has a list of amenity items: a separate kitchen, a bath or shower, an indoor flushing toilet, hot running water, central heating or electric storage heaters, and a place to sit outside. A PDI was constructed according to the proportion of the population (adults and children) who lived in households without each item. Individuals were disadvantaged if their score was below 80 per cent of the median weighted score of all individuals.
Neighbourhood perception	*Individual lives in a household below relative neighbourhood disadvantage threshold.* - Respondents were asked whether or not the household suffers from: noise from neighbours or outside, pollution caused by traffic or industry, and crime or vandalism in the area. A PDI was constructed according to the proportion of the population (adults and children) who lived in households without each item. Individuals were disadvantaged on this index if their score was below 60 per cent of the median weighted score of all individuals.
Social relations	*Individual below relative social relations threshold.* - Respondents (adults only) were asked about their levels of social support networks: the frequency of seeing friends or relatives, how often they spoke to their neighbours and whether they were a member of a club or organization. A PDI was constructed according to the proportion of the population (adults only) who lacked each form of social contact (e.g. saw friends or relatives less than once a month). Individuals were disadvantaged on this index if their score was below 60 per cent of the median weighted score of all working-age adults.

Table 7.2   (continued)

Physical health	*Individual has physical health problems.*
	- Respondents were asked a series questions about their physical ill health: a subjective assessment of general health and whether they were hampered in daily activities. A PDI was constructed according to the proportion of the population (adults only) who suffered from ill health. Individuals were disadvantaged on this index if their score was below 70 per cent of the median weighted score of all working-age adults.
Mental health	*Individual has mental health problems.*
	- Respondents were asked a series questions about their mental ill health: whether they felt they had to cut down on the things they usually do around the house, at work, or in their free time due to emotional or mental health problems and satisfaction levels with various aspects of their daily life (housing circumstance, financial situation and leisure time). A PDI was constructed according to the proportion of the population (adults only) who suffered from ill health. Individuals were disadvantaged on this index if their score was below 70 per cent of the median weighted score of all working-age adults.

Establishing the magnitude of disadvantage across Europe

Ensuring the set of social exclusion indicators is valid across countries requires a number of quality assessment procedures.[13] A common assessment procedure is to verify that each indicator is actually measuring the concept of disadvantage that it purports to measure in each country and that the indicator is identifying disadvantaged individuals. This validation procedure was undertaken in Chapter 3 by comparing the BHPS indicators with other questions from the survey that covered similar concepts. A similar method is used here with the ECHP data (see Table 7.3).

---

[13] The quality assessment procedures included choosing a disadvantaged response to a question or questions for each social exclusion domain in each country, and ensuring that information required to construct each indicator is present and of useable quality in each of the three waves of the survey. Despite such procedures the comparability of the indicators may be hindered by factors outside the control of the researcher. For example, although the ECHP is a highly harmonized survey differences may appear between countries due to problems in translation of centrally designed questions and cultural differences in answering subjective questions (European Commission, 1996).

Table 7.3 Magnitude of disadvantage by social exclusion dimension, disadvantaged working-age adults,[a] ECHP, 1996, cell per cent

Disadvantage item	Be	De	Fr	Ge	Gr	Ir	It	Lu	Ne	Po	Sp	UK	EU-12
							Country						
Financial													
Poverty line (x100)[b]	7.5	7.9	7.2	7.7	4.3	5.4	5.2	11	6.9	3.8	4.5	6.8	5.9
Poverty gap (x100)[c]	2.2	2.1	1.9	2.4	1.4	1.2	1.9	2.8	2.4	1.4	1.5	1.8	2.0
Financial difficulties[d]	29	30	42	20	78	59	38	28	38	54	62	42	48
Repayment arrears[e]	24	[10]	24	7	57	24	15	*	9	7	16	33	21
Cannot afford holiday[f]	49	28	65	26	82	72	69	40	35	82	79	69	66
Cannot afford furniture[g]	52	41	65	41	92	47	81	41	48	88	80	67	70
Cannot afford clothes[h]	21	[9]	23	27	44	24	26	*	32	61	18	33	30
Cannot afford meat[i]	*	*	15	10	63	10	13	*	[7]	12	5	20	16
Cannot afford to host[j]	26	*	27	21	92	35	31	[15]	20	27	30	30	34
Material													
Cannot afford phone[k]	35	[10]	14	11	21	44	25	*	*	57	41	*	33
Cannot afford TV[l]	*	[11]	12	[6]	12	*	11	*	*	20	3	*	10
Housing													
No bath/shower[m]	[12]	25	12	20	8	16	5	*	[14]	34	9	*	16
Financial burden[n]	53	[19]	31	20	32	52	65	*	[15]	37	51	49	41
Neighbourhood													
Crime/vandalism[o]	82	46	72	79	66	65	80	44	56	79	86	47	73
Neighbourhood noise[p]	81	93	99	93	81	99	87	98	89	99	91	99	92
Social relations													
Very little contact[q]	41	19	62	48	59	*	36	53	16	65	25	42	42
No communication[r]	*	*	[7]	*	*	*	31	*	--	20	*	*	17

Table 7.3 (continued)

Physical health

Cut down on activity[s]	74	88	55	88	57	86	59	81	86	69	79	88	77
Chronic illness[t]	57	58	72	64	84	61	63	62	57	84	58	67	67
Mental health													
Cut down on activity[u]	34	22	16	18	8	17	5	42	24	36	18	43	20
Dissatisfied (financial)[v]	29	30	37	51	39	55	41	[40]	30	45	70	45	45
Dissatisfied (housing)[w]	25	37	28	16	38	46	37	[39]	27	45	52	43	36
Dissatisfied (leisure)[x]	52	53	63	32	63	55	70	[32]	62	36	50	31	52

Notes:

[a] Table includes only those adults disadvantaged according to each dimension of social exclusion. For example, the magnitude of financial disadvantage applies only to individuals below the income poverty line (i.e. those in financial disadvantage). For Belgium, of those below the poverty line, 29 per cent were experiencing financial difficulties, 24 per cent were in arrears with repayments etc. Likewise, the magnitude of material disadvantage applies only to individuals defined as being in material disadvantage. For Belgium, of those experiencing material disadvantage, 35 per cent could not afford a phone, and so on.

[b] Poverty line is drawn at 60 per cent of annual median household income for all individuals (adults and children) in each country. The poverty line is expressed in terms of the Purchasing Power Standard (PPS). The PPS is used to make income comparable across countries. National monetary units cannot be made directly comparable, by using exchange rates alone for example, as the difference in purchasing power of a particular monetary unit in the different countries will not be taken into account. The PPS uses conversion rates that take both rates of exchange and differences in purchasing power into account. The resulting common reference unit can buy the same amount of goods and services across the countries in a specific year.

[c] The poverty gap is defined as the difference between the income poverty line and household income averaged across all poor working-age adults. The poverty gap is expressed in terms of PPS.

[d] Individuals with difficulty or great difficulty in making ends meet.

[e] Individuals in arrears with utility (electricity, gas, water) bills and/or housing costs (mortgage payments or rent) during the past 12 months.

[f] Individual living in a household that cannot afford paying for a week's annual holiday away from home.

[g] Individual living in a household that cannot afford replacing worn-out furniture.

[h] Individual living in a household that cannot afford to buy new rather than second-hand clothes.

[i] Individual living in a household that cannot afford eating meat (or alternative) every second day, if wanted.

[j] Individual living in a household that cannot afford to have friends or family for a drink or dinner once a month.

Notes to Table 7.3 continued:

k Individual living in a household that wants but cannot afford a telephone.

l Individual living in a household that wants but cannot afford a television.

m Individual living in a household that has no bath or shower.

n Individual living in a household where housing costs are a heavy financial burden.

o Individual living in a household where there is crime or vandalism in the area.

p Individual living in a household where there is noise from neighbours or outside.

q Individual meets other people less often that once a month.

r Individual has not spoken to someone outside the household (even by telephone) in the last week. There is no information available for the Netherlands.

s Individual has had to cut down on things s/he usually does around the house, at work or in free time because of illness or injury.

t Individual has a chronic health problem, illness or disability.

u Mean satisfaction score (work or main activity), 1=not satisfied, 6=fully satisfied.

v Mean satisfaction score (financial situation), 1=not satisfied, 6=fully satisfied.

w Mean satisfaction score (housing situation), 1=not satisfied, 6=fully satisfied.

x Mean satisfaction score (amount of leisure time), 1=not satisfied, 6=fully satisfied.

One of the major criticisms of the relative approach to measuring poverty is that arbitrary thresholds of disadvantage are constructed which often fail to stand up to any justification or validity of a level of decency in terms of living standards (Townsend, 2000). The same criticism can be applied to indicators of social exclusion that are constructed using the PDI approach. To illustrate the validity of each indictor constructed here, Table 7.3 also includes statistics from some of the questions used to create the indicators to illustrate the actual levels of disadvantage in each country, something often hidden in a composite index.

Table 7.3 displays a range of information on individuals who were disadvantaged according to each of the seven social exclusion indicators. It is important to remember that as these indicators are constructed to reflect levels of disadvantage across a range of variables in relation to average levels of prosperity in the population, they may represent different absolute levels of disadvantage in different countries. However what is clear from the table is that the indicators are identifying individuals who experienced quite severe forms of disadvantage in each country and that severity was consistent according to a number of measures.

There is a noticeable difference in disadvantage levels and types between countries. For example, working-age adults in Greece who experienced income poverty were particularly likely to have had other financial difficulties, including feeling unable to afford a number of often considered necessities (such as a holiday and new clothes). In Denmark however the income poor were less likely to face such problems, despite living on relatively low income. The level of the poverty line in the respective countries (measured using the Purchasing Power Standard) may explain such differences; it was almost twice as high in Denmark as in Greece.

The information presented in Table 7.3 also shows how the composite indices used to create the indicators perform in each country. As the indices take account of the relative inequality of disadvantage in each country the statistics show which component contributes most in their construction. For example, taking those excluded on the neighbourhood indicator, it is clear that neighbourhood noise was more of an issue than crime and vandalism across the EU-12, particularly in Denmark, Luxembourg and the UK.

Another useful validation procedure is to compare estimates of social exclusion from the ECHP with estimates from external national sources. Researchers at Eurostat performed an external validity of ECHP income poverty statistics for France, the Netherlands and the UK. The preliminary conclusion from this exercise was that the quality of the ECHP data was satisfactory (European Commission, 2000). To date there have been very few external validations of ECHP non-income statistics. Comparing the indicators for the UK with the indicators constructed for Great Britain using the BHPS in Chapter 3 revealed some marked differences (see Appendix D for details). In particular, the ECHP findings report higher levels of neighbourhood disadvantage and lower levels of both forms of health disadvantage. Reasons for these disparities are mainly due to the different questions used in the surveys (minor differences could be found because of dissimilarities in survey sampling and weighting procedures).

Investigating social exclusion in Europe

Having performed various procedures for checking the validity and quality of the ECHP indicators, the analysis can proceed to an investigation of the nature of social exclusion across the EU-12. This analysis will consider the multi-dimensional and longitudinal features of social exclusion across Europe, in particular the prevalence of current and persistent one-dimensional disadvantage and the pattern of relationships between indicators across countries.

Longitudinal aspects of social exclusion

The investigation of social exclusion begins with a look at that prevalence of current and persistent one-dimensional disadvantage, for each of the seven social exclusion indicators, across the EU-12. Current one-dimensional disadvantage is measured at a point in time using the latest available wave of the ECHP (1996). Given that only three waves of the ECHP survey are available, introducing a longitudinal aspect to the investigation of social exclusion is somewhat limited. Mejer and Linden (2000) used the same span of data for their analysis of poverty in the EU-12, defining persistent income poverty as being below a low-income threshold in all of the three waves. A similar method will be used here to define persistent one-dimensional disadvantage. Table 7.4 presents the prevalence of current and persistent one-dimensional disadvantage in the EU-12 and also includes statistics on the persistent disadvantage share – that is the proportion of those who were disadvantaged in 1996 who were in a similar position in 1995 and 1994 also.

A comparison of the rates of current disadvantage shows the percentage of working-age adults in disadvantage in the latest available wave of the ECHP survey. In terms of economic dimensions of disadvantage, the southern European countries (Italy, Portugal, Spain and Greece) register the highest proportions of income poverty, with Portugal also recording the highest proportion of adults in material and housing deprivation. Countries that record low proportions of working-age economic disadvantage include Denmark, the Netherlands and Luxembourg.

The UK records levels of current income poverty slightly below the EU-12 average. Similar studies of income poverty have found the UK to record one of the highest poverty rates in Europe (for example Mejer and Linden, 2000). The reason why this research does not do so is because it focuses on working-age adults only. Poverty rates for children and adults over retirement age were particularly high for the UK, mainly due to the low level of financial welfare benefits aimed at these groups of the population (McKay and Rowlingson, 1999). Material and housing disadvantage is also below the EU-12 average for working age adults in the UK.

Table 7.4 Prevalence of current[a] and persistent[b] one-dimensional disadvantage in the EU-12, working-age adults, ECHP, 1996, 1994-1996, cell per cent[c]

Disadvantage type	Country												
	Be	De	Fr	Ge	Gr	Ir	It	Lu	Ne	Po	Sp	UK	EU
Financial													
Current	16	9	15	14	18	16	19	12	12	17	18	15	16
Persistent	7	2	6	6	7	7	9	4	4	9	8	5	7
Persistent share	44	22	40	43	39	44	47	33	33	53	44	33	44
Material													
Current	7	8	9	8	17	19	9	6	4	22	18	6	12
Persistent	2	2	3	2	7	7	2	[2]	1	15	10	3	5
Persistent share	29	25	33	25	41	37	22	[33]	25	68	56	50	42
Housing													
Current	10	6	10	6	13	7	10	5	5	22	6	8	10
Persistent	4	[1]	4	2	5	2	3	[2]	1	14	2	1	4
Persistent share	40	[17]	40	33	38	29	30	[40]	20	64	33	13	40
Neighbourhood													
Current	10	5	10	7	5	7	17	6	12	11	13	11	10
Persistent	3	[1]	4	3	2	2	6	[1]	2	4	4	4	4
Persistent share	30	[10]	40	43	40	43	35	17	17	36	31	36	40
Social													
Current	9	10	12	5	3	5	13	7	10	14	7	4	9
Persistent	[2]	2	2	1	*	*	5	[1]	3	4	[1]	*	2
Persistent share	22	20	17	20	*	*	38	14	30	29	14	*	22

Table 7.4 (continued)

Physical

Current	11	18	10	13	5	9	4	11	17	12	16	10
Persistent	3	4	3	3	1	2	1	3	4	4	4	3
Persistent share	27	22	30	23	20	22	25	27	24	33	25	30

Mental

Current	9	4	7	12	8	10	8	4	4	10	7	8
Persistent	1	1	1	1	1	2	1	1	*	*	2	1
Persistent share	11	25	14	8	13	20	13	25	*	*	43	13

Notes:

[a] Current disadvantage denotes the number of indicators disadvantaged on in 1996.

[b] Persistent disadvantage denotes the number of indicators disadvantaged on in all three waves (1994, 1995 and 1996).

[c] Example – In Belgium 16 per cent of working-age adults were disadvantaged according to financial situation (income poverty) in 1996 and 7 per cent were disadvantaged according to financial situation (income poverty) in 1994, 1995 and 1996. Hence, 44 per cent of those who were disadvantaged according to financial situation in 1996 were in a similar position in 1995 and 1994 also.

It is clear from Table 7.4 that not everybody who was living in a disadvantaged household in 1996 had also been a member of a disadvantaged household in the previous two waves. For example, across the EU-12 as a whole just over two in five (44 per cent) working-age adults who were living in low-income households in 1996 had been doing so in both 1994 and 1995. This represents approximately 7 per cent of all working-age adults across the EU-12. This finding is comparable to that of Mejer and Linden (2000) who found a similar proportion of all individuals (adults and children) to have experienced persistent income poverty over the same years.

The propensity to live in persistent income poverty clearly differs between countries, but does so in a similar manner to patterns of current income poverty. Across the EU-12 those most likely to experience persistent poverty lived in southern European countries such as Portugal, Spain and Italy. For example, more than every second poor working-age person in Portugal in 1996 had also been living in poor households in the previous two waves. On the other hand the persistent poor in Denmark, the Netherlands and Luxembourg represent a small proportion of the current poor, suggesting that as well as having low current poverty rates these countries had very few working-age adults who experienced poverty continuously over a number of waves. These patterns remain when looking at the other two indicators associated with economic aspects of disadvantage. Portugal clearly records the highest levels of both current and persistent material possessions and housing circumstance disadvantage. The other two southern European countries do not lie too far behind.

In terms of neighbourhood and social dimensions of social exclusion, the cross-national levels of disadvantage differ from analysis of the economic indicators. Although southern European countries again appear to contain a high proportion of disadvantaged working-age adults, in particular Italy, other countries such as the Netherlands (for neighbourhood perception disadvantage) and France (for social relations disadvantage) have rates higher than the EU-12 average. The relationship between current and persistent disadvantage appears weaker, especially for social relations, although these patterns are likely to be distorted by the low proportion in disadvantage in certain countries.

Given the relatively low levels of poor health across the EU-12, as a consequence of excluding adults over retirement age, differences between countries are more difficult to detect. Denmark, Portugal and the UK record the highest prevalence of current physical health problems and these countries also have persistent rates higher than the EU-12 average. Germany tops the list of countries with high rates of mental health problems, although, as was found with the BHPS data, the propensity for such problems to last persistently was very low.

The analysis of non-economic indicators in the UK again shows that rates are markedly below the EU-12 average for social relations disadvantage and markedly above for physical ill health. Rates for neighbourhood perception disadvantage and mental ill health are around the EU-12 average. What is clear is that the analysis of non-economic indicators of social exclusion in particular provides a picture of disadvantage that differs to traditional income poverty analysis for the UK and indeed all the countries under investigation.

Patterns of social exclusion across Europe: a cluster analysis

Overall, the UK records levels of disadvantage around the EU-12 average for the majority of dimensions of social exclusion presented in Table 7.5. Ranking the countries according to the proportion of the working-age population disadvantaged on the indicators, either currently or persistently, shows southern European countries such as Portugal, Spain and Italy as the most disadvantaged. At the other end of the scale, working-age adults in Luxembourg face the least likelihood of experiencing the various forms of social exclusion.

A more scientific grouping of the countries according to the prevalence of persistent disadvantage, crucial to the notion of social exclusion, is presented in Table 7.5. The analysis uses a statistical procedure (cluster analysis) that groups objects that share similar characteristics – the prevalence of persistent disadvantage. Cluster analysis measures the 'distance' between cases (countries in this analysis) on a combination of dimensions (the seven social exclusion indicators) and uses this to identify groups of cases within which there is considerable homogeneity and between which there are clear boundaries.

Table 7.5   Grouping the EU-12 countries according to persistent disadvantage, ECHP, 1994-1996, cluster analysis[a]

---

1. Portugal

2. Italy

3. Greece, Ireland, Spain

4. Belgium, France, Germany, UK

5. Denmark, Luxembourg, Netherlands

Notes:
[a] Based on k-means cluster analysis performed with k=5. See Appendix E for further details.

Table 7.5 provides a more robust evidence of the grouping of countries according to social exclusion characteristics alluded to in the interpretation of Table 7.4. Portugal and Italy stand as clusters on their own, mainly due to the high incidence on the majority of indicators (particularly Portugal). The remaining two southern European countries (and Ireland) form another cluster with high incidence of disadvantage, followed by a cluster including the UK. As suggested earlier Luxembourg is in the final cluster, containing countries with relatively low levels of disadvantage. The cluster analysis procedure provides evidence of which dimensions contribute most to differentiating between clusters. The evidence (not presented in Table 7.8, see Appendix E for details) suggests that the economic dimensions of social exclusion (financial situation, material possessions and housing circumstance) and social relations are the most distinguishing characteristics.

Such grouping of countries is not dissimilar to Gallie and Paugam's (Eds. 2000) analysis that constructs models of family residence and unemployment welfare regimes in their study of unemployed individuals in eight European countries. Using the ECHP survey and data from national sources the study sought to test a number of hypothesize, most notably that living standards of the unemployed depend to a considerable extent on the nature and form of intervention of the welfare state, and, that their degree of social integration depend on the form and stability of family structures. This study is particularly relevant to the findings presented here as the focus is on individuals of working age. Also social as well as financial outcomes are considered and the labour market is seen as an important predictor of social exclusion status.

Gallie and Paugam constructed the family residence model according to the degree of stability of the family and the role the family plays in contributing to the welfare of its members. As a result three family types were detected – an extended dependence type, where different generations are brought together in the same household, offering everyone minimum protection but restricting individual autonomy (common in the southern European countries and Ireland); a family type that represents relative autonomy between generations, where adult children living with their parents are under an obligation to be actively preparing for entry into the labour market (common in countries such as France and Belgium); and a family type that represents advanced inter-generational autonomy, which contrasts with the extended dependence family type, as the self-realization of the young adult is regarded as inconceivable without acquiring autonomy from the parents (common in countries such as the UK, the Netherlands, Germany, Denmark and Sweden).

The welfare regime model was constructed according to the degree of coverage, the level and duration of financial cover, and the extent of development of active employment policies. Taking these three criteria it was possible to distinguish four unemployment regimes in Europe: ranging from the sub-protective regime which offers the unemployed less than the minimum level of protection needed for subsistence and a virtually non-existent active employment policy (common to southern European countries) through the liberal/minimal regime (Ireland and the UK) and the employment-centred regime (France, Belgium, Netherlands and Germany), to the universalistic regime which offers high level comprehensive coverage and an ambitious active employment policy (common in Scandinavian countries). The link between the two models is not clear-cut. For example, it is not justifiable to attribute the decisive role in the creation of family residence models to the type of unemployment welfare regime that prevails in each country.

Although it is not the intention of this research to perform a detailed analysis of European family and welfare regimes, such models[14] are useful to refer to when interpreting the prevalence and nature of disadvantage. For example, analysis of the financial situation and material possessions indicators (see Table 7.4) reveals that the southern European countries experience the highest levels of economic deprivation. Such a finding appears rational when referring back to the welfare regime model, which places these countries in the sub-protective regime – a regime that offers few welfare benefits to the unemployed and for those that are offered the amount is low.

---

[14] Of course other attempts to model welfare regimes across Europe have been attempted, most notably by Esping-Anderson (1990).

Table 7.6 Number of indicators of social exclusion on which individuals were currently[a] and persistently[b] disadvantaged, working-age adults, ECHP, row per cent

Country		*Number of indicators disadvantaged on*				
		0	1	2	3	4 to 7
Belgium	Current	56	28	11	4	[2]
	Persistent	82	14	3	*	*
Denmark	Current	59	29	9	3	*
	Persistent	88	11	[1]	*	0
France	Current	56	27	11	4	2
	Persistent	83	14	3	1	*
Germany	Current	56	29	9	4	2
	Persistent	85	13	2	[1]	0
Greece	Current	54	30	12	4	1
	Persistent	81	15	3	1	*
Ireland	Current	56	28	10	4	2
	Persistent	83	13	3	*	*
Italy	Current	50	31	12	5	2
	Persistent	78	18	3	1	*
Luxembourg	Current	67	22	9	[2]	*
	Persistent	89	9	[2]	*	0
Netherlands	Current	56	31	9	2	1
	Persistent	87	11	1	*	0
Portugal	Current	39	32	17	8	4
	Persistent	64	23	10	3	[1]
Spain	Current	51	29	14	5	2
	Persistent	79	16	4	1	*
UK	**Current**	**57**	**28**	**10**	**3**	**2**
	Persistent	**84**	**13**	**3**	*	*
EU-12	Current	53	29	12	4	2
	Persistent	80	15	3	1	<1

Notes:
[a] Current disadvantage denotes the number of indicators disadvantaged on in 1996.
[b] Persistent disadvantage denotes the number of indicators disadvantaged on for all three waves (1994, 1995 and 1996).

Multi-dimensional aspects of social exclusion

The previous section explored the prevalence of current and persistent one-dimensional disadvantage across the EU-12 countries. This analysis revealed that disadvantage was widespread, albeit in varying forms, across the EU-12 and that it tended to be concentrated in southern European countries, particularly Portugal. The focus of this section is an investigation of the nature of multi-dimensional disadvantage across the EU-12. Methodological techniques applied in previous chapters are employed to investigate whether multi-dimensional disadvantage exists and to what degree, and the relationship between dimensions of social exclusion. The analysis in this section begins with a look at the propensity for working-age adults to face disadvantage in several domains. The number of indicators on which individuals were disadvantaged in 1996 is presented in Table 7.6.

In general, the likelihood of an individual experiencing multi-dimensional disadvantage was related to the levels of disadvantage on separate domains of social exclusion in their country. Such a finding appears intuitive, but provides evidence to suggest that there were substantial groups of working-age individuals who experienced more than one form of disadvantage at any one time.

As well as recording high levels of disadvantage (see Table 7.4) Portugal stands out as a country where working-age adults were likely to experience a number of forms of disadvantage (individuals in Luxembourg were the least likely to do so). In 1996 approximately one in twenty working-age adults in Portugal experienced disadvantage on four or more of the seven social exclusion indicators, twice as many as the EU-12 average. Only two in five working-age adults in Portugal experienced no disadvantage, suggesting that disadvantage was widespread but also particularly problematic for a subset of this population. Working-age adults in Italy and Spain also faced rates of multi-dimensional disadvantage above the EU-12 average. Again levels in the UK were around the EU-12 average.

Although Table 7.6 has revealed that multi-dimensional disadvantage does exist, albeit to a varying degree, across the EU-12, the analysis does not provide any information on the nature of such disadvantage – in particular which array of indicators of social exclusion were most commonly experienced. Table 7.7 illustrates the combination of indicators on which those suffering from current and persistent multi-dimensional disadvantage were particularly likely to be disadvantaged. This is presented in the form of a summary of findings from a factor analysis[15] on the seven dimensions of social exclusion, by country.

It is clear from Table 7.7 that various patterns of association between dimensions of disadvantage exist across the EU-12. At an EU-12 level the association between the seven indicators replicates that found for Great Britain using the BHPS data in Chapter 2. This suggests a grouping of indicators, for both current and persistent disadvantage, according to a notion of *household economic deprivation* (comprising of the financial situation, material possessions and housing circumstance indicators), *personal civic exclusion* (comprising of the neighbourhood perception and social relations indicators) and *personal health exclusion* (comprising of the physical health and mental health indicators). However these groupings vary slightly across countries and according to whether current or persistent disadvantage is used.

---

[15] Factor analysis was used in a similar way to group indicators of social exclusion for Britain using the BHPS in Chapter 4. See Appendix C for further details.

Table 7.7   Multi-dimensional relationships between indicators of social exclusion (current[a] and persistent[b]), working-age adults, ECHP, 1994-1996, factor analysis grouping[c]

Country		*Dimension of social exclusion*						
		Fin	Mat	Hou	Nei	Soc	Phy	Men
Belgium	Current	1 3	1	1	1	3	2	2
	Persistent	2	2	2 3	3	3	1	1
Denmark	Current	1	1	1	1		2	2
	Persistent	3	3	1	1	4	2	2 4
France	Current	1	1	1	1		2	2
	Persistent	1	1	1	3	3	2	2
Germany	Current	2	2	3	3	3	1	1
	Persistent	2	2	1 2	1	1	3	3
Greece	Current	1	1	1	3	2 3	2	2
	Persistent	2	2	2		1	1	1
Ireland	Current	1	1	1	1 3	3	2	2
	Persistent	1	1	1	1 3	3	2	2
Italy	Current	1	1	1	1	2	2	2
	Persistent	1	1	1		3	2 3	2
Luxembourg	Current	2	2 3	3	3	2	1	1
	Persistent	1 3	1	1	3	3	2	2
Netherlands	Current	1	1	3	3	3	2	2
	Persistent	1	1	1	1 3	3	2	2
Portugal	Current	1	1	1	3	3	2	2
	Persistent	1	1	1	2	2	2	2
Spain	Current	1	1	1	3	3	2	2
	Persistent	1	1	1 3	3	2 3	2	2
UK	**Current**	1	1	1 3	3	3	2	2
	Persistent	1	1	2	2	2	3	3
EU-12	Current	1	1	1	3	3	2	2
	Persistent	1	1	1	3	3	2	2

Notes:

[a] Current disadvantage denotes the number of indicators disadvantaged on in 1996.

[b] Persistent disadvantage denotes the number of indicators disadvantaged on for all three waves (1994, 1995 and 1996).

[c] Number denotes with factor group an indicator is a member of. A factor group is a set of indicators that form a group due to strong associations between them. Factor group 1 explains the largest amount of variance and so on. An indicator can be a member of more than one factor group. See Appendix C for factor analysis statistics.

In general the strongest relationship between the indicators exists between the economic indicators of disadvantage. When using current disadvantage, in 10 of the 12 countries the factor analysis reveals that working-age adults who were disadvantaged on one of the financial, material and housing dimensions were likely to be disadvantaged on the other two as well. Where the three economic indicators do not appear in the same group they appear linked to disadvantage according to neighbourhood perception, and, sometimes, social relations as well. For example, at a persistent disadvantage level in Denmark, the financial and material indicators are grouped together but the housing indicator is grouped with neighbourhood disadvantage. The same is found in the Netherlands for current disadvantage, but this time the housing and neighbourhood indicators are grouped with the social relations disadvantage indicator.

Associations between the two indicators of poor health (physical and mental) show up in all 12 countries at both current and persistent levels. In the southern European countries poor health is also associated with a lack of social relationships. The relationship between the neighbourhood indicator and other indicators appears to vary across the EU-12, veering between associations with housing and social dimensions of disadvantage. In Germany, Ireland, the Netherlands and the UK working-age adults were likely to be disadvantaged on all three of the housing, neighbourhood and social indicators. In the southern European countries neighbourhood disadvantage was linked to social relations, and hence the notion of civic exclusion identified at an EU-12 level is particularly relevant here, as suggested by Gallie and Paugam's (Eds. 2000) family residence model.

Identifying social exclusion in Europe

The previous two sections have investigated the multi-dimensional and longitudinal nature of disadvantage across the EU-12. The emphasis of this section now moves on to combine both approaches to allow an identification of the prevalence of social exclusion and the socio-demographic characteristics of the socially excluded in each country. To enable this exploration a measure of social exclusion is adopted that allows for valid comparisons across the EU-12 countries. The construction of the measure of social exclusion is detailed below. It involves three steps: the selection of indicators, the creation of a Proportional Social Exclusion Index (PSEI) and the choice of social exclusion threshold.

The first step in the construction of a comparative measure of social exclusion involves the selection of indicators. The theoretical and empirical investigations in this book to date have stressed the importance of adopting both a multi-dimensional *and* longitudinal approach to the identification of social exclusion. Consequently the definition of social exclusion adopted here uses information on the range of social exclusion indicators and concentrates on persistent disadvantage – which is disadvantage experienced in all three waves of the available ECHP data.

The second step details the creation of a Proportional Social Exclusion Index (PSEI). When constructing indicators to compare separate domains of disadvantage across countries the importance of adopting a relative approach was emphasized. Likewise it is essential that a measure of social exclusion is relative and reflects any cultural or resource-based differences that may occur between countries.

Following on from the method used to define cross-country indicators of social exclusion, the PSEI is constructed using a similar approach to that applied in the creation of the Proportional Disadvantage Index. Using the PSEI approach means that a measure of social exclusion is constructed which weights the domain of disadvantage according to the proportion of the population who experienced it in each country. This means that if a particular form of disadvantage is very rare (common) it is given a high (low) weight in the index.[16]

The final stage of the index construction is to decide on a threshold to distinguish those who experience social exclusion from those who do not. This decision is difficult to make without some degree of arbitrariness. In particular it would be difficult to identify a level for the index that would be considered as a critical point that distinguishes the socially excluded. As the index is constructed as a continuous variable, a percentage of those with the lowest scores could be taken to identify the socially excluded, or a percentage of the average (mean or median) score could be used as a threshold. Alternatively, a threshold could be determined by disadvantage on a number of indicators or disadvantage on certain indicators in particular. In keeping with the notion of a relative definition of social exclusion and with the aim of identifying individuals excluded from 'mainstream' society, a percentage of the average level will be used as a threshold (a similar approach was taken by Barnes et al, 2002). The threshold is set at 70 per cent of the median PSEI score.[17] Therefore to have experienced social exclusion according to this definition, an individual needs to have been below the country-specific PSEI threshold in all three available waves of the ECHP data.

The prevalence of social exclusion in EU-12 countries

The prevalence of social exclusion in EU-12 countries is calculated as the percentage of working-age individuals below each country-specific social exclusion score threshold (set at 70 per cent of the median PSEI score) in all three available waves of the ECHP. The rates of social exclusion across these countries are illustrated in Figure 7.1.

---

[16] The PSEI is converted so that a low score represents a high level of disadvantage (and vice-versa) so to allow the standard convention of defining those below the threshold to be of interest.

[17] Alternative thresholds between 50 per cent and 80 per cent of the median were assessed for suitability but they produced either too few individuals to allow valid analysis or so many individuals that the notion of social exclusion was questioned.

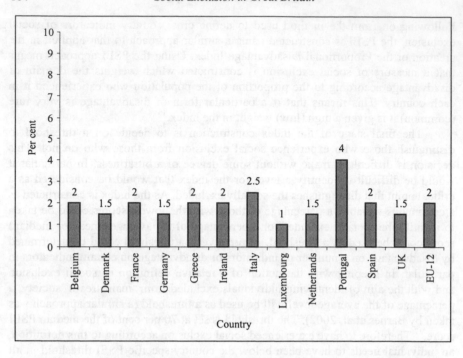

Figure 7.1   The prevalence of social exclusion in the EU-12, working-age adults, ECHP, 1994-1996

Figure 7.1 shows that the prevalence of social exclusion amongst working-age adults was low in all countries across the EU-12 in the mid-1990s.[18] The EU-12 average stands at just 2 per cent and this varied very little between the 12 countries. It is clear from Figure 7.1 however that Portugal stands out as the country where working-age adults were most likely to experience social exclusion. Here the rate of social exclusion was twice that of the EU-12 average. The other country with a rate of social exclusion higher than the EU-12 average was Italy. Portugal was also the only country where rates of one-dimensional persistent disadvantage were higher than the EU-12 average for every one of the seven social exclusion indicators (see Table 7.4 above). The association between rates of one-dimensional persistent disadvantage and social exclusion (see Figure 7.1) demonstrate the validity of the composite social exclusion measure.

The rate of social exclusion in the UK lies slightly below the EU-12 average. In fact ranking countries according to rates of social exclusion sees the UK in joint eighth place along with Denmark, Germany and the Netherlands. This is not surprising given that the UK did not record any rates of persistent disadvantage markedly above the EU-12 average on the seven separate social exclusion indicators (see Table 7.4). Indeed rates of social exclusion for working-age adults

---

[18] It must be remembered that the prevalence of social exclusion is to some degree dependent on the threshold used to define social exclusion.

in the UK were notably lower than rates of current income poverty, reinforcing once again the need for a multi-dimensional and longitudinal approach to measuring social exclusion.

Figure 7.1 suggests that there existed a small subset of socially excluded working-age individuals in each of the EU-12 countries. Although the low prevalence of social exclusion rather restricts a comparison of rates in Europe the composite measure can be used to identify the socio-demographic characteristics of the socially excluded in each country and to make comparisons of these groups across countries.

Socio-demographic characteristics of individuals who experience social exclusion in Europe

Having established that social exclusion exists across the EU-12, albeit to varying degree and nature, the focus of attention now switches to an investigation of the characteristics of working-age adults particularly likely to suffer such forms of disadvantage in each country. Previous studies have shown that rates of income poverty vary according to individual and household characteristics both within and across countries in the EU For example, an investigation of the low-income population (all adults) by Mejer (2000) found that across the EU-12 in general, single parent households, elderly people and large families were disproportionately found to be living in income poverty. This type of analysis is developed in this section to identify which groups of working-age individuals were particularly likely to suffer from social exclusion in countries in the EU-12.

The strict definitions imposed during the construction of the seven social exclusion indicators, and the resultant composite index of social exclusion, meant that only the most severely and persistently disadvantaged individuals were identified. Analysis above has shown that only a minority of working-age adults across the EU-12 experienced social exclusion. The limitations of the ECHP database means that a breakdown of the risk of social exclusion by socio-demographic characteristic is not possible. Instead a multivariate analysis is performed[19] to identify the odds ratios for the effects of various socio-demographic characteristics[20] (most notably family circumstances and individual status) on the probability of experiencing social exclusion. Table 7.8 presents the findings of this analysis.

---

[19] The logistic regression technique is based on linear models, which does not require such large sample sizes to produce robust results.
[20] Socio-demographic characteristics are recorded from the 1996 wave.

Table 7.8 Odds[a] of experiencing social exclusion[b] by individual and household socio-demographic characteristic, working-age adults, ECHP, 1994-1996, logistic regression model

Socio-demographic characteristics (1996)	Country												
	Be	De	Fr	Ge	Gr	Ir	It	Lu	Ne	Po	Sp	Uk	Eu
Sex													
Male	ref	ref	ref	ref	ref	ref	ref	ref	ref	ref	ref	ref	ref
Female	1.0	0.3	1.1	0.8	1.1	1.5	1.1	0.5	2.0	0.8	1.2	**2.2**	1.0
Age group													
16-29 years	1.0	4.0	0.9	3.8	1.6	1.0	0.9	0.7	2.9	0.7	1.2	0.7	1.1
30-44 years	ref	ref	ref	ref	ref	Ref	ref	ref	ref	ref	ref	ref	ref
45-59/64 years	0.8	2.7	0.8	3.0	1.1	0.5	1.2	0.2	0.4	0.9	1.2	1.0	1.0
Household type													
Single	3.7	0.5	2.6	4.2	4.5	9.9	2.1	*	1.8	8.2	3.3	2.9	3.6
Couple, no children	0.4	0.1	0.6	0.5	1.0	5.5	0.9	*	0.3	2.5	3.3	0.7	1.2
Couple, dependent children only	ref	ref	ref	ref	ref	Ref	ref	ref	ref	ref	ref	ref	ref
Couple, some non-dependent children	1.9	0.1	1.9	1.6	1.3	1.5	1.7	*	0.7	2.8	3.0	1.9	2.0
Lone parent, dependent children only	0.4	1.4	2.0	3.6	8.3	1.8	1.0	*	1.0	9.9	*	1.7	2.9
Lone parent, some non-dependent children	3.5	*	1.3	1.3	1.0	1.3	3.4	*	2.0	8.5	2.4	3.5	3.2
Other	0.1	*	0.9	0.9	2.4	0.2	2.0	*	*	3.1	2.2	1.5	2.2
Number of children													
None	0.2	0.8	0.6	0.4	1.6	0.2	0.5	*	0.5	1.1	0.1	0.2	0.7
One	ref	ref	ref	ref	ref	ref	ref	ref	ref	ref	ref	ref	ref
Two	0.7	2.2	1.5	2.3	1.4	1.2	1.7	*	0.8	2.2	2.9	1.0	1.7
Three or more	0.4	*	2.0	4.8	1.8	2.9	5.4	1.7	1.7	6.1	9.9	1.9	4.1

Table 7.8 (continued)

Education level													
High	0.7	1.1	0.9	0.7	0.4	0.8	0.5	*	0.3	0.9	0.5	0.5	0.6
Medium	ref	ref	ref	ref	ref	ref	ref	ref	ref	ref	ref	ref	ref
Low	1.3	*	**3.0**	1.1	**8.9**	2.1	**3.7**	1.7	1.4	**9.9**	**3.8**	0.8	**3.8**
Main activity status													
Employed full time	1.1	0.3	0.7	0.6	2.1	0.6	1.4	0.2	1.2	**0.6**	0.8	0.7	0.9
Employed part time	**5.7**	*	0.9	*	*	*	3.6	*	*	2.3	3.4	*	1.6
Unemployed	1.4	0.3	**2.2**	**3.3**	**2.0**	1.2	**3.8**	4.7	0.7	1.2	**4.7**	1.4	**1.8**
Care of home/family	ref	ref	ref	ref	ref	ref	ref	ref	ref	ref	ref	ref	ref
Education/training	0.1	0.9	**4.2**	0.9	0.9	0.1	1.6	*	0.5	0.4	0.5	*	0.8
Other inactive	**5.3**	*	0.4	*	**6.9**	1.8	**3.1**	*	1.5	**5.3**	**4.0**	**9.9**	**3.8**
Number in household in employment													
None	**9.9**	1.7	**6.6**	**4.0**	**3.2**	**7.4**	1.6	0.8	**9.9**	1.6	**2.5**	**5.0**	**2.6**
One	ref	Ref	ref	ref	ref	ref	ref	ref	ref	ref	ref	ref	ref
Two or more	**0.2**	0.1	**0.3**	0.7	**0.2**	0.2	**0.3**	1.3	**0.1**	**0.5**	**0.5**	0.2	**0.5**

Notes:
[a] Odds ratios higher (lower) than 1 imply that the socio-demographic characteristic is associated with an increased (decreased) odds of experiencing the event (social exclusion) compared to the reference category (ref). Bold text indicates a statistically significant ($p<0.05$) coefficient.
[b] Social exclusion means being below the PSEI threshold in 1994, 1995 and 1996.

Just as the prevalence of social exclusion varied across the EU-12 so did the risk according to socio-demographic characteristic. At an EU-12 level the following socio-demographic characteristics were significantly ($p<0.05$) related to an increase in odds of social exclusion (with respect to the reference category, see Table 7.8 for details): living alone, living in a couple with non-dependent children household, living in a lone parent household, living in an 'other' household (likely to be students and non-related adults), living in a household with two or three or more children, having low education, being unemployed or 'other' inactive (likely to be ill or disabled people) and living in a household where no one is in employment. Conversely, living in a household with no children, having high education and living in a household where two or more members were in employment is significantly ($p<0.05$) related to a decrease in the odds of experiencing social exclusion.

Table 7.8 illustrates that the risk of social exclusion according to socio-demographic characteristic varies both between and within member states. Portugal was the country with the highest prevalence of social exclusion and within this country people living alone, lone parents and those with low education were particularly at risk. Young adults in Portugal appear less likely to face social exclusion, probably a result of the protective role of the family associated with this and other southern European countries. In the UK; females, the 'other' inactive (likely to be ill or disabled people) and those who lived in a household where no one was in employment carried the highest risk of social exclusion.

The magnitude of risk of social exclusion for these population groups can clearly differ according to the country in question. For example, those with low education appear particularly likely to have experienced social exclusion in Greece and Portugal, less so in Ireland and education appears to have little or no affect in countries such as Belgium and Germany.

Conclusion

Although there have been initiatives to promote the concept of social exclusion in social policy discourse at an EU level, empirical investigations have been far and few between. The introduction of the ECHP survey has meant that information on the social, demographic and economic aspects of individuals in EU Member States is available in a truly comparable format for the first time. This chapter has made use of the ECHP information to construct a set of robust indicators of social exclusion, and a composite social exclusion index, for working-age adults in the EU-12 countries. A composite index was an appropriate comparative measure of social exclusion, particularly given that the relationship between indicators suggested that the three integral elements of social exclusion found for Great Britain with BHPS data (see Chapter 4) were not found consistently amongst the EU-12 countries. Procedures to verify the validity of these measures have shown that although thresholds have been arbitrarily defined, using a relative approach most suitable for comparative analysis, the thresholds identify appropriate levels of disadvantage in each country.

As would be expected, the prevalence of social exclusion across the EU-12 is lower than for disadvantage measured according to single domains, most notably when compared to other studies of low income. However there were still significant numbers of working-age adults (and often their household members) who suffer from a combination of social exclusion related problems, particularly in southern Europe.

An analysis of the prevalence of social exclusion across the EU-12, using analysis of both separate indicator and composite index methods, has shown that countries suffering similar aggregate levels of disadvantage cluster together, particularly in terms of economic disadvantage (financial situation, material possessions and housing circumstance). Portugal stands alone as suffering the most disadvantage across a variety of indicators, followed by other of the southern European countries. Luxembourg in particular can be found at the other end of the scale. The UK sits around the EU-12 average, but exhibits particularly high rates of physical ill health.

Such stringent definitions of social exclusion act to identify the most severe and permanently disadvantaged individuals in each country. The risk of social exclusion according to the socio-demographic characteristics of these individuals was investigated using logistic regression analysis. Age group, household type, number of children, education level and main activity each had an affect on the probability of experiencing social exclusion. The risk of social exclusion according to socio-demographic characteristic clearly varies between countries, perhaps as a consequence of differing cultural aspects and the intervention of state and social institutions in maintaining appropriate levels of welfare.[21]

The analysis suggests that applying multi-dimensional and longitudinal techniques to the investigation of social exclusion across the EU-12 is essential to understand the prevalence, nature and those most at risk of such experiences. Although traditional methods of identifying static income poverty should be retained (given the role low income plays in predetermining other forms of disadvantage and the importance it has in prevention and alleviation policies), such procedures failure to expose the extent and features of hardship that the most disadvantaged in societies across the EU-12 experience. In summary, it is evident that an empirical operationalization of social exclusion at a European level helps to distinguish between those individuals who may suffer from one or few components of social exclusion (and perhaps only short-term) and those who experience (or are on the journey to) a multi-faceted assortment of disadvantage.

---

[21] The analysis suggests that variations between countries in the level and pattern of deprivation would benefit from a more focussed analysis on the role of such welfare and institutional customs and conventions, something beyond the scope of this research.

Chapter 8

Operationalizing Social Exclusion: Implications for Research and Policy

> ... [Adopting the notion of social exclusion] indicates that we have developed a sharper understanding of social problems and the complex links between them. We now place emphasis on 'joining up' policy between government departments and taking a long-term approach. ... And this better understanding means we can develop policies more effectively, and implement them in new ways to bring real change on the ground (John Prescott, deputy prime minister, 2002, p. 3).

Introduction

This final chapter assembles the main methodological and substantive findings from the research and discusses the implications of operationalizing social exclusion for research and policy. The chapter begins with a succinct account of the key empirical findings. It then moves on to discuss the context in which these findings should be regarded, concentrating in particular on methodological considerations and the limitations of survey data. There follows a discussion of the significance of the main findings for policy analysis and policy making, with particular reference to recommendations for improvements to the government's *Opportunity for all* indicators. The chapter concludes with a final reflection on the implications for defining and measuring social exclusion in this manner and themes for future research.

Key empirical findings

The overall aim of the research was to build upon theoretical discussions of social exclusion to construct an empirical model, using quantitative survey data, to investigate the nature and extent of social exclusion amongst working-age adults living in private households in Great Britain in the 1990s and to compare findings for Great Britain with other European Union member states. To achieve this aim six research objectives were constructed. Each objective was tackled in turn and covered in sequential chapters of the book (the third objective – to examine in detail the nature of social exclusion in Great Britain, in particular its multi-dimensional and longitudinal characteristics – in fact covered two chapters). To ensure that a discussion of the implications of this research is located in context of the main research findings, the first section of this chapter presents a concise summary of the key theoretical and empirical analysis.

The first objective was to clarify the conceptual properties of social exclusion. In addressing this research objective an extensive assessment of the academic and political social exclusion literature was undertaken. A concept of social exclusion was adopted that draws in particular on the theory of Room (Ed. 1995, 1998, 2000) and refers to the multi-dimensional and longitudinal consequences of being shut out, fully or partially, from the economic, social and cultural systems that determine the social integration of a person in society. This concept of social exclusion is much more complex than the traditional notion of 'poverty', which focuses on the dearth of financial resources, primarily income, at a point in time; and of the notion of 'deprivation', which centres on a combination of the dearth of financial resources and other non-monetary economic forms of disadvantage such as poor housing and lack of material possessions, again at a point in time.

The next stage of the research process, and indeed the second research objective, was to operationalize this notion of social exclusion using empirical models based on quantitative survey data. To ameliorate previous, albeit limited attempts to operationalize social exclusion, a framework for a quantitative investigation of social exclusion was outlined. This framework detailed the functional, theoretical and methodological criteria for an investigation using quantitative social indicators, emphasizing in particular the need for a thorough understanding of the multi-dimensional and longitudinal nature of social exclusion. Seven indicators of social exclusion were chosen: financial situation (a measure of income poverty), material possessions, housing circumstance, neighbourhood perception, social relations, physical health and mental health. Four distinct models were devised that would highlight the important methodological developments of research into social exclusion. These models reflect current one-dimensional disadvantage (incorporating the notion of 'income poverty'); persistent one-dimensional disadvantage; current multi-dimensional disadvantage and persistent multi-dimensional disadvantage (incorporating the notion of 'social exclusion').

The seven indicators of social exclusion were constructed, and validated, for Great Britain using nine waves (1991 to 1999) of the British Household Panel Survey. The indicators were constructed using a similar methodology to the recent *Poverty and Social Exclusion* (PSE) survey in Great Britain (Gordon et al, 2000). The PSE survey used an *absolute* approach to investigate the levels of individual dimensions of disadvantage but also a *relative* approach in the sense that the dimensions reflect the population's judgement on what is essential to have in modern British society.

The third objective was to examine in detail the nature of social exclusion in Great Britain, in particular its multi-dimensional and longitudinal characteristics. The analysis of the BHPS data began with a focus on models of current one-dimensional disadvantage. The seven indicators of social exclusion separately identified between eight and 21 per cent of the working-age population at any one time during the 1990s. For example, in 1996 16 per cent were living in households below the poverty line (£187 per week in 2001 prices), 11 per cent lived in poor housing and 10 per cent had psychological health problems. As the indicators were constructed using a part-absolute approach, they exhibited some variation across the decade. The economic indicators in particular showed a marked decline, clearly reflecting the prosperous condition of the British economy of the 1990s.

The separate analysis of the social exclusion indicators at a cross-sectional level revealed not only a diverse range of disadvantage prevalent in British society, but also that which affected particular subgroups of the working-age population to varying extent. For example, age was related to an individual's risk of experiencing disadvantage in different ways – young adults were at risk of economic and neighbourhood forms of disadvantage, whilst older adults were at risk of health and social related problems. Groups of the working-age population that were at particular risk of a number of different forms of disadvantage were people living alone, lone parents, people with no education, unemployed people and people who lived in a household where no one works.

Analysis of current multi-dimensional disadvantage explored the likelihood of experiencing disadvantage on a number of indicators and the relationship between the indicators at a given observation (data from the 1996 wave was used as this corresponded to the most recent wave of data from the ECHP survey). This analysis showed that approximately half the working-age population was disadvantaged on at least one indicator at a point in time, although very few individuals were likely to be disadvantaged on a large number of indicators. Although two-fifths of the working-age population was disadvantaged on two or more indicators, less than 3 per cent were disadvantaged on four or more and none were disadvantaged on all seven.

Individuals who were disadvantaged on any of the economic indicators (financial situation, material possessions and housing circumstance) or the mental health indicator were more likely to have faced disadvantage on at least one other indicator. An investigation of the relationship between the indicators, using factor analysis, revealed three distinctive and integral elements of social exclusion – *household economic deprivation* (comprising the financial situation, material possessions and housing circumstance indicators), *personal civic exclusion* (comprising the neighbourhood perception and social relations indicators) and *personal health exclusion* (comprising the physical and mental health indicators). The relationship between the health indicators proved strongest followed by the relationship between the economic indicators.

Household economic deprivation (defined as income poverty and at least one other form of economic disadvantage) was experienced by approximately 5 per cent of the working-age population. In general, experiences of *household economic deprivation* were linked most heavily to being out of work and living in households where no one worked. Employment was the factor most associated with the avoidance of *household economic deprivation*, probably as a means of attaining and accumulating economic resources. The groups of individuals most likely to have faced *household economic deprivation* were lone parents, households with children, and those living alone, each of which may have experienced obstacles to work (such as childcare) and/or had no other potential workers to rely on (because of living with children or alone) and/or had to provide for other non-working household members (such as children).

Personal civic exclusion (defined as disadvantage according to neighbourhood perception and social relations) was experienced by approximately 4 per cent of the working-age population. Although those in income poverty were three times more likely than those above the poverty line to have faced civic exclusion, multivariate analysis revealed that low income was not significantly associated with civic exclusion. The experience of *personal civic exclusion* was most heavily linked to living in a lone-parent household and being unemployed, although also with poor housing and physical ill health. The finding that unemployment was linked to a lack of social relationships and dissatisfaction with the neighbourhood, as well as low income and economic deprivation, suggests that attempts to include individuals into the labour market may be well founded. However, although the labour market may be a mechanism to promote civic ties, having good quality housing, perhaps in which to host social occasions, and good physical health, perhaps with which to attend social activities away from the household, also appear to be crucial.

Personal health exclusion (defined as disadvantage according to physical health and mental health) was experienced by approximately 3 per cent of the working-age population. Again a relationship with income poverty seem prevalent, as the income poor were twice as likely to have experienced *personal health exclusion* than the non income-poor. In fact income poverty was significantly associated with the experience of *personal health exclusion*, perhaps a reflection of the inability to work and consequently the reliance on health-related benefits, as was lack of social relations (a relationship discussed above), having a low education (possibly linked to more physically demanding employment) and being female (possibly as women are more inclined than men to seek health advice).

The method chosen to identify wide-ranging forms of current multi-dimensional disadvantage was based on the premise that the most severe forms of multiple disadvantage would be that which cut across all three integral elements of social exclusion. A measure of wide-ranging current multi-dimensional disadvantage – disadvantage on at least one indicator in all three of the integral elements of social exclusion – revealed only a very small subset of afflicted individuals. Only approximately 3 per cent of the working-age population was disadvantaged on at least one indicator in all three elements at any one time. The sub-group of the working-age population most prone to such experiences was lone parents with dependent children. The level of education seemed to be a useful predictor of wide-ranging disadvantage also, as did main activity status. Those with a degree or higher education were disproportionately likely to avoid such experiences, the opposite being the case for those with no academic education at all. Having a connection to the labour market suggested the avoidance of such widespread forms of disadvantage, particularly so for those in full-time work.

Important insights into the nature of social exclusion can result from making time explicit in conceptualization, definition and measurement (Walker, 1995). Models of longitudinal one-dimensional disadvantage were constructed using nine waves of the BHPS to categorize individual's experiences of disadvantage during the 1990s. The analysis began by considering the number of observations in which individuals were disadvantaged, for each of the seven separate indicators. For each indicator, the prevalence of disadvantage over time was greater than that recorded at just one observation, indicating that disadvantage affected a range of individuals during the decade. Income poverty and mental health problems were the areas of disadvantage that touched the highest proportion of working-age individuals during the 1990s – approximately two-fifths of the working-age population experienced one or other of these forms of disadvantage at least once during the decade.

Certain forms of disadvantage were more likely to have been experienced for a long overall duration, such as housing disadvantage and physical health (25 per cent and 18 per cent respectively, did so for seven observations or more) and certain forms for a short duration, such as neighbourhood perception and mental health (77 per cent and 84 per cent respectively, did so for one, two or three observations). Housing circumstance and social relations disadvantage stood out as domains where individuals would experience only one spell of disadvantage during the decade, with low income and health problems most likely to be repeated. Consequently housing circumstance recorded the longest average first spell duration (3.7 years) whilst mental health recorded the lowest (1.5 years).

Such complex analysis of the duration and sequence of disadvantage events led to the formation of five summary categories of longitudinal disadvantage pattern: none, occasional, recurrent, short-term persistent and long-term persistent. This is similar to the categorizations of income poverty used by Jenkins and Rigg (2001) but it is the first time this approach has been applied to other indicators of disadvantage. As expected from the previous analysis, neighbourhood perception and mental health were most likely to be experienced for occasional or recurrent periods (67 per cent and 72 per cent of individuals did so, respectively), material possessions and social relations for short-term persistent periods (42 per cent and 53 per cent respectively), and housing circumstance and physical health for long-term persistent periods (23 per cent and 18 per cent respectively). Income poverty was spread most equally between the categories.

Towards the end of the Chapter 4 the investigation focussed on the most wide-ranging form of disadvantage, as this was earlier deemed an integral feature of the notion of social exclusion. Likewise enduring disadvantage was seen as paramount to the experience of social exclusion, so the investigation at the end of Chapter 5 focussed on the prevalence and make-up of long-term persistent disadvantage. The magnitude of the relationship between current and long-term persistent disadvantage was found to be highest for the housing circumstance indicator – two thirds of the currently disadvantaged in 1999 had experienced long term persistent disadvantage during the decade.

From an empirical viewpoint, adopting a longitudinal method does not generate an entirely different profile of disadvantaged individuals compared to an approach that measures disadvantage at a point in time. However, although some socio-demographic and economic factors pervade certain groups of long-term and persistently disadvantaged individuals, most notably education and labour market status, certain characteristics, such as age and household type, were particularly associated with certain domains of social exclusion. For example, older working-age adults were significantly less likely than younger adults to have experienced economic forms of disadvantage, but more likely to have experienced physical health problems. This analysis is therefore particularly useful for modifying the relative risk of disadvantage attributed to the different groups according to the area of social exclusion under investigation.

The fourth research objective was to identify the prevalence of social exclusion in Great Britain and the socio-demographic characteristics associated with increased odds of social exclusion. Methodologies introduced in previous chapters were combined to form various estimates of longitudinal multi-dimensional disadvantage. Almost nine in ten working-age individuals experienced at least one observation of disadvantage on at least one indicator during the decade, although less than one in ten (8 per cent) experienced six or more observations of multi-dimensional disadvantage (on any combination of indicators) and just over one in twenty (6 per cent) experienced long-term persistent disadvantage on any two or more indicators.

Factor analysis revealed that the relationships between the seven indicators found at a cross-sectional level were replicated at a longitudinal level, thereby substantiating the notion of three integral elements of social exclusion – *household economic deprivation*, *personal civic exclusion* and *personal health exclusion*. Within these three elements, relationships between indicators at a longitudinal revealed relatively little multi-dimensional and longitudinal disadvantage – measured according to long-term persistent disadvantage on two or more indicators – less than 5 per cent for each element.

The final task of Chapter 6 was to create a working model of social exclusion that identified the most comprehensive and enduring forms of disadvantage. A definition was adopted that identified long-term persistent disadvantage on at least one indicator in each of the three integral elements of social exclusion. This analysis revealed that very few working-age adults, less than 2 per cent, experienced social exclusion, so defined, in Great Britain in the 1990s. Certain socio-demographic characteristics were linked to increased odds of social exclusion defined in this way, most notably living in a lone parent household, living alone, living in a household with two or more children and living in a household where no one works. The low number of individuals identified as socially excluded in the BHPS dataset meant more extensive analysis was not possible.

The European Community Household Panel (ECHP) survey provided an appropriate dataset for undertaking the fifth research objective – to compare the extent of social exclusion and the characteristics of the socially excluded in Great Britain with other EU member states. Although the investigation was limited, given the availability of only three waves of ECHP data, measures of multi-dimensional disadvantage, using indicators of the same domains used in the BHPS analysis, and persistent disadvantage, disadvantage in all three waves of the survey, were constructed.

The UK recorded rates of current income poverty slightly below the EU-12 average, as it did for indicators of material possessions, housing circumstance, social relations and mental health. The UK also recorded below EU-12 average rates of persistent disadvantage for all three economic indicators. UK rates for current physical ill health were well above the EU-12 average. Other countries were much more likely to record disadvantage rates above the EU-12 average, Portugal and Italy in particular. Cluster analysis of countries according to persistent disadvantage revealed a grouping of countries similar to findings of Gallie and Paugam (Eds. 2000). Their analysis grouped countries according to the stability and role of the family (the family residence model); and the coverage, level and duration of financial assistance, and the extent of development of active employment policies (the welfare regime model). According to their analysis the UK was placed with countries characterized by relatively weak family and welfare support.

Analysis of the multi-dimensional nature of social exclusion in Europe revealed that the extent of multiple disadvantage varied across Europe in much the same way as rates of individual domains of disadvantage. Portugal stood out as the country where working-age adults were most likely to have experienced multiple disadvantage, with the UK just below the EU-12 average. Factor analysis of BHPS data revealed three integral elements of social exclusion – *household economic deprivation*, *personal civic exclusion* and *personal health exclusion*. A similar analysis of the ECHP data revealed the same grouping at a EU-12 level, although groupings at a national level did vary for some countries. For example, in the Southern European countries indicators of neighbourhood disadvantage and social relations were most strongly linked, reaffirming the family residence model identified in Gallie and Paugam's (Eds. 2000) study.

To identify the prevalence of social exclusion in Europe a proportional social exclusion index (PSEI) was constructed that incorporates persistent disadvantage – that is disadvantage in all three waves – with disadvantage on a number of indicators. The PSEI adopts a relative measure of social exclusion to ensure comparability between countries. This is achieved by weighting the seven different domains of social exclusion according to the prevalence of each in the population of each country. This is a modern technique used in very few comparative studies of disadvantage.

Akin to analysis of social exclusion for working-age adults in Great Britain, using the BHPS, the prevalence of social exclusion across the EU-12 was low – the EU-12 average was just 2 per cent. However there were still significant numbers of working-age adults (and, consequently, often their household members too) who suffered from a combination of social exclusion related problems. This was particularly true for southern Europe countries. Rates of social exclusion in Portugal were twice the EU-12 average. Great Britain again was slightly below the EU-12 average. Luxembourg was found at the other end of the scale, recording rates of social exclusion of just 1 per cent.

Methodological limitations

There are always two major problems with quantifying social phenomena: definition and measurement. The definition and, in particular, the measurement of social exclusion have been the main foci of this research. Both have contributed to the quantification of social exclusion in Great Britain and other European Union member states. A consequence of quantifying social phenomena is that crucial methodological decisions are often influenced by procedures involved with using survey data. These procedures often involve arbitrary decisions that can affect the outcome of the research investigation. The following section therefore reflects on methodological limitations and the consequences for theoretical research.

Before the investigation of social exclusion could take place a decision had to be made on the conceptual foundation on which measurement was to be based. This decision was not straightforward given the multitude of conceptual theories of social exclusion present in the contemporary discourse (see Chapter 2 for an outline of the principal conceptual theories). Although it was never the intention of this research to formulate a new concept of social exclusion, but simply to elucidate and utilize existing theories, this choice was likely to shape the investigation of social exclusion. This of course has consequences for how to measure social exclusion.

The research sought to represent the integration and consolidation of key elements of the concept that is crucial to valid measurement. A number of issues arise from the research that has implications for the construction of a measure of social exclusion. These centre around, in particular, the identification of domains of social exclusion, the creation of appropriate indicators of these domains, an investigation of the relationship between these indicators and how they behave over time and, using the results of these investigations, the final classification of social exclusion.

The first stage of concept operationalization involved selecting a number of domains from which to create a comprehensive measure of social exclusion. After careful evaluation of the poverty and social exclusion literature, seven domains were chosen to represent social exclusion in this investigation; financial situation, material possessions, housing circumstance, neighbourhood perception, social relations, physical health and mental health. The inclusion of domains of neighbourhood perception and social relations in particular, distinguished an intention to measure social exclusion from a traditional economic-focussed measure of poverty.

After domains had been decided upon the next stage in the operationalization of social exclusion was to create appropriate indicators of these domains. Each indicator was constructed to denote a valid outcome measure of the domain it was designed to represent. For example, an individual with below 60 per cent median income was deemed to have a disadvantaged financial situation. The choice of information from which to construct each indicator was therefore crucial to this process and to some extent dependant on the range and quality of survey data.

Although an array of information is collected in both the BHPS and ECHP surveys, much of which is relevant to the investigation of social exclusion, still gaps remain. These gaps meant that social exclusion could not be operationalized to the extent and degree to which one would have hoped. For example, both surveys lack information on aspects of social relations, such as social interaction and networks, particularly with respect to quality and purpose. They also lack information on the neighbourhood, local services and community actions, something crucial to Room's notion of social exclusion. The coverage of material possessions and consumer durable items is not as broad as in some other surveys (most notably the *Poverty and Social Exclusion survey*). Neither do the surveys ask whether, if the household does not possess a material item, such as a television, it is because the household does not want it or because the household cannot afford it (although the ECHP does ask this for non-monetary possessions).

Also crucial to the construction of indicators is a decision on the threshold to determine disadvantage status. The indicators constructed using the BHPS made use of responses to a number of questions and tried to follow conventions used in other studies, such as the *Poverty and Social Exclusion survey*. An integral part of this methodology was to determine disadvantage status based on knowledgeable judgements of what constitutes disadvantage for each domain. Where possible for Great Britain, this decision was determined in relation to views of the general public as to what constitutes disadvantage, using evidence from the PSE survey.

The cross-national indicators created from the ECHP were constructed slightly differently. Here a proportional disadvantage index was calculated that made use of an array of items on a particular domain along with the possession or participation rates of each item in each country. Disadvantage thresholds for each indicator were based on a relative cut-off point on the distribution of the index amongst each national population (in much the same way as relative income thresholds are calculated). Both of the threshold judgements for each type of indicator were to some degree arbitrary, the BHPS thresholds based on knowledge that is not necessarily objective and ECHP thresholds based on a percentage of the average index score.

The final stage in the operationalization of social exclusion was to decide on a classification of social exclusion. For Great Britain, this decision was based on the theory that social exclusion was an experience that cut across the three integral elements of social exclusion (*household economic deprivation, personal civic exclusion* and *personal health exclusion*) and also lasted for persistent periods of time. Again this decision was somewhat arbitrary. Although the three integral elements of social exclusion were based on factor analysis, there is no evidence to suggest a period of time suffering three unrelated forms of disadvantage is any worse than a period of time suffering on a number of related forms. However it is reasonable to suggest that disadvantage that cuts across a multitude of disadvantage areas is more troublesome than that which is focussed in just one area, and which, in turn, may lead to exclusionary processes.

There is also little justification for selecting a seven to nine wave period of disadvantage as signifying long-term persistent disadvantage. This categorization was based on the work of Jenkins and Rigg (2001), also derived from (again arbitrary) nine waves of panel data. Conducting longitudinal analysis also poses a number of other methodological problems. Data collected over time is only useful if it is collected regularly and consistently. To be able to build up a longitudinal picture of an individual, and their household, a wide-range of information asked in the same way, in most, if not every, wave is necessary. Information has to be regularly collected to be able to pick up any short-term changes and consistent to be comparable from one time point to the next. The BHPS in particular contains a wealth of information, but some of this is not appropriate for longitudinal analysis because of sporadic and inconsistent occurrences across waves. For similar reasons having only three waves of the ECHP survey severely hindered an understanding of social exclusion at a European level.

Also relevant to the analysis of longitudinal data is lost information, caused by attrition and non-response. In terms of attrition, a comparison of cross-sectional and longitudinal samples in the BHPS concluded that those who appeared more likely to drop out of the survey included those who were young, lived in lone parent with dependent children households, lived in rented accommodation, had no qualifications or were inactive. These are characteristics attributed to individuals likely to be at high risk of social exclusion (the findings of this research have confirmed this). Missing data analysis caused by non-response also revealed the loss of respondents at high risk of social exclusion. Missing data was a particular problem given that longitudinal analysis relied on repeated observations of a variable and multi-dimensional analysis relied on a combination of different variables.

Methodological limitations also affected the comparative analysis of social exclusion. Although the ECHP survey covered a wide range of social exclusion related topics, certain domains were rather thinly covered and some were omitted altogether. For some countries and for some information in particular, the data was of different or insufficient quality, for example due to large numbers of missing records, differences in variable definition and question wording, and absence of the question in the questionnaire. Also some of the information was not comparable over time, because of changes to the questionnaire and routing.

The final problem with using secondary data to classify social exclusion is incomplete survey coverage. Household surveys such as the BHPS and ECHP cover only individuals in private households. Therefore they exclude the very individuals that a considered measure of social exclusion is likely to identify. These people include the homeless and those living in institutions. A consequence of this is that estimates are likely to underestimate the prevalence of social exclusion and overlook subgroups of the population most at risk.

Implications for policy

Constructing a conceptually valid definition of social exclusion has implications for policy, especially relevant at a time when social exclusion is being readily incorporated into the philosophy and strategy of governments and policy makers. This section considers the contribution of this research to political concepts and measures of social exclusion. This begins with a brief discussion of how the main findings contribute to overall policy analysis and design, before focusing in more depth on how the approach to operationalize social exclusion can be developed to improve the government's *Opportunity for all* indicators.

Policy analysis and design

There can be little doubt that the introduction of the notion of social exclusion into the political arena has had an effect on the theories that shape policies introduced to alleviate and avert such conditions. The notion of social exclusion has been firmly adopted by the New Labour government and tackling poverty and social exclusion made a policy priority. The formation of the Social Exclusion Unit, set up to organize the government's social exclusion strategy, is further evidence that tackling poverty and social exclusion is high up on the government's political agenda.

Within the social exclusion agenda, and evident in the *Opportunity for all* report particularly, New Labour place emphasis on the role low income plays in generating disadvantage. The emphasis on low income is not misplaced and is evident in much of the findings in this research. Combining this with the fact that income related policies are traditionally at the forefront of much social policy, and will continue to be so, suggests that income assistance should continue to play an important part in the alleviation and prevention of poverty and social exclusion.

Much of the income related policies aimed at eradicating poverty and social exclusion are also linked to tackling the disincentives to work. The empirical findings of this research have suggested that New Labour is correct in adopting policies that encourage individuals to work. Employment, particularly full-time employment, was seen as a factor that reduces the likelihood of a number of social exclusion related problems, economic problems especially. However this research has also revealed that whereas full-time work is associated with an avoidance of poverty and social exclusion the same cannot be said for part-time work, which is often associated with low-pay, insecurity and job dissatisfaction. This suggests dangers with concentrating on reinsertion into work *per se* as the major policy to combat social exclusion.

Moving away from the link between the labour market and income, the analysis has revealed that disadvantage does not simply affect people on a single domain but can happen in more than one domain at a time and over a period of time. Policies therefore need to be aware of such multi-dimensional and longitudinal disadvantage and pay particular attention to the relationships that formed the three integral elements of social exclusion; *household economic deprivation*, *personal civic exclusion* and *personal health exclusion*. Analysis also showed that multi-dimensionality can only really be understood, and therefore tackled, by adopting a longitudinal perspective. Too often in the past, policy has been based on a static understanding of disadvantage, which can conceal the real nature of social exclusion. In particular, without a longitudinal perspective the relationship between different dimensions of disadvantage is hard to understand. This can lead to confusion about the likely duration of disadvantage, which domains are likely to occur simultaneously and which are likely to lead to other forms of disadvantage. These findings suggest that policies need to focus on processes for a range of social exclusion related problems, not just low income, to identify problems and options for improvements.

By creating a measure that can focus attention on the genuinely poor or socially excluded, something a static measure of low income is unlikely to do, there is greater prospect for identifying subgroups of the population most at risk and, perhaps more importantly, the domains and patterns of disadvantage which affect them most. Analysis has shown that there are certain subsets of the working-age population, such as lone parents, sick and disabled people and those out of the labour market, at particular risk of poverty and social exclusion. Similar studies of poverty, although not restricted to working-age adults, have highlighted the adverse position of various other population groups, such as children (Vleminckx and Smeeding, (Eds.) 2001), the elderly (Tsakloglou, 1996) and women (Millar, 1997). The analysis has also shown that various forms of disadvantage affect various individuals in different ways. This analysis is necessary to be able to disentangle the various causes and consequences of disadvantage and exclusion and has obvious importance for successful and effective policy design. For example, the research has suggested a number of areas in which policy could focus to reduce the likelihood of disadvantage, such as increasing education and involvement with the labour market.

At a EU level, the Amsterdam Treaty saw the term social exclusion treated explicitly in a political legal context, defining social exclusion as a process that prevents people from fully participating in society, as well as from becoming socially integrated. Within Eurostat, the statistical arm of the European Commission, a taskforce has been made responsible for developing a measure of social exclusion at a EU level (Eurostat, 1998). To date the taskforce has not arrived at a precise statistical definition of social exclusion, instead choosing to outline a number of indicators that span a number of diverse aspects of life (Social Protection Committee, 2001; Atkinson et al, 2002).

The work in Chapter 7 makes considerable progress in the empirical operationalization of social exclusion at a European level using the ECHP survey. The methodology of the Proportional Social Exclusion Index, which reflects any cultural and resourced-based differences between countries, has meant a comparable, multi-dimensional and longitudinal measure of social exclusion is possible. This meant the research was able to estimate the levels of social exclusion in Europe and identify sub-groups of the population at particular risk. This analysis provides evidence of the nature of social exclusion at a national level, crucial for countries without national surveys, as well as confirmation of the disparity of social exclusion both within and between countries.

Opportunity for all and measuring poverty

Opportunity for all outlines the key policy areas that the government has highlighted to tackle poverty and social exclusion. The report contains a number of indicators that are used to measure, and monitor progress in tackling, poverty and social exclusion. It is these indicators that have attracted most attention from the public, politicians and academics alike. The indicators have been criticized on a number of points: for lacking a theoretical foundation, for failing to adequately measuring poverty and social exclusion – the multi-dimensional and longitudinal characteristics of the phenomena especially – and, for failing to distinguish between outcomes and risk factors (see Chapter 2 for a more detailed discussion). Such criticisms led the government to seek consultation from experts in the field of poverty and social exclusion measurement on how best to construct and employ indicators appropriate for monitoring progress of attempts to tackle poverty and social exclusion (DSS, 2001c; DWP, 2002).[1]

From these consultations emerged four options for the design of indicators of poverty.[2] The first option is to use a number of multi-dimensional headline indicators to capture outcomes from the important dimensions of poverty. The second option is to create a one-figure index that summarizes headline indicators of poverty. The third option is to create a measure of 'consistent poverty' that strives to capture a valid measure of living standards. The fourth and final option is to use a measure of consistent poverty alongside other key indicators, such as absolute low income and relative low income, which can be monitored in the long-term. Each of these approaches has limitations of course, both methodological and practical, and these, along with political considerations, are likely to have influenced the government's choice of method to improve the indicators. The findings of this research are relevant to the choice of method to improve these indicators. Although not set up specifically to evaluate the four options the government is considering, the research has illustrated the main features of each approach.

The first approach, a range of headline indicators covering different dimensions of poverty, was outlined in Chapter 4. Using a range of headline indicators illustrated the extent of each form of disadvantage and a breakdown by socio-demographic characteristic showed types of individuals most at risk. However this approach failed to determine either the multi-dimensional or longitudinal experience of disadvantage and therefore is most useful for looking at current incidence and, if repeated over time, trends of various forms of disadvantage in society. Important judgements to be made during this approach are to decide which dimensions of poverty are important, how to measure them and how to decide on the disadvantage thresholds. These decisions are particularly important given that the indicators present a suite of information that requires ease of comprehension and interpretation. This approach can be seen to be a refinement of the original *Opportunity for all* indicators.

The second approach, a single composite index, was used for cross-national investigations of social exclusion in Chapter 7. This approach was used to create a one-figure summary of the seven social exclusion indicators for each of the EU-12

---

[1] These consultations have in fact focussed on indicators for measuring child poverty but are relevant to this discussion.

[2] The consultation paper does not explicitly distinguish between the notions of poverty and social exclusion and hence no consistent differentiation between indicators of poverty and social exclusion is apparent. Consequently the language of poverty will be used to outline the government's approach, even though some of the indicators, although relatively few, refer to non-economic aspects of disadvantage.

countries.[3] The index was easy to present, for example it allowed for a comparison of social exclusion rates across the countries, but interpretation of the index was difficult without further knowledge of the behaviour of the separate indicators, both at a multi-dimensional and longitudinal level. The methodology involved in the construction of the index was complex, but necessary to be able to create a relative measure of social exclusion crucial for cross-country comparisons. However, as alluded to above, the complexity of the index meant conditions of transparency might fail. Also, as with separate indicator construction the index still relied on somewhat arbitrary decisions on dimensions of social exclusion to be included, the choice of weighting procedure and a threshold to identify the socially excluded.

The third approach, a poverty definition that incorporates low income and other forms of material deprivation to obtain a consistent measure of living standards, was created in the operationalization of the notion of *household economic deprivation* in Chapter 4. Acknowledgement of the relationship between income and non-monetary indicators of economic deprivation by researchers at ESRI (Nolan and Whelan, 1996) has consequently been used to produce the Irish government's national anti-poverty strategy (Inter-Departmental Policy Committee, 1997). This strategy aims to reduce the number of people below 60 per cent of median income *and* experiencing deprivation on a number of basic household items such as heating, a substantial diet and new clothing (approximately one in twenty of the working-age population in Great Britain according to the definition employed in this research). By definition this approach adopts a more severe measure of poverty than that which uses an income measure alone (if the same income threshold is applied in both measures) by aligning low income with resource forfeiture. However this definition again relies heavily on methodological decisions, such as the choice of low-income threshold and deprivation indicators. There are also dangers with using a method that combines absolute and relative measures in this way. As has been shown in Ireland in recent times a paradox is created when living standards improve (meaning fewer people living in absolute poverty) alongside greater inequality (meaning more people living in relative poverty). In such circumstances presenting and interpreting a measure of consistent poverty could be perplexing for the public and politicians alike (Nolan, 2001).

The fourth and final option considered by the government is to present a measure of consistent poverty alongside two other key indicators – absolute low income and relative low income – which can be monitored in the long-term. The government sees this approach as appropriate for presenting a gradient of progress in tackling poverty and also for international comparisons. This approach is useful for the emphasis it places on time in understanding poverty. Using this measure poverty can be seen to be falling when all three indicators show a reduction in the proportion of poor families. Chapter 4 showed that a presentation of trends of the various dimensions of disadvantage could be used to assess changes in levels of disadvantage over time. Analysis such as this of course has to take into account

---

[3] This approach is also appropriate for a relative measure of disadvantage at a country-specific level.

any contemporaneous changes in absolute definitions of disadvantage, such as the deprivation indicators chosen to represent living standards. Just as important as making definitions consistent over time is the need to make them consistent between countries in cross-national comparisons. The analysis of social exclusion in Europe between 1994 and 1996, presented in Chapter 7, applied a relative approach that took into account differences between countries and changes in the incidence of various forms of disadvantage that occurred from one wave to the next. Applying an absolute approach to cross-national comparisons of poverty would require an in-depth knowledge of wave-on-wave country-specific minimum living standards and the construction of a measure that not only took both of these requirements into account but also produced presentable and meaningful statistics.

As stated earlier, the approach adopted by the government is likely to be guided by both methodological and political constraints. From a purely methodological perspective this research has advocated an approach to measurement that adopts both multi-dimensional and longitudinal methods. A multi-dimensional approach is required to cover a range of outcomes relevant to poverty (dependent on course on the definition of what poverty is) and, perhaps more importantly, to identify the number of people who experience disadvantage on a number of indicators at any one time. A longitudinal approach is required to look at trends in indicators over time and to identify the number of people who experience disadvantage on one indicator, or a number of indicators simultaneously, for different time periods and patterns. An analysis of characteristics of the disadvantaged population has also advocated an approach that captures and distinguishes between outcomes and risk factors. A breakdown of poverty information by individual, household or area characteristics can reveal prevalence patterns and whether aggregate level changes in indicators occur at a more detailed level, both of which contribute to a more detailed monitoring procedure and can also provide useful pointers for policy if indicators go down when anti-poverty policies succeed (and vice-versa).

Information used in *Opportunity for all* is derived from a variety of sources and therefore unsuitable for the construction of multi-dimensional and longitudinal indicators of poverty and social exclusion. To enable a detailed measurement and monitoring program, the indicators would need to come from an appropriate complex, panel survey. The British Household Panel Survey has been suitable for most of the analysis in this book, some of which would be too elaborate for a set of government indicators, although limitations of the dataset have been exposed in terms of comprehensiveness, consistency, time-span, geographical detail, survey coverage, attrition and sample size.[4] If the government wish to make use of the BHPS to construct indicators of poverty these limitations would need to be resolved, as would the speed in which data is available for dissemination. An alternative to enhancing the BHPS would be the design of a new poverty survey that would incorporate the methodological requirements outlined in this book. One

---

[4] A possible alternative is the Families and Children Survey, administered by the National Centre for Social Research (see http://www.natcen.ac.uk), which over-sampled low-income families in 1999 and 2000.

advantage of retaining the BHPS however is that it has been in operation since 1991, meaning many waves of rich data are readily available, including that relevant to the previous Conservative government's period in office – a period in which New Labour are eager to demonstrate they have improved upon.

From a purely political perspective, setting an overall standard against which success or failure in tackling poverty can be assessed is a responsible and committed act. However this act is likely to lack substance unless targets are specifically defined and policy declarations given appropriate content and meaning. The first stage of such actions is to agree on a notion of poverty, although evidence from Ireland suggests that obtaining widespread agreement on a definition is not a major obstacle (Nolan, 2001). Rather more difficult is to create a measure of poverty that receives public and political credibility.

Creating a poverty indicator that shifts attention from a focus on low income alone is unlikely to receive too much political condemnation given the widely accepted criticism of that approach. In any case, a measure of poverty based only on low income can be too easily dismissed whereas a range of measures cannot. Furthermore, to inform both policy-makers and the public as fully as possible requires the use of a range of information. However, if targets to poverty reduction are to be set then there needs a headline indicator, or at least very few indicators, against which success or failure is to be judged. Without clarity of definition and purpose attempt to measure and monitor poverty are likely to become confused and misinterpreted.

Each of the four approaches to improve the *Opportunity for all* indicators outlined above retains low income as an integral part of the measure of poverty. Income is clearly a critical element of both the conceptualization and measurement of poverty, and plays a significant role in anti-poverty policy design, so maintaining its presence in indicator construction is appropriate. This raises issues of how income should be measured and how to decide on a threshold to determine when income is insufficient. The question of income measurement covers topics such as whether income should be calculated before or after housing costs, which equivalence scale should be used to account for household size and composition, and whether the value of public services (the 'social wage') should be incorporated into income statistics (Hills, 2001).

Insufficient income is most commonly defined using a purely relative measure, such as below a fraction of the average contemporary income; an approach applied in the HBAI series. Although the poverty line drawn from this approach is often arbitrary, an absolute measure of low income is complicated by decisions of how to define participation in society and how to cost this in income terms. These decisions also need regular revision in line with changing societal standards and costs. Issues of low-income duration and pattern also need to be considered given that persistent or repeated low income is likely to be more problematic than transitory low income.

If poverty is defined as an inability to participate in society because of insufficient income and a lack of other financial resources, an indicator of low income needs to be complemented with other measures. These other measures should include the other financial resources that can affect participation in society, in particular resource-based assets. In this respect the government's choice to adopt option four – a tiered approach incorporating absolute low income, relative low income and a measure of 'consistent poverty' (Department for Work and Pensions, 2003) – appears justifiable, as it considers low income alongside material assets to identify poverty resulting from lack of resources. To construct an absolute measure of poverty based on a relative standard of participation in society this approach requires an appropriate participation level, income threshold and set of deprivation indicators, which need to be revised regularly to take into account society's costs, values and perceptions. Although this measure does not cover many of the issues raised in this research, for example the relational aspects of social exclusion, it represents a marked improvement to the indicators offered in *Opportunity of all* as they currently stand.

The value of social exclusion: definition and measurement

The aim of this research was to build upon theoretical discussions of social exclusion to construct an empirical model, using quantitative survey data, to investigate the nature and extent of social exclusion in Great Britain and to compare findings for Great Britain with other European Union member states. The operationalization of social exclusion has thus been accomplished and implications of this for theory and policy discussed. The final section of this chapter pulls together the main findings of the research to consider the overall value of a valid and robust definition and measure of social exclusion.

In terms of definition, the book built upon theoretical discussions of social exclusion, and poverty, to opt for a theory that emphasizes the multi-dimensional, longitudinal and relative features of social exclusion. This definition is similar to Room's (Ed. 1995, 1998, 2000) notion of social exclusion and also to what Levitas (1998) calls the *redistributive discourse* on social exclusion. In this discourse social exclusion is seen to differ from traditional notions of poverty in that it captures the multi-dimensional character of social disadvantage and also refers to a process rather than a static concept. This discourse also sees social exclusion as a consequence of poverty, something that was investigated in this research by examining the relationship between the financial situation indicator and other indicators of disadvantage.

Because the definition of social exclusion is not new, but rather an amalgamation of current theoretical discourse, it cannot offer a great deal in terms of precise conceptualization. In fact, it could be argued that the notion of social exclusion assumed here is not markedly different from many of the more elaborate notions of poverty. The notion of poverty has often been misrepresented as a static, one-dimensional measure of financial disadvantage but there are numerous examples of it being taken to a conceptually higher plane; Rowntree's (1901) discussion of life-stages and Townsend's (1979) premise of a range of inadequate resources that can restrict participation are examples that originate from two of the most influential poverty theories.

If the two notions are broadly similar, the contribution of social exclusion to theoretical discourse of disadvantage over and above that of poverty must be questioned. Indeed, Micklewright (2002) believes that the conceptual advances social exclusion appears to have made would have happened anyway as a consequence of the evolution of poverty discourse. Nolan and Whelan (2001) on the other hand offer a response to the merits of distinguishing between poverty and social exclusion. They reason that poverty can be multi-dimensional, longitudinal and relative, and refer to a lack of resources or inability to participate, but, and here is the crux of their argument, poverty refers to such conditions only when caused by insufficient income and other financial resources.

Nolan and Whelan's argument that financial resources should remain at the heart of the notion of poverty, and the causal properties of poverty in particular, suggest that poverty research should focus on investigations of the effect of low income and other forms of monetary scarcity on the ability to achieve a minimum living standard and full participation in the life of society. The first action of such investigations should be to define minimum living standards and full participation (something beyond the scope of this discussion). Investigations should then consider which standards and participatory events are caused directly by insufficient financial resources. This research has shown that low income is associated with a range of disadvantage situations, particularly economic related, both at a point in time and longitudinally. However, the association between income and other aspects of economic disadvantage was not particularly strong.

The effect of low income on non-economic related forms of disadvantage appears less straightforward. It is at this point that research that only considers the effects of financial hardship is likely to be deficient, as it is likely to overlook a variety of other forms of disadvantage in society. Here the notion of social exclusion appears appropriate. Thus, the notion of social exclusion should be applied to the realization of minimum living standards and full participation in society (as is the notion of poverty), but to consider outcomes caused by factors other than, but also including, financial hardship. Thereby social exclusion will bring non-economic forms of disadvantage into the spotlight, particularly those concerned with issues of social, civil and political rights. It will also concentrate on the relationship between all these forms of disadvantage, how and why multi-dimensional disadvantage occurs and longitudinal patterns of such experiences. All these are features of disadvantage often misrepresented by the notion of poverty. The notion of social exclusion therefore provides an opportunity to progress the conceptualization of disadvantage.

This does not address the issue of whether there is a place for both poverty and social exclusion in disadvantage discourse. If social exclusion considers the realization of minimum living standards and full participation in society according to a variety of causal factors, including financial situation, with poverty incorporated into this notion, is not the notion of poverty superseded by the notion of social exclusion? Although logically this may be the case, there are a number of reasons to retain both notions. Perhaps the most pertinent reason is because to many, politicians and the public alike, the word poverty implies unacceptable adversity and the moral imperative that something should be done to eradicate such problems. Poverty is also a worldwide concept and the stalwart of disadvantage vocabulary. As already explained, although not as powerful and effectual at present, the notion of social exclusion is crucial to the conceptualization of features of disadvantage often overlooked in poverty discourse.

Although very few theorists have agreed on a distinct conceptualization of social exclusion, many agree that the introduction of the term has shifted debate on measurement towards consideration of a number of fundamental features of disadvantage that are often overlooked in traditional poverty research (for example see Micklewright, 2002). A common criticism of poverty research is that although poverty has been conceptualized as complex, dynamic, relative and communal, it has not been adequately measured. In other words, low income at a point in time is not a satisfactory measure of poverty. Using an unsatisfactory measure to represent the notion of poverty can have consequences both for research, where attempts to understand the true nature of poverty are likely to be restricted, and policy, where policies that are based on such misinformed research are likely to be misguided.

This research has concentrated on the operationalization of social exclusion in a manner that is different from that of traditional measures of poverty and in accord with the conceptual definition of social exclusion employed – a multi-dimensional and dynamic process of being shut out, fully or partially, from the economic, social and cultural systems that determine the social integration of a person in society (Walker, 1997). The measurement concentrated principally on two of the main elements of the concept – the multi-dimensional and longitudinal nature of social exclusion whilst also using indicators that detect an individual's perception of their neighbourhood and that value an individual's social relationships.

From a theoretical standpoint there are two main implications for research. First, the study of disadvantage, whether conceptualized as poverty or social exclusion, should not focus on low income only. Evidence from this research has suggested that using only income as an indicator of disadvantage restricts an understanding of poor people's circumstances. Secondly, and a consequence of the first implication, to understand disadvantage fully it has to be conceptualized and measured using both a multi-dimensional *and* longitudinal approach. Evidence from this research has demonstrated diverse relationships between different dimensions of disadvantage. Coupled with a need to depict the multiple difficulties faced by the most disadvantaged individuals is the requirement to represent the duration of such hardship. Often measures such as poverty and deprivation concentrate only on disadvantage at a point in time. Such information can be misleading because situations may alter which could have major repercussions of lifestyle and also, perhaps more importantly, because people amass resources over time which affect their opportunities and their ability to cope during difficult periods. Longitudinal information allows a classification of the currently disadvantaged according to duration of disadvantage making it possible to highlight those less able to cope with such unfortunate circumstances.

One of the most significant findings to emerge from this research was the identification of three integral elements of social exclusion. Factor analysis of the seven social exclusion indicators using BHPS data identified, at both a cross-sectional and longitudinal level, a grouping of indicators according to notions of *household economic deprivation, personal civic exclusion* and *personal health exclusion*. Although the identification of these three elements depends to some degree on the choice and construction of indicators in this study, it does provide a useful framework for the analysis of social exclusion for Great Britain.

The financial situation (income poverty), material possessions and housing circumstance indicators showed associations at both cross-sectional and longitudinal levels to suggest identification of a *household economic deprivation* element of social exclusion. This element appears close to traditional notions of income poverty, although perhaps closer still to the approach of Nolan and Whelan (1996) who combined both income and direct indicators of deprivation. Akin to Nolan and Whelan's findings, this research has shown that the relationship between income and non-monetary indicators of economic hardship was not striking, especially at a cross-sectional level. Although the BHPS data failed to take into account differences in choice, it is unlikely that the main distinction between the low-income economically deprived and the low-income non-economically deprived were living standard preferences. Instead there were likely to be other factors that influenced their circumstances, such as the accumulation and erosion of resources over time. What the findings imply however is that income should not be taken as the sole indicator either of poverty or social exclusion.

Notions of *personal civic exclusion* and *personal health exclusion* were formed from the relationships between the remaining four indicators – in fact the strongest relationship between the seven social exclusion indicators was for the physical and mental health indicators. The implications of finding only a limited overlap between income and other indicators of social exclusion were to discourage further the use of income as the only indicator of social exclusion, particularly when non-economic outcomes are considered, as well as the need to distinguish between different dimensions of disadvantage.

Other evidence that promotes the need to distinguish different elements of social exclusion was how explanatory variables, defined according to certain socio-demographic household- and individual-level variables, related differently to the individual and composite disadvantage measures. For example, young adults were particularly likely to complain about their neighbourhood, especially when combined with *household economic deprivation*, older adults were linked with physical health problems, lone parents to low income and so on.

This evidence supports an idea that methods to measure social exclusion should take into consideration the population under investigation. For example indicators relevant to certain populations groups should not be made applicable across the entire population. This also applies to cross national investigations. Analysis of the ECHP survey showed that although the three integral notions of social exclusion were identifiable across the EU as a whole, this did vary between countries. This suggests that a framework for investigating social exclusion applicable to one country may not be applicable to another. The construction of the Proportional Social Exclusion Index ensured these differences were taken into consideration in a comparative social exclusion analysis.

Summary and themes for future research

If social exclusion is the destination on a journey through various experiences of disadvantage, both multifaceted and enduring, then this research has found that social exclusion in Great Britain, and other European Union member states, was relatively uncommon amongst the working-age population living in private households in the 1990s. Analysis of complex panel data also revealed that these experiences were associated with certain individual and household economic and socio-demographic characteristics. This investigation has also enhanced methodological developments in the operationalization of social exclusion. Multi-dimensional and longitudinal methodology applied to the development of an operational definition of social exclusion suggested a framework for measuring social exclusion in Great Britain that involves notions of *household economic deprivation*, *personal civic exclusion* and *personal health exclusion*. At a European level advances were made in a cross-national measure of social exclusion that used a relative approach to ensure comparability between countries.

A number of implications for research and policy arose from these findings. The notion of social exclusion, and the multidimensional, longitudinal, relative, participative and relational form of disadvantage that it implies, offers advantages to both theory and policy making. Social exclusion as conceptualized and operationalized in this book is complex, does occur over time and does involve more than financial shortage. Consequently attempts to measure and to understand social exclusion should be designed to take into account these features. So, for example, a measure of consistent poverty, developed according to a notion of *household economic deprivation*, should be a preferred approach to low-income as an indicator of poverty in the *Opportunity for all* report. Likewise policy strategies that do not take into account these features of social exclusion are likely to be too simplistic to comprehend and tackle the complex phenomena of disadvantage in society. Although combating social exclusion is high on the agenda of many European countries and has been made an explicit objective of the European Community, only recently have Governments begun to acknowledge that social exclusion is a deep-rooted, complex problem that requires long-lasting, well-structured policies.

This research has opened up various routes for further analysis. Understanding the processes by which individuals become socially excluded, and the patterns of their experiences, is likely to be crucial to the formulation of preventative policies designed to reverse such trajectories. In particular there is the need to investigate the sequencing and relationship between indicators of social exclusion; if the severity, length and pattern of disadvantage spells are dependent on the characteristics of earlier spells; and the factors that reduce the likelihood of disadvantage risk. To understand how social exclusion operates within a time perspective many waves of comprehensive, wide-ranging, good quality panel data is required. To assess household and household member conditions for example, it is necessary to determine how these resources have developed over time and the likelihood that they can be deployed in the future. An obvious restriction of such proposals is the availability of such data. Therefore efforts need to be put into the formation of datasets able to allow such investigations to develop.

Thorough investigations into social exclusion are still relatively uncommon. This research has contributed to these investigations, in particular by providing evidence to enhance the operationalization of social exclusion at a national and cross-national level. These investigations need to continue, not only to assist analysis of disadvantage in society, and its complex and dynamic features, but also to contribute to efforts to minimize the experiences that can blight the living standards of individuals, households and communities.

Bibliography

6, Perri (1997) *Escaping poverty*, London: Demos.

Abel-Smith, B. and Townsend P. (1965) *The poor and the poorest*, London: Bell.

Alcock, P. (1993) *Understanding poverty*, London: Macmillan.

Apospori, E. and Millar, J. (Eds.) (2002) *The dynamics of social exclusion in Europe*, Cheltenham: Edward Elgar.

Ashworth, K., Hill, M.S. and Walker, R. (1991) *The severity and duration of childhood poverty in the USA*, Centre for Research in Social Policy, working paper 144, Loughborough: Loughborough University of Technology.

Ashworth, K., Hill, M.S. and Walker, R. (2000) 'A new approach to poverty dynamics', in Rose, D. (Ed.) *Researching social and economic change: the uses of household panel studies*, London: Routledge.

Ashworth, K. and Walker, R. (1994) 'Measuring claimant populations', in Buck, N., Gershuny, J., Rose, D. and Scott, J. (Eds.) *Changing households: The British Household Panel Survey 1990-1992*, Colchester: ESRC Research Centre on Micro-Social Change.

Atkinson, A.B. (1989) *Poverty and social security*, London: Harvester Wheatsheaf.

Atkinson, A.B., Cantillon, B., Marlier, E. and Nolan, B. (2002) *Social indicators: The EU and social inclusion*, Oxford: Oxford University Press.

Atkinson, A.B. and Hills, J. (Eds.) (1998) *Exclusion, employment and opportunity*, CASEpaper, CASE/4, London: London School of Economics.

Bajekal, M. and Purdon, S. (2001) *Social capital and social exclusion: development of a condensed module for the Health Survey of England*, London: National Centre for Social Research.

Bane, M. and Ellwood, D. (1986) 'Slipping in and out of poverty: the dynamics of spells', *Journal of Human Resources*, Vol. 21, No. 1, pp. 1-23.

Barclay, P. (2000) 'Foreword', in Gordon, D., Townsend, P., Levitas, R., Pantazis, C., Payne, S., Patsois, D., Middleton, S., Ashworth, K. and Adelman, L. *Poverty and social exclusion in Britain*, York: Joseph Rowntree Foundation.

Bardesi, E., Jenkins, S.P. and Rigg, J. (2001) *Documentation for derived current and annual net household income variables*, BHPS waves 1-9, ISER working paper, University of Essex: ISER.

Barnes, M. (2002) 'Social exclusion and the life course', in Barnes, M., Heady, C., Millar, J., Middleton, S., Tsakloglou, P., Papadopoulos, F. and Room, G. *Poverty and Social Exclusion in Europe*, Cheltenham: Edward Elgar.

Barnes, M., Heady, C., Millar, J., Middleton, S., Tsakloglou, P., Papadopoulos, F. and Room, G. (2002) *Poverty and social exclusion in Europe*, Cheltenham: Edward Elgar.

Barnes, M. and Middleton, S. (2002) 'Introduction: analysing poverty and social exclusion', in Apospori, E. and Millar, J. (Eds.) *The dynamics of social exclusion in Europe*, Cheltenham: Edward Elgar.

Benzeval, M. (1997) 'Health', in Walker, A. and Walker, C. (Eds.) *Britain divided: the growth of social exclusion in the 1980s and 1990s*, London: CPAG.

Benzeval, M. and Judge, K. (2000) 'Income and health: The time dimension', *Social Science and Medicine,* Vol. 52, pp. 1371-1390.

Berghman, J. (1995) 'Social exclusion in Europe: Policy context and analytical framework', in Room, G. (Ed.) *Beyond the Threshold: The Measurement and Analysis of Social Exclusion*, Bristol: The Policy Press.

Berthoud, R. (2000) 'A measure of changing health', in Berthoud, R. and Gershuny, J. (Eds.) *Seven years in the lives of British families: evidence on the dynamics of social change from the British Household Panel Study*, Bristol: Policy Press.

Bradbury, B. and Markus, J. (2001) 'Child poverty across the industrialized world: Evidence from the Luxembourg Income Study', in Vleminck, K. and Smeeding, T.M. (Eds.) *Child wellbeing, child poverty and child policy in modern nations*, Bristol: Policy Press.

Bradshaw, J. (Ed.) (1993) *Budget standards for the United Kingdom*, Aldershot: Avebury.

Bradshaw, J. (1999) 'Child poverty in comparative perspective', *European Journal of Social Security*, Vol. 1, No. 4, pp. 383-404.

Bradshaw, J. (Ed.) (2000) *Poverty: The outcomes for children*, London: Family Policies Institute.

Bradshaw, J. (2001) 'Poverty: the outcomes for children', in, *Indicators of progress: A discussion of approaches to monitor the government's strategy to tackle poverty and social exclusion*, Report of the workshop held on 19 July 2000 organized by Department of Social Security and Centre for Analysis of Social Exclusion, LSE, CASEreport 13, London: London School of Economics.

Bradshaw, J. and Finch, N. (2001) *Core poverty*, paper for a seminar at the Centre for Analysis of Social Exclusion, London School of Economics, York: Social Policy Research Unit.

Bryman, A. and Cramer, D. (1997) *Quantitative data analysis with SPSS for windows: A guide for social scientists*, London: Routledge.

Buck, N., Ermisch, J.F. and Jenkins, S.P. (1995) *Choosing a longitudinal survey design: the issues*, ESRC Centre on Micro-Social Change: University of Essex.

Burchardt, T. (2000) 'Social exclusion: concepts and evidence', in Gordon, D. and Townsend, P. (Eds.) *Breadline Europe: the measurement of poverty*, Bristol: The Policy Press.

Burchardt, T., Le Grand, J., Piachaud, D. (1999) 'Social Exclusion in Britain 1991-1995', *Social Policy and Administration*, Vol. 33, No. 3, pp. 227-244.

Callan, T. and Nolan, B. (1994) 'The meaning and measurement of poverty', in Callan, T. and Nolan, B. (Eds.) *Poverty and policy in Ireland*, Dublin: Gill and Macmillan Ltd.

Callan, T., Nolan, B. and Whelan, C.T. (1993) 'Concepts of poverty and the poverty line: a critical survey of approaches to measure poverty', *Journal of Economic Surveys*, Vol. 5, pp. 243-262.

Carley, M. (1981) 'Definitions and dimensions of social indicators', *Social measurement and social indicators: Issues of policy and theory*, Contemporary social research series: 1, London: George Allen & Unwin Ltd.

Clasen, J., Gould, A. and Vincent, J. (1997) *Long-term unemployment and the threat of social exclusion: a cross-national analysis of the position of long-term unemployed people in Germany, Sweden and Britain*, Bristol: Policy Press.

Clémenceau, A. and Verma, V. (1996) 'Methodology of the European Community Household Panel', *Statistics in Transition*, Vol. 2, No. 7, pp. 1023-1062.

Daniel, W.W. (1990) *The unemployed flow*, London: Policy Studies Institute.

Davey Smith, G., Hart, C., Blane, D., Gillis, C. and Hawthorne, V. (1997) 'Lifetime socio-economic position and mortality: Prospective observational study', *British Medical Journal*, Vol. 314, pp. 547-552.

Denzin, N.K. (1989) *The research act: A theoretical introduction to sociological methods*, New Jersey: Prentice-Hall.

Department of Health (1998) *Independent inquiry into inequalities in health report*, London: The Stationery Office.

Department of Social Security (1996) *Households Below Average Income: Methodological review*, Report of a working group, London: The Stationery Office.

Department of Social Security (1998) *New ambitions for our country: A new contract for welfare*, London: The Stationery Office.

Department of Social Security (1999a) *Opportunity for all: Tackling poverty and social exclusion*, London: The Stationery Office.

Department of Social Security (1999b) *Opportunity for all, Indicators of success: definitions, data and baseline information*, annex to the first report, London: The Stationery Office.

Department of Social Security (2000a) *Opportunity for all: One year on, making a difference*, London: The Stationery Office.

Department of Social Security (2000b) *Opportunity for all – one year on: making a difference, Indicators of progress: definitions, data, baseline and trends information, annex to the second annual report*, London: London School of Economics.

Department of Social Security (2001a) *Households Below Average Income – a statistical analysis 1994/5 to 1998/9*, London: The Stationery Office.

Department of Social Security (2001b) *Households Below Average Income – 1999/00*, London: The Stationery Office.

Department of Social Security (2001c) *Indicators of progress: A discussion of approaches to monitor the government's strategy to tackle poverty and social exclusion*, Report of the workshop held on 19 July 2000 organized by Department of Social Security and Centre for Analysis of Social Exclusion, LSE, CASEreport 13, London: London School of Economics.

Department of the Environment, Trade and the Regions (1999) *A better quality of life: A strategy for sustainable development for the United Kingdom*, London: The Stationery Office.

Department of the Environment, Trade and the Regions (2000) *Survey of English Housing*, London: The Stationery Office.

Department of Work and Pensions (2002) *Measuring child poverty: A consultation document*, London: The Stationery Office.

Department of Work and Pensions (2003) *Measuring child poverty*, London: The Stationery Office.

Desai, M. and Shah, A. (1988) 'An econometric approach to the measurement of poverty', *Oxford Economic Papers*, Vol. 40, No. 3, pp. 505-522.

Dirven, H. and Bergham, J. (1991) *Poverty, insecurity of subsistence and relative deprivation in the Netherlands*, Tilburg: IVA/Department of Social Security Studies.

Dunn, J., Hodge, I., Monk, S. and Kiddle, C. (1998) *Developing indicators of rural disadvantage*, Research report No. 36, Salisbury: Rural Development Commission.

EEC (1981) *Final report from the Commission to the Council on the first programme of pilot schemes and studies to combat poverty*, Brussels: Commission of the European Communities.

EEC (1985) 'On specific community action to combat poverty', (Council decision of 19 December 1984) 85/8/EEC, *Official journal of the EEC*, 2/24.

Esping-Anderson, G. (1990) *The three worlds of welfare capitalism*, Oxford: Polity Press.

European Commission (1990) *Poverty in figures: Europe in the early 1980s*, Luxembourg: Office for Official Publications of the European Communities.

European Commission (1994) *Poverty statistics in the late 1980s: Research based on micro-data*, Luxembourg: Office for Official Publications of the European Communities.

European Commission (1996) *European Community Household Panel (ECHP): Survey methodology and implementation*, Luxembourg: Office for Official Publications of the European Communities.

European Commission (1999a) *European Community Household Panel (ECHP): Selected indicators from the 1995 wave*, Luxembourg: Office for Official Publications of the European Communities.

European Commission (1999b) *European Community Household Panel longitudinal user's database manual*, Luxembourg: Eurostat.

European Commission (2000) *European social statistics: Income, poverty and social exclusion*, Luxembourg: Office for Official Publications of the European Communities.

Eurostat (1998) *Recommendations on poverty and social exclusion statistics*, Luxembourg: Eurostat.

Evans, M. (1995) *Out for the count: The incomes of the non-household population and the effect of their exclusion from national income profiles*, Welfare State Programme Discussion Paper No. WSP/111, London: London School of Economics.

Fielding, J. and Gilbert, N. (2000) *Understanding social statistics*, London: SAGE.

Fisher, G.M. (1992) 'The development and history of the poverty thresholds', *Social Security Bulletin*, Vol. 55, No. 4, pp. 3-14.

Forrest, R. and Gordon, D. (1993) *People and places: a 1991 Census atlas of England*, SAUS, University of Bristol.

Forssen, K. (1998) *Child poverty and family policy in the OECD countries*, Luxembourg Income Study working papers, No. 178, Luxembourg: LIS.

Gallie, D. and Paugam, S. (Eds.) (2000) *Welfare regimes and the experience of unemployment in Europe*, Oxford: Oxford University Press.

Gillies, P. (1997) 'Social capital: recognising the value of society', *Healthlines*, Vol. 45, pp. 15-17.

Ginsburg, N. (1997) 'Housing', in Walker, A. and Walker, C. (Eds.) *Britain divided: the growth of social exclusion in the 1980s and 1990s*, London: CPAG.

Goldberg, D. (1972) *The detection of psychiatric illness by questionnaire*, Oxford: Oxford University Press.

Goodin, R.E., Headey, B., Muffels, R. and Dirven, H.D. (1999) *The real worlds of welfare capitalism*, Cambridge: Cambridge University Press.

Gordon, D. and Pantazis, C. (Eds.) (1997) *Breadline Britain in the 1990s*, Aldershot: Ashgate.

Gordon, D. and Pantazis, C. (Eds.) (2000) *Tackling inequalities: where are we now and what can be done?*, Bristol: The Policy Press.

Gordon, D., Townsend, P., Levitas, R., Pantazis, C., Payne, S., Patsois, D., Middleton, S., Ashworth, K. and Adelman, L. (2000) *Poverty and social exclusion in Britain*, York: Joseph Rowntree Foundation.

Gough, I. (2001) 'Social assistance regimes: a cluster analysis', *Journal of European Social Policy*, Vol. 11, pp. 165-170.

Green, H. and Hansbro, J. (1995) *Housing in England: A report of the 1993/4 survey of English housing*, London: The Stationery Office.

Gregg, P. and Wadsworth, J. (1998) *Unemployment and non-employment: Unpacking economic inactivity*, London: Employment Policy Institute.

de Haan, A. and Maxwell, S. (Eds.) (1998) Poverty and social exclusion in North and South, *IDS bulletin*, University of Sussex: IDS.

Hallerod, B. (1995) 'The truly poor: direct and indirect consensual measurement of poverty in Sweden', *Journal of European Social Policy*, Vol. 5, No. 2, pp. 111-129.

Hallerod, B. (1998) 'Poor Swedes, poor Britons: A comparative analysis of relative deprivation', in Andress, H.-J. (Ed.) *Empirical poverty research in a comparative perspective*, Aldershot: Ashgate.

Hauser, R., Nolan, B., Morsdorf, K. and Strengmann-Klein, W. (2000) 'Unemployment and poverty: change over time', in Gallie, D. and Paugam, S. (Eds.) *Welfare regimes and the experience of unemployment in Europe*, Oxford: Oxford University Press.

Hill, M. and Jenkins, S.P. (2001) 'Poverty amongst British children: chronic or transitory?', in Bradbury, B., Jenkins, S.P. and Micklewright, J. *The dynamics of child poverty in industrialized countries*, Cambridge: Cambridge University Press.

Hills, J. (1998) *Income and wealth: The latest evidence*, York: Joseph Rowntree Foundation.

Hills, J. (2001) 'The British approach', in *Indicators of progress: A discussion of approaches to monitor the government's strategy to tackle poverty and social exclusion*, Report of the workshop held on 19 July 2000 organized by Department of Social Security and Centre for Analysis of Social Exclusion, LSE, CASEreport 13, London: London School of Economics.

HM Treasury (2001) *Saving and assets for all, The modernization of Britain's tax and benefit system*, Paper eight, London: The Stationery Office.

Home Office (1977) *The costs of industrial change*, London: Home Office.

Howarth, C., Kenway, P., Palmer, G. and Miorelli, R. (1999) *Monitoring poverty and social exclusion 1999*, York: Joseph Rowntree Foundation.

Howarth, C., Kenway, P., Palmer, G. and Street, C. (1998) *Monitoring poverty and social exclusion: Labour's inheritance*, York: Joseph Rowntree Foundation.

Inter-Departmental Policy Committee (1997) *Sharing in progress: National anti-poverty strategy*, Dublin: The Stationery Office.

Jarman, B. (1984) 'Identification of underprivileged areas', *British Medical Journal*, Vol. 286, pp. 1705-1709.

Jarvis, S. and Jenkins, S.P. (1995) *Do the poor stay poor? New evidence about income dynamics from the British Household Panel Study*, Occasional paper No. 95-2, ESRC Research Centre on Micro-Social Change, Colchester: University of Essex.

Jarvis, S. and Jenkins, S.P. (1996) *Changing places: Income mobility and poverty dynamics in Britain*, Working papers of the ESRC Research Centre on Micro-Social Change, 98-19, Colchester: University of Essex.

Jarvis, S. and Jenkins, S.P. (1998a) 'How much income mobility is there in Britain?', *Economic Journal*, Vol. 108, No. 447, pp. 237-254.

Jarvis, S. and Jenkins, S.P. (1998b) *Net family income dataset. ESRC Data Archive*, Colchester: University of Essex.

Jarvis, S. and Jenkins, S.P. (2000a) 'Low-income dynamics in 1990s Britain', in Rose, D. (Ed.) *Researching social and economic change: the uses of household panel studies*, London: Routledge.

Jarvis, S. and Jenkins, S.P. (2000b) 'Dynamics of household incomes', in Berthoud, R. and Gershuny, J. (Eds.) *Seven years in the lives of British families: Evidence on the dynamics of social change from the British Household Panel Survey*, Bristol: The Policy Press.

Jenkins, S.P. and Rigg, J.A. with the assistance of Devicienti (2001) *The dynamics of poverty in Britain*, Department of Work and Pensions research report 157, Leeds: Corporate Document Services.

Kangas, O. and Ritakallio, V.-M. (1998) 'Different measures – different results? Approaches to multi-dimensional poverty', in Andress, H.-J. (Ed.) *Empirical poverty research in a comparative perspective*, Aldershot: Ashgate.

Kempson, E. et al (1994) *Hard times*, Policy Studies Institute: London.

Layte, R., Maitre, B., Nolan, B. and Whelan, C, (2000) *Explaining levels of deprivation in the European Union*, EPAG working paper 12, Institute for Social and Economic Research, Essex: University of Essex.

Lazarsfeld, P.F. (1958) 'Evidence and inference in social research', *Daedalus*, Vol. 87, pp. 99-130.

Lee, P. and Murie, A. (1997) *Poverty, housing tenure and social exclusion*, Bristol: The Policy Press.

Leisering, L. and Walker, R. (Eds.) (1998) *The dynamics of modern society: Poverty, policy and welfare*, Bristol: The Policy Press.

Levitas (1998) *The inclusive society? Social exclusion and New Labour*, Basingstoke: Macmillan.

Link, B. and Phelan, J. (1995) 'Social conditions as fundamental causes of disease', *Journal of Health and Social Behaviour*, pp. 80-94.

Lynch, J.W. and Kaplan, G.A. (1997) 'Understanding how inequality in the distribution of income affects health', *Journal of Health Psychology*, Vol. 2, pp. 1889-1895.

Mack, J. and Lansley, S. (1985) *Poor Britain*, London: Allen and Unwin.

Marsh, A., Gordon, D., Pantazis, C. and Heslop, P. (1999) *Home sweet home? The impact of poor housing on health*, Bristol: The Policy Press.

Marshall, T.H. (1950) *Citizenship and social class*, Cambridge: Cambridge University Press.

Martinez, R. and Ruiz-Huerta, J. (1999) *Income, multiple deprivation and poverty: An empirical analysis using Spanish data*, paper presented at the 26th general conference of The International Association for Research in Income and Wealth, Cracow, Poland.

McKay, S., Barnes, M. and Walker, R. (1996) *Pensions analysis and the working lives survey: A programme of research*, Loughborough: CRSP.

McKay, S. and Rowlingson, K. (1999) *Social Security in Britain*, Basingstoke: Macmillan.

McLaughlin, E., Millar, J. and Cooke, K. (1989) *Work and welfare benefits*, Aldershot: Gower.

Mejer, L. (2000) 'Social exclusion in the EU member states', *Statistics in Focus*, theme 3, No. 1, Luxembourg: Eurostat.

Mejer, L. and Linden, G. (2000) 'Persistent income poverty and social exclusion in the European Union', *Statistics in Focus*, Population and social conditions, Theme 3 – 13/2000, Luxembourg: Eurostat.

Micklewright, J. (2002) *Social exclusion and children: A European view for a US debate*, CASEPaper 54, London: London School of Economics.

Middleton, S., Ashworth, K. and Braithwaite, I. (1997) *Small fortunes*, London: CPAG.

Millar, J. (1997) 'Gender', in Walker, A. and Walker, C. (Eds.) *Britain divided: the growth of social exclusion in the 1980s and 1990s*, London: CPAG.

Millar, J. and Glendinning, C. (1989) 'Gender and poverty', *Journal of Social Policy*, Vol. 18, No. 3, pp. 363-81.

Muffels, R., Berghman, J. and Dirven, H-J. (1992) 'A multi-method approach to monitor the evolution of poverty', *Journal of European Social Policy*, Vol. 2, pp. 193-213.

Mulgan, G. (1998) 'Social exclusion: joined up solutions to joined up problems', in Oppenheim, C. (Ed.) *An inclusive society: Strategies for tackling poverty*, London: Institute for Public Policy Research.

Mumford, K. (2001) *Talking to families in East London: A report on the first stage of the research*, CASEreport 09, London: London School of Economics.

Murie, A. (2000) 'How can we end inequalities in housing?', in Pantazis, C. and Gordon, D. (Eds.) *Tackling inequalities: Where are we now and what can be done?*, Bristol: The Policy Press.

National Anti-Poverty Strategy (1997) *Sharing in progress*, Stationery Office, Dublin.

Nolan, B. (1999) 'Targeting poverty: The Irish example', *New Economy*, Vol. 6, No. 1, pp. 44-49.

Nolan, B. (2001) 'Measuring and targeting poverty: The Irish example', in, *Indicators of progress: A discussion of approaches to monitor the government's strategy to tackle poverty and social exclusion*, Report of the workshop held on 19 July 2000 organized by Department of Social Security and Centre for Analysis of Social Exclusion, LSE, CASEreport 13, London: London School of Economics.

Nolan, B. and Whelan, C.T. (1996) 'Measuring poverty using income and deprivation indicators: Alternative approaches', *Journal of European Social Policy*, Vol. 6, pp. 225-240.

Office for National Statistics (2001a) *Retail Price Index: All items index*, London: The Stationery Office.

Office for National Statistics (2001b) *Social trends*, London: Office for National Statistics.

Oppenheim, C. and Harker, L. (1996) *Poverty: The facts*, 3rd edition, London: Child Poverty Action Group.

Pantazis, C. (2000) 'Tackling inequalities in crime and social harm', in Pantazis, C. and Gordon, D. (Eds.) *Tackling inequalities: Where are we now and what can be done?*, Bristol: The Policy Press.

Parker, H. (Ed.) (1998) *Low cost but acceptable: A minimum income standard for the UK: Families with young children*, Bristol: Policy Press.

Paugam, S. (1995) 'The spiral of precariousness', in Room, G. (Ed.) *Beyond the Threshold: The Measurement and Analysis of Social Exclusion*, Bristol: The Policy Press.

Paugam, S. (1996) Poverty and social disqualification: A comparative analysis of cumulative social disadvantage in Europe, *Journal of European Social Policy*, Vol. 6, pp. 287-303.

Piachaud, D. (1981) 'Peter Townsend and the holy grail', *New Society*, Vol. 10, pp. 419-421.

Piachaud, D. (1987) 'Problems in the definition and measurement of poverty', *Journal of Social Policy*, Vol. 16, No. 2, pp. 147-164.

Percy-Smith, J. (2000) 'Introduction: The contours of social exclusion', in Percy-Smith, J. (Ed.) *Policy responses to social exclusion: Towards inclusion?*, Buckingham: Open University Press.

Power, A. (1999) 'Area problems and multiple deprivation', in *Persistent poverty and lifetime inequality: The evidence*, Report of a seminar organized by HM Treasury and CASE, CASEreport 5, London: CASE.

Prescott, P. (2002) 'The heart and soul of the nation', *The Guardian*, Society section, Wednesday 16 January, p. 3.

Putnam, R.D. (1995) 'Bowling alone: America's declining social capital', *Journal of Democracy*, Vol. 6, No. 1., pp. 65-78.

Rahman, M., Palmer, G. and Kenway, P. (2001) *Monitoring poverty and social exclusion 2001*, York: Joseph Rowntree Foundation.

Rahman, M., Palmer, G., Kenway, P. and Howarth, C. (2000) *Monitoring poverty and social exclusion 2000*, York: Joseph Rowntree Foundation.

Ramprakash, D. (1994) 'Poverty in the countries of the European Union: A synthesis of Eurostat's statistical research on poverty', *Journal of European Social Policy*, Vol. 4, No. 2, pp. 117-128.

Ringen, S. (1985) 'Toward a third stage in the measurement of poverty', *Acta Sociologica*, Vol. 28, No. 2, pp. 99-113.

Ringen, S. (1988) 'Direct and indirect measures of poverty', *Journal of Social Policy*. Vol. 17, pp. 351-366.

Robson, B., (1995), 'The Development of the 1991 Local Deprivation Index', in Room, G. (Ed.) *Beyond the Threshold: The Measurement and Analysis of Social Exclusion*, Bristol: The Policy Press.

Room, G. (1995) 'Conclusions', in Room, G. (Ed.) *Beyond the Threshold: The Measurement and Analysis of Social Exclusion*, Bristol: The Policy Press.

Room, G. (Ed.) (1995) *Beyond the Threshold: The Measurement and Analysis of Social Exclusion*, Bristol: The Policy Press.

Room, G. (1998) 'Social exclusion, solidarity and the challenge of globalization', *International Journal of Social Welfare*, Vol. 8, No. 3, pp. 166-74.

Room, G. (2000) 'Trajectories of social exclusion', in Gordon, D. and Townsend, P. (Eds.) *Breadline Europe*, Bristol: The Policy Press.

Rowlingson, K., Whyley, C. and Warren, T. (1999) *Wealth in Britain. A life-cycle perspective*, London: Policy Studies Institute.

Rowntree, B.S. (1901) *Poverty: A study of town life*, London: Macmillan.

Rowntree, B.S. (1941) *Poverty and progress*, London: Longmans Green.

Saunders, P. (1994) *The role, value and limitations of poverty research*, SPRC Discussion papers 53, The University of New South Wales.

Schaber, G. (1993) *Developing comparative databases: Comparative research on household panel studies*, PACO Document No. 2, Luxembourg: CEPS.

Sen, A. (1983) 'Poor, relatively speaking', *Oxford Economic Papers*, Vol. 35, No. 2, pp. 153-169.

Social Exclusion Unit (2000a) *National Strategy for Neighbourhood Renewal: a framework for consultation*, London: The Stationery Office.

Social Exclusion Unit (2000b) *The social exclusion leaflet*, http://www.cabinet-office.gov.uk/seu/index.htm.

Social Protection Committee (2001) *Report on indicators in the field of poverty and social exclusion*, Brussels: European Union Social Protection Committee.

Spicker, P. (1991) 'Solidarity', in Room, G. (Ed.) *Towards a European welfare state?*, Bristol: SAUS.

Taylor, A. (1994) 'Appendix: Sample characteristics, attrition and weighting', in Buck. N., Gershuny, J., Rose, D. and Scott, J. (Eds.) *Changing households: The British Household Panel Survey 1990-1992*, University of Essex: ESRC Research Centre on Micro-Social Change.

Taylor, M. (2000) 'Work, non-work, jobs and job mobility', in Berthoud, R. and Gershuny, J. (Eds.) *Seven years in the lives of British families: Evidence on the dynamics of social change from the British Household Panel Survey*, Bristol: The Policy Press.

Taylor, M., Keen, M., Buck, N. and Corti, L. (1994) 'Income welfare and consumption', in Buck. N., Gershuny, J., Rose, D. and Scott, J. (Eds.) *Changing households: The British Household Panel Survey 1990-1992*, University of Essex: ESRC Research Centre on Micro-Social Change.

Townsend, J. (1995) 'The burden of smoking', in Benzeval, M., Judge, K. and Whitehead, M. (Eds.) *Tackling inequalities in health: An agenda for action*, pp. 82-94 King's Fund.

Townsend, P. (1979) *Poverty in the United Kingdom*, Harmondsworth: Penguin.

Townsend, P. (1985) 'A sociological approach to the measurement of poverty – a rejoinder to Professor Amaryta Sen', *Oxford Economic Papers*, Vol. 37, No. 4, pp. 659-668.

Townsend, P. (2000) 'The case for poverty surveys', in *Measuring social exclusion*, proceedings of a joint seminar hosted by the Statistics and Research Branch, Department for Societal Development and the Social Security Research Group, School of Sociology and Social Policy, Queen's University, Belfast, pp. 57-66.

Townsend, P., Phillimore, P. and Beattie, A. (1988) *Health and deprivation: Inequality and the North*, London: Croom Helm.

Tsakloglou, P. (1996) 'Elderly and non-elderly in the European Union: A comparison of living standards', *Review of Income and Wealth*, Vol. 42, pp. 271-291

Tsakloglou, P. and Panopoulou, G. (1998) 'Who are the poor in Greece?: Analysing poverty under alternative concepts of resources and equivalence scales', *Journal of European Social Policy*, Vol. 8, No. 3, pp. 229-252.

Tsakloglou, P. and Papadopoulos, F. (2002) 'Poverty, material deprivation and multi-dimensional disadvantage during four life stages: evidence from the ECHP', in Barnes, M., Heady, C., Millar, J., Middleton, S., Tsakloglou, P., Papadopoulos, F. and Room, G. *Poverty and social exclusion in Europe*, Cheltenham: Edward Elgar.

UN (1995) *The Copenhagen declaration and programme of action: World summit for social development 6-12 March 1995*, New York: United Nations Department of Publications.

Veit-Wilson, J. (1986) 'Paradigms of poverty: A rehabilitation of B.S. Rowntree', *Journal of Social Policy*, Vol. 15, No. 1, pp. 69-99.

Veit-Wilson, J. (1998) *Setting adequacy standards: How governments define minimum incomes*, Bristol: The Policy Press.

Vleminckx, K. and Smeeding, T.M. (Eds.) (2001) *Child Well-Being, Child Poverty and Child Policy in Modern Nations*, Bristol: The Policy Press.

Walker, A. (1997) 'Introduction: the strategy of inequality', in Walker, A. and Walker, C. (1997) *Britain divided: the growth of social exclusion in the 1980s and 1990s*, London: CPAG.

Walker, A. and Walker, C. (Eds.) (1997) *Britain divided: the growth of social exclusion in the 1980s and 1990s*, London: CPAG.

Walker, R. (1995) 'The dynamics of poverty and social exclusion', in Room, G. (Ed.) *Beyond the Threshold: The Measurement and Analysis of Social Exclusion*, Bristol: The Policy Press.

Walker, R. and Ashworth, K. (1994) *Poverty dynamics: Issues and examples*, Aldershot: Avebury.

Webb, S. (1995) 'Poverty and health', in Benzeval, M., Judge, K. and Whitehead, M. (Eds.) *Tackling inequalities in health: An agenda for action*, London: King's Fund.

Whelan, B.J. and Whelan, C.T. (1995) 'In what sense is poverty multi-dimensional?', in Room, G. (Ed.) *Beyond the Threshold: The Measurement and Analysis of Social Exclusion*, Bristol: The Policy Press.

Whelan, C.T., Layte, R. and Maitre, B. (2001) *What is the scale of multiple deprivation in the European Union?*, EPAG working paper 19, Colchester: University of Essex.

Appendices

Appendix A   Income inflation adjustments

The income poverty line constructed in the *Poverty and Social Exclusion survey* (Gordon et al, 2000) was used as the threshold of the financial situation indicator in this research. The PSE threshold was set at £178 for an individual living alone in 1999. For the purpose of this research this threshold was modified to take into account other households according to household size and composition in line with conventional HBAI equivalization procedures (DSS, 2001a). To retain the concept of absolute poverty over time, the PSE threshold was converted to year of survey prices using the Retail Price Index (ONS, 2001a). The down rating calculations are presented in Table A.1.

Table A.1   Down rating calculations for PSE absolute income poverty line for individual living alone, BHPS,[a] RPI[b]

Wave	Year	RPI	Deflation factor	Poverty line
A	1991	134.6	0.810	£144
B	1992	139.4	0.839	£149
C	1993	141.9	0.854	£152
D	1994	145.0	0.872	£155
E	1995	150.6	0.906	£161
F	1996	153.8	0.925	£165
G	1997	159.3	0.958	£171
H	1998	164.4	0.989	£176
I	1999	166.2	1.00	£178

Notes:
[a] Calculations based on data for September each year, the month when the majority of the BHPS interviews took place.
[b] Source: Retail Price Index, Office for National Statistics (2001a).

Appendix B   Missing data analysis

Various types of analysis were performed in the investigation of social exclusion, most notably analysis at a cross-sectional level to examine the multi-dimensional nature of social exclusion and analysis at a longitudinal level to examine the longitudinal nature and prevalence of social exclusion. The cross-sectional and longitudinal analysis was based on different samples of working age-adults. The cross-sectional analysis was based on working-age adults present in a particular wave of the survey (1996 for both the BHPS and ECHP) and the longitudinal analysis was based on a panel sample of working-age adults present in all available waves of the survey (1994-1996 for the ECHP and 1991-1999 for the BHPS).

Whether these samples were representative of the population from which they were drawn was considered in the main text of the research. This analysis found only negligible differences between the samples and the populations they were estimated to be drawn from, although characteristics of socially excluded individuals were over-represented in those omitted from the longitudinal sample in particular.

Another form of bias from the analysis of survey data can occur if survey respondents record a differential amount of missing data. Missing data analysis helps address several concerns caused by incomplete data. Cases with missing data that are systematically different from cases without missing data can obscure results. Also, missing data may reduce the precision of calculated statistics because there is less information than originally planned. This is particularly relevant to this investigation because missing data is magnified when combing information from a number of variables (multi-dimensional analysis) and when using repeated observations (longitudinal analysis).

The following analysis examines the prevalence and type of missing data amongst respondents selected for investigation in this research. The analysis is divided into two sections, that for Britain using the BHPS and that for EU-12 countries using the ECHP. Within each section cross-sectional and longitudinal analysis is considered separately.

BHPS missing data analysis

Cross-sectional missing data analysis
In Chapter 3 the selection and validation of the BHPS sample for cross-sectional analysis was performed. The majority of cross-sectional analysis, presented in Chapter 4, was performed on the 1996 wave of the BHPS. A sample of working-age adults was chosen to minimize missing data by ensuring that each individual, and their household, had completed a full interview. A total of 6520 working-age individuals satisfied these criteria. However, because cross-sectional analysis of social exclusion required complete information on a number of disadvantage domains, an individual was determined to have missing data if any of variables used in this analysis was missing. This meant that approximately one in ten of the working-age cross-sectional sample had missing data (see Table B.1.1).

Table B.1.1   Cross-sectional missing data status, working-age adults, BHPS 1996

Missing data status	Frequency	Per cent
Missing	708	11
Not missing	5812	89
Total	6520	100

Table B.1.2 presents an analysis of the relationship between missing data status and socio-demographic characteristic. The analysis shows that individuals excluded from the investigation because of missing data were more likely to have been male, younger or older rather than middle aged, lived in a household with non-relatives, were out of the labour market (particularly in education or training) and lived in a household where no one works. These characteristics were associated with individuals at most risk of social exclusion and hence analysis was likely to underestimate the prevalence of social exclusion due to the under-representation of these 'at risk' groups.

Table B.1.2   Relationship between cross-sectional missing data status and socio-demographic characteristic, working-age adults, BHPS 1996, column per cent within category

Socio-demographic characteristic	Missing data status	
	Missing	Not missing
Sex		
Male	58	50
Female	42	50
Age group		
16-29 years	54	30
30-44 years	22	39
45-59/64 years	25	31
Household type		
Single	9	9
Couple no children	17	26
Couple, dep children only	34	39
Couple, some non-dep children	10	14
Lone parent, dep children only	6	6
Lone parent, some non-dep children	5	3
Other	19	3
Number of dependent children		
None	59	55
One	21	21
Two or more	20	24

Table B.1.2   (continued)

Education level		
Degree or higher	16	19
A-level	20	22
O-level	30	29
CSE level	8	7
None of these	26	23
Main activity status		
Employed full time	**50**	**67**
Employed part time	4	5
Unemployed	5	3
Care of home/family	14	18
Education/training	**27**	**6**
Other inactive	<1	<1
No. in household in employment		
None	18	11
One	26	28
Two or more	56	61
Base	708	5812

Note:
Bold text indicates statistically significant relationship (p<0.05) between socio-demographic characteristic and missing data status.

Longitudinal missing data analysis
The selection and validation of the BHPS sample for longitudinal analysis was performed meant a sample of working-age adults was chosen to minimize missing data by ensuring that each individual, and their household, had completed a full interview at each of the nine observations used in longitudinal analysis. A total of 3106 working-age individuals satisfied these criteria. Because longitudinal analysis relied on nine repeated observations for each data item (variable) for each individual, the likelihood of missing data was increased. The likelihood of missing data was further increased because multi-dimensional analysis required complete information on all variables used. An individual was determined to have missing data if any of the nine observations on a variable was missing or if any of the variables required for multi-dimensional analysis was missing. This meant that one quarter of the working-age panel sample had missing data (see Table B.2.1).

Table B.1.3   Longitudinal missing data status, working-age adults panel sample, BHPS 1991-1999

Missing data status	Frequency	Per cent
Missing	768	25
Not missing	2338	75
Total	3106	100

Table B.2.2 presents an analysis of the relationship between missing data status and socio-demographic characteristic. The analysis shows that individuals excluded from the investigation because of missing data were more likely to have been male, younger or older rather than middle aged, lived alone, lived without dependent children, had no educational qualifications, were out of the labour market and lived in a household where no one works. Again it is these characteristics than were associated with individuals at most risk of social exclusion, although the magnitude of difference between missing and non-missing data status was less than at a cross-sectional level. Hence analysis was likely to slightly underestimate the prevalence of social exclusion due to the under-representation of these 'at risk' groups.

Table B.1.4   Relationship between longitudinal missing data status and socio-demographic characteristic, working-age adults panel sample, BHPS 1991-1999, column per cent within category

Socio-demographic characteristic (1999)	*Missing data status*	
	Missing	Not missing
Sex		
Male	53	49
Female	47	51
Age group		
16-29 years	12	10
30-44 years	40	47
45-59/64 years	48	43
Household type		
Single	13	9
Couple no children	26	27
Couple, dep children only	35	42
Couple, some non-dep children	17	15
Lone parent, dep children only	5	4
Lone parent, some non-dep children	3	2
Other	2	1
Number of dependent children		
None	59	54
One	17	18
Two or more	24	28
Education level		
Degree or higher	20	22
A-level	19	21
O-level	27	28
CSE level	6	7
None of these	28	22
Main activity status		
Employed full time	67	72
Employed part time	6	7

Table B.1.4   (continued)

Unemployed	1	1
Care of home/family	24	19
Education/training	1	1
Other inactive	1	<1
No. in household in employment		
None	15	9
One	29	27
Two or more	56	64
Base	768	2338

Note:
Bold text indicates statistically significant relationship (p<0.05) between socio-demographic characteristic and missing data status.

ECHP missing data analysis

Chapter 7 contained cross-national analysis of social exclusion in the EU-12 using data from the ECHP survey. As with the BHPS analysis, the ECHP sample focussed on working-age adults who had information from completed full individual and household interviews. The selection of the sample was intended to minimize missing data given the requirements of multi-dimensional and longitudinal analysis. Despite this, some missing data was still apparent in the sample. The following analysis details the amount and make-up of this missing data and discusses whether it was likely to have had an effect on findings.

Cross-sectional missing data analysis
The cross-sectional analysis of social exclusion in the EU-12 used data from the 1996 wave of the ECHP. Because cross-sectional analysis of social exclusion required complete information on a number of disadvantage domains, an individual was determined to have missing data if any of variables used in this analysis was missing. This meant that approximately one in twenty of the working-age cross-sectional sample had missing data across the EU-12 as a whole. This varied between countries; Greece did not record any cross-sectional missing data whilst had 17 per cent of cases that recorded missing data. The UK also recorded a high amount of missing data (14 per cent). Table B.2.1 details the amount of cross-sectional missing data per country.

Table B.2.2 presents the relationship between cross-sectional missing data status and socio-demographic characteristic for each of the EU-12 countries. At an EU-12 level those excluded from the investigation because of missing data were more likely to be male, aged 16 to 29 years, live in a couple with at least one non-dependent child household, be in education or training and live in a household where one person is in employment. Again the characteristics of individuals with missing data varied across countries, but the negligible amount of missing data in the majority of countries meant it was unlikely to affect the main findings.

Longitudinal missing data analysis

The magnitude of missing data in the longitudinal analysis exceeded that at a cross-sectional level but was still relatively low (8 per cent) for the EU-12 as a whole. Again missing data varied between countries; Greece still recorded no missing data and Ireland recorded levels as high as 30 per cent. The UK again recorded high levels of missing data, almost one in five individuals doing so (see Table B.2.3).

Table B.2.4 presents the relationship between longitudinal missing data status and socio-demographic characteristic for each of the EU-12 countries. At an EU-12 level those excluded from the investigation because of missing data were more likely to be male, aged 16 to 29 years and in education or training. Again the characteristics of individuals with missing data varied across countries. These characteristics were associated with individuals at most risk of social exclusion, so this should be taken into account when interpreting findings, although the negligible amount of missing data in the majority of countries meant it was unlikely to affect the main results.

Table B.2.1 Cross-sectional missing data status, working-age adults, ECHP 1996

Country Missing data status	Frequency	Per cent
Belgium		
Missing	349	7
Not missing	4448	93
Denmark		
Missing	174	4
Not missing	3753	96
France		
Missing	414	4
Not missing	9861	96
Germany		
Missing	140	2
Not missing	6659	98
Greece		
Missing	0	0
Not missing	8374	100
Ireland		
Missing	1046	17
Not missing	5069	83
Italy		
Missing	108	1
Not missing	13968	99
Luxembourg		
Missing	17	1
Not missing	1562	99
Netherlands		
Missing	23	<1
Not missing	7547	99
Portugal		
Missing	97	1
Not missing	8612	99
Spain		
Missing	197	2
Not missing	11563	98
UK		
Missing	**739**	**14**
Not missing	**4581**	**86**
EU-12		
Missing	3304	4
Not missing	89301	96

Table B.2.2   Relationship between cross-sectional missing data status and socio-demographic characteristic, working-age adults, ECHP 1996, increase/decrease risk indicator[a]

Socio-demographic characteristics (1996)	Country												
	Be	De	Fr	Ge	Gr	Ir	It	Lu	Ne	Po	Sp	Uk	Eu
Sex													
Male		⇧			-	⇧		*	*	⇧	⇧	**⇧**	**⇧**
Female		⇩			-	⇩		*	*	⇩	⇩	**⇩**	**⇩**
Age group													
16-29 years	⇧		⇧		-	⇧		*	*	⇧	⇧	**⇧**	**⇧**
30-44 years	⇩		⇩	⇩	-	⇩		*	*	⇩			
45-59/64 years	⇧			⇧	-			*	*	⇩		**⇩**	
Household type													
Single					-			*	*				
Couple no children		⇩			-			*	*				
Couple, dep ch only			⇩		-		⇩	*	*	⇩	⇩		
Couple, some ndep ch	⇧	⇧			-		⇧	*	*	⇧			⇧
Lone par, dep ch only					-			*	*				
Lone par, some ndep					-		⇧	*	*	⇧			
Other					-			*	*	⇩		⇧	
Number of children													
None		⇩	⇧	⇧	-		⇧	*	*	⇧	⇧		
One					-			*	*	⇩			
Two		⇧			-		⇩	*	*	⇩			
Three or more					-			*	*				
Education level													
High		⇩			-			*	*				
Medium		⇧	⇩		-		⇩	*	*	⇧			
Low	⇧		⇧		-		⇧	*	*	⇩			
Main activity status													
Employed full time		⇧	⇩		-		⇩	*	*	⇩	⇩	**⇧**	
Employed part time					-			*	*				
Unemployed					-			*	*				
Care of home/family		⇩	⇧		-	⇩		*	*	⇩	⇩	**⇩**	**⇩**
Education/training	⇧				-	⇧		*	*	⇧	⇧	**⇧**	**⇧**
Other inactive					-		⇧	*	*	⇧	⇧		
No. of hh in employmnt													
None	⇧	⇧	⇧		-			*	*				
One	⇧	⇧	⇩	⇧	-		⇧	*	*	⇧			⇧
Two or more	⇩	⇩		⇩	-		⇩	*	*	⇩			⇩

Notes:
[a] ⇧ indicates increased missing data risk by socio-demographic characteristic. ⇩ indicates decreased missing data risk by socio-demographic characteristic. Bold arrow indicates statistically significant (p<0.05) relationship between socio-demographic characteristics and missing data status.

Table B.2.3 Longitudinal missing data status, working-age adults panel sample, ECHP 1994-1996

Country Missing data status	Frequency	Per cent
Belgium		
Missing	703	17
Not missing	3494	83
Denmark		
Missing	191	6
Not missing	3167	94
France		
Missing	850	9
Not missing	8194	91
Germany		
Missing	397	6
Not missing	5904	94
Greece		
Missing	0	0
Not missing	7188	100
Ireland		
Missing	1572	30
Not missing	3737	70
Italy		
Missing	341	3
Not missing	12046	97
Luxembourg		
Missing	71	5
Not missing	1391	95
Netherlands		
Missing	56	1
Not missing	6249	99
Portugal		
Missing	140	2
Not missing	7225	98
Spain		
Missing	625	6
Not missing	9366	94
UK		
Missing	**924**	**19**
Not missing	**3902**	**81**
EU-12		
Missing	5870	8
Not missing	71863	92

Table B.2.4   **Relationship between longitudinal missing data status and socio-demographic characteristic, working-age adults panel sample, ECHP 1994-96, increased/decreased risk indicator[a]**

Socio-demographic characteristics (1996)	Be	De	Fr	Ge	Gr	Ir	It	Lu	Ne	Po	Sp	Uk	Eu
Sex													
Male					-	⇑		⇑	⇑	⇑	⇑	⇑	⇑
Female					-	⇓		⇓	⇓	⇓	⇓	⇓	⇓
Age group													
16-29 years					-	⇑			⇑	⇑	⇑	⇑	⇑
30-44 years	⇑		⇑		-	⇓				⇓	⇓		
45-59/64 years		⇓			-	⇓			⇓	⇓	⇓	⇓	
Household type													
Single					-								
Couple no children					-								
Couple, dep ch only			⇓		-	⇓	⇓		⇓	⇓	⇓		
Couple, some ndep ch	⇑	⇑			-	⇑	⇑		⇑	⇑	⇑		
Lone par, dep ch only		⇓			-								
Lone par, some ndep					-					⇑			
Other					-			⇓	⇑	⇓			
Number of children													
None		⇑			-		⇑	⇓			⇑		
One					-		⇑	⇑	⇑				
Two	⇓	⇑			-			⇓	⇓	⇓	⇓		
Three or more	⇓				-				⇓				
Education level													
High		⇓			-				⇓	⇑			
Medium		⇑	⇓		-						⇑		
Low			⇑	⇑	-				⇑	⇓			
Main activity status													
Employed full time		⇓			-		⇓		⇓	⇓	⇓	⇑	
Employed part time					-								
Unemployed													
Care of home/family					-	⇓					⇓	⇓	⇓
Education/training					-	⇑				⇑	⇑		⇑
Other inactive					-					⇑	⇑		
No. of hh in employmnt													
None		⇑			-				⇑				
One	⇑				-			⇓	⇓	⇑			
Two or more	⇓	⇑			-				⇑		⇓		

Notes:
[a] ⇑ indicates increased missing data risk by socio-demographic characteristic. ⇓ indicates decreased missing data risk by socio-demographic characteristic. Bold arrow indicates statistically significant (p<0.05) relationship between socio-demographic characteristics and missing data status.

Appendix C   Factor analysis statistics

Chapter 4 concentrated on the multi-dimensional nature of social exclusion in Great Britain (Chapter 7 contained a similar, although more brief, analysis with ECHP data). One of the objectives of this analysis was to investigate whether disadvantage on an indicator was associated with disadvantaged on another or others. Factor analysis was used in this investigation to bring order to the multiple disadvantage experienced by individuals by determining which of the indicators were related and which were not. It is a technique that identifies underlying variables, or factors, which explain the pattern of association within a set of observed variables (in this case the seven poverty and social exclusion indicators) that suggest the formation of groups of distinct concepts.

Factor analysis is primarily concerned with describing the variation or variance that is shared by scores of people on three or more variables. It extracts a factor according to the largest amount of variance accounted for by a combination of variables. The second factor consists of the next largest amount of variance that is not related to or explained by the first one. The third factor extracts the next largest amount of variance and so on. The larger the variance explained by a factor the more important it is in explaining relationships between the variables.

There are as many factors as variables. The number of factors to de decided upon is based on the amount of variance they account for. By default SPSS selects factors that explain more variance than a single variable. In other words, a factor that explains less variance than a single variable is excluded from the final factor result. In this research, factors have been selected using an orthogonal rotation technique that produces factors that are unrelated to each other.

The relationship between each variable (indicator) and a factor is expressed as a correlation or loading. The loading therefore implies the direction and strength of the relationship between an indicator and the factor. Conventionally items that load less than 0.3 with a factor are omitted from consideration since they account for such little variance and so are not important.

The following tables present details of the number of factors, the total variance explained by each factor and the size of the loading of each indicator to the respective factor. The analysis is split into two sections, one for analysis of the BHPS data and one for analysis of the ECHP data. Within each section is detailed the factor analysis performed at a cross-sectional and longitudinal level. It was the 1996 wave of each survey that was used in the majority of cross-sectional analysis presented in the research.

BHPS factor analysis statistics

Factor analysis was performed at a current and longitudinal level using data from the BHPS. From this analysis notions of *household economic deprivation* (comprising the financial situation, material possessions and housing circumstance indicators), *personal civic exclusion* (comprising the neighbourhood perception and social relations indicators) and *personal health exclusion* (comprising the physical health mental health indicators) were formed. As Tables C.1.1 and C.1.2

show, for the 1996 wave (presented in Chapter 4) the notion of *household economic deprivation* was derived from one factor, whilst the factor loadings of the first factor determined the conceptualization of the other two notions. The relationship between the factors was present in the majority of waves. Three distinct factors were actually found from the factor analysis in the 1997 wave.

Table C.1.1   Factor analysis statistics, current disadvantage, working-age adults, BHPS, 1991-1999

| Year | *Rotated factor matrix loading* | |
Indicator	Factor 1	Factor 2
1991		
Financial situation	0.576	--
Material possessions	0.661	--
Housing circumstance	0.691	--
Neighbourhood perception	--	0.304
Social relations	--	0.442
Physical health	--	0.635
Mental health	--	0.735
Percentage of variance	19%	19%
1992		
Financial situation	0.545	--
Material possessions	0.657	--
Housing circumstance	0.667	--
Neighbourhood perception	--	--
Social relations	--	0.371
Physical health	--	0.654
Mental health	--	0.748
Percentage of variance	20%	16%
1993		
Financial situation	--	0.562
Material possessions	--	0.688
Housing circumstance	--	0.697
Neighbourhood perception	0.348	--
Social relations	0.500	--
Physical health	0.622	--
Mental health	0.718	--
Percentage of variance	21%	17%
1994		
Financial situation	0.537	--
Material possessions	0.666	--
Housing circumstance	0.715	--
Neighbourhood perception	--	0.319
Social relations	--	0.444
Physical health	--	0.662
Mental health	--	0.699
Percentage of variance	20%	17%

Table C.1.1 (continued)

1995		
Financial situation	--	0.588
Material possessions	--	0.641
Housing circumstance	--	0.695
Neighbourhood perception	0.345	--
Social relations	0.486	--
Physical health	0.621	--
Mental health	0.733	--
Percentage of variance	21%	17%
1996		
Financial situation	--	0.509
Material possessions	--	0.716
Housing circumstance	--	0.669
Neighbourhood perception	0.327	--
Social relations	0.413	--
Physical health	0.682	--
Mental health	0.703	--
Percentage of variance	20%	16%
1997		
Financial situation	0.635	--
Material possessions	0.664	--
Housing circumstance	0.629	--
Neighbourhood perception	--	--
Social relations	--	0.484
Physical health	--	0.671
Mental health	--	0.748
Percentage of variance	20%	16%
1998		
Financial situation	--	0.483
Material possessions	--	0.694
Housing circumstance	--	0.693
Neighbourhood perception	--	--
Social relations	0.363	--
Physical health	0.717	--
Mental health	0.704	--
Percentage of variance	20%	16%
1999		
Financial situation	--	0.542
Material possessions	--	0.670
Housing circumstance	--	0.635
Neighbourhood perception	--	--
Social relations	--	--
Physical health	0.726	--
Mental health	0.709	--
Percentage of variance	19%	16%

Table C.1.2   Factor analysis statistics, persistent disadvantage, working age adults, BHPS, 1991-1999

Indicator	Rotated factor matrix loading	
	Factor 1	Factor 2
Financial situation	--	0.518
Material possessions	--	0.695
Housing circumstance	--	0.738
Neighbourhood perception	0.369	--
Social relations	0.500	--
Physical health	0.716	--
Mental health	0.749	--
Percentage of variance	25%	18%

ECHP factor analysis statistics

As Tables C.2.1 and C.2.2 show, the three integral notions of social exclusion were presents at an EU-12 level for both current and persistent disadvantage. However there were differences between countries when analysis was performed at a national level. The results for the UK were similar to that found with the BHPS data, although the ECHP analysis displays three distinct factors rather than two. These relationships were found in the 1996 wave (illustrated below) and the 1994 and 1995 waves (statistics for these two waves are not presented below for reasons of space consideration).

Table C.2.1   Factor analysis statistics, current disadvantage, working-age adults, ECHP 1996

Country Indicator	Rotated factor matrix loading		
	Factor1	Factor2	Factor3
Belgium			
Financial situation	0.432	----	----
Material possessions	0.627	----	----
Housing circumstance	0.685	----	----
Neighbourhood perception	0.616	----	----
Social relations	----	----	0.839
Physical health	----	0.799	----
Mental health	----	0.787	----
Percentage of variance	23%	17%	14%

Table C.2.1   (continued)

Denmark			
Financial situation	0.621	----	
Material possessions	0.641	----	
Housing circumstance	0.634	----	
Neighbourhood perception	0.452	----	
Social relations	----	----	
Physical health	----	0.781	
Mental health	----	0.788	
Percentage of variance	22%	17%	
France			
Financial situation	0.669	----	
Material possessions	0.702	----	
Housing circumstance	0.560	----	
Neighbourhood perception	0.373	----	
Social relations	----	----	
Physical health	----	0.748	
Mental health	----	0.759	
Percentage of variance	22%	17%	
Germany			
Financial situation	----	0.776	----
Material possessions	----	0.745	----
Housing circumstance	----	----	0.656
Neighbourhood perception	----	----	0.778
Social relations	----	----	0.401
Physical health	0.785	----	----
Mental health	0.771	----	----
Percentage of variance	21%	17%	15%
Greece			
Financial situation	0.644	----	----
Material possessions	0.729	----	----
Housing circumstance	0.652	----	----
Neighbourhood perception	----	----	0.908
Social relations	----	0.443	0.344
Physical health	----	0.758	----
Mental health	----	0.778	----
Percentage of variance	21%	19%	15%
Ireland			
Financial situation	0.580	----	----
Material possessions	0.674	----	----
Housing circumstance	0.631	----	----
Neighbourhood perception	0.532	----	0.363
Social relations	----	----	0.888
Physical health	----	0.791	----
Mental health	----	0.795	----
Percentage of variance	22%	17%	14%

Table C.2.1 (continued)

Italy			
Financial situation	0.600	----	
Material possessions	0.627	----	
Housing circumstance	0.685	----	
Neighbourhood perception	0.475	----	
Social relations	----	0.352	
Physical health	----	0.748	
Mental health	----	0.741	
Percentage of variance	22%	17%	
Luxembourg			
Financial situation	----	0.759	----
Material possessions	----	0.607	0.339
Housing circumstance	----	----	0.809
Neighbourhood perception	----	----	0.593
Social relations	----	0.496	----
Physical health	0.753	----	----
Mental health	0.790	----	----
Percentage of variance	22%	16%	13%
Netherlands			
Financial situation	0.779	----	----
Material possessions	0.787	----	----
Housing circumstance	----	----	0.662
Neighbourhood perception	----	----	0.743
Social relations	----	----	0.398
Physical health	----	0.793	----
Mental health	----	0.782	----
Percentage of variance	21%	17%	15%
Portugal			
Financial situation	0.587	----	----
Material possessions	0.789	----	----
Housing circumstance	0.718	----	----
Neighbourhood perception	----	----	0.845
Social relations	----	----	0.459
Physical health	----	0.774	----
Mental health	----	0.794	----
Percentage of variance	23%	17%	15%
Spain			
Financial situation	0.683	----	----
Material possessions	0.748	----	----
Housing circumstance	0.575	----	----
Neighbourhood perception	----	----	0.804
Social relations	----	----	0.569
Physical health	----	0.774	----
Mental health	----	0.769	----
Percentage of variance	21%	17%	15%

Table C.2.1   (continued)

UK			
Financial situation	0.769	----	----
Material possessions	0.717	----	----
Housing circumstance	0.428	----	0.496
Neighbourhood perception	----	----	0.553
Social relations	----	----	0.745
Physical health	----	0.782	----
Mental health	----	0.765	----
Percentage of variance	23%	16%	14%
EU-12			
Financial situation	0.675	----	----
Material possessions	0.745	----	----
Housing circumstance	0.622	----	----
Neighbourhood perception	----	----	0.775
Social relations	----	----	0.636
Physical health	----	0.779	----
Mental health	----	0.784	----
Percentage of variance	21%	17%	15%

Table C.2.2   Factor analysis statistics, persistent disadvantage, working-age adults, ECHP, 1994-1996

Country	Rotated factor matrix loading		
Indicator	Factor1	Factor2	Factor3
Belgium			
Financial situation	----	0.662	----
Material possessions	----	0.709	----
Housing circumstance	----	0.487	0.418
Neighbourhood perception	----	----	0.690
Social relations	----	----	0.615
Physical health	0.790	----	----
Mental health	0.776	----	----
Percentage of variance	19%	17%	15%
Denmark			
Financial situation	----	----	----
Material possessions	----	----	----
Housing circumstance	0.727	----	----
Neighbourhood perception	0.716	----	----
Social relations	----	----	0.902
Physical health	----	0.770	----
Mental health	----	0.615	0.348
Percentage of variance	17%	15%	14%

Table C.2.2   (continued)

France			
Financial situation	0.742	----	----
Material possessions	0.713	----	----
Housing circumstance	0.463	----	----
Neighbourhood perception	----	----	0.812
Social relations	----	----	0.542
Physical health	----	0.703	----
Mental health	----	0.711	----
Percentage of variance	19%	16%	14%
Germany			
Financial situation	----	0.367	----
Material possessions	----	0.774	----
Housing circumstance	0.463	0.541	----
Neighbourhood perception	0.682		----
Social relations	0.670	----	----
Physical health	----	----	0.724
Mental health	----	----	0.746
Percentage of variance	17%	16%	14%
Greece			
Financial situation	----	0.635	
Material possessions	----	0.724	
Housing circumstance	----	0.609	
Neighbourhood perception	----	----	
Social relations	0.686	----	
Physical health	0.609	----	
Mental health	0.705	----	
Percentage of variance	21%	18%	
Ireland			
Financial situation	0.635	----	----
Material possessions	0.700	----	----
Housing circumstance	0.574	----	----
Neighbourhood perception	0.328	----	0.665
Social relations	----	----	0.780
Physical health	----	0.787	----
Mental health	----	0.802	----
Percentage of variance	21%	19%	15%
Italy			
Financial situation	0.668	----	----
Material possessions	0.690	----	----
Housing circumstance	0.616	----	----
Neighbourhood perception	----	----	0.655
Social relations	----	----	0.677
Physical health	----	0.731	----
Mental health	----	0.734	----
Percentage of variance	19%	17%	15%

Table C.2.2   (continued)

Luxembourg			
Financial situation	0.380	----	----
Material possessions	0.771	----	----
Housing circumstance	0.723	----	----
Neighbourhood perception	----	----	----
Social relations	----	----	0.543
Physical health	----	0.787	0.707
Mental health	----	0.770	----
Percentage of variance	19%	19%	16%
Netherlands			
Financial situation	0.529	----	----
Material possessions	0.659	----	----
Housing circumstance	0.633	----	----
Neighbourhood perception	0.313	----	----
Social relations	----	----	0.880
Physical health	----	0.751	----
Mental health	----	0.755	----
Percentage of variance	18%	17%	14%
Portugal			
Financial situation	0.596	----	----
Material possessions	0.774	----	----
Housing circumstance	0.701	----	----
Neighbourhood perception	----	----	0.856
Social relations	----	----	0.517
Physical health	----	0.733	----
Mental health	----	0.755	----
Percentage of variance	21%	16%	14%
Spain			
Financial situation	0.706	----	----
Material possessions	0.763	----	----
Housing circumstance	0.512	----	0.370
Neighbourhood perception	----	----	0.736
Social relations	----	----	0.464
Physical health	----	0.717	----
Mental health	----	0.649	----
Percentage of variance	20%	16%	14%
UK			
Financial situation	0.610	----	----
Material possessions	0.700	----	----
Housing circumstance	0.366	----	0.403
Neighbourhood perception	----	----	0.462
Social relations	----	----	----
Physical health	----	0.472	0.627
Mental health	----	0.659	----
Percentage of variance	18%	15%	15%

Table C.2.2 (continued)

EU-12			
Financial situation	0.632	----	----
Material possessions	0.749	----	----
Housing circumstance	0.632	----	----
Neighbourhood perception	----	----	0.813
Social relations	----	----	0.576
Physical health	----	0.738	----
Mental health	----	0.745	----
Percentage of variance	20%	16%	15%

Appendix D   Comparison of Great Britain/UK social exclusion indicators with BHPS and ECHP data

As indicators of social exclusion were constructed from both the BHPS and ECHP surveys, it is possible to compare findings for Great Britain/United Kingdom (see Table D.1). It is clear from Table D.1.1 that estimates of current disadvantage for the UK/Great Britain according to the two surveys were not identical. In particular, the ECHP findings report higher levels of neighbourhood disadvantage and lower levels of both forms of health disadvantage.

Table D.1.1   Incidence of current disadvantage in the UK,[a] working-age adults, ECHP, BHPS, 1996, cell per cent

Social exclusion indicator	Survey	
	ECHP	BHPS
Financial situation	15	13
Material possessions	6	9
Housing circumstance	8	10
Neighbourhood perception	19	12
Social relations	6	10
Physical health	6	16
Mental health	3	10

Note:
[a] The ECHP data refers to the whole of the UK while the BHPS data refers to Great Britain only.

Even though the same domains of social exclusion were used when constructing indicators from the BHPS and ECHP datasets, the two sets of indicators were not identical. Because the two surveys contain slightly different information, as a consequence of asking slightly different questions, the indicators were not constructed in the same way. Also, different thresholds were used to distinguish disadvantage from non-disadvantage. The ECHP indicators used the Proportional Social Exclusion Index approach whilst the BHPS indicators were constructed using an absolute approach based on a relative notion of disadvantage in society. It is also likely that minor differences between the indicators could be found because of dissimilarities in survey sampling and weighting procedures.

Appendix E   Cluster analysis statistics

In Chapter 7 an analysis was performed to group countries according to the prevalence of persistent disadvantage. Cluster analysis is a statistical procedure that groups cases, or variables, into clusters according to their similarity on a number of variables (the seven social exclusion indicators in this case). It measures the distance between cases, or variables, on a combination of dimensions and uses this to identify groups within which there is considerable homogeneity and between which there are clear boundaries.

There are a number of cluster analysis techniques available to the researcher. The cluster analysis technique used in this investigation is called k-means cluster analysis (KCA). This technique allows the researcher to specify *a priori* the number of clusters (k) to be created. The technique also offers a good range of information to help evaluate the empirical adequacy of the clusters and to interpret results (for further information on the cluster analysis technique in comparative analysis see Gough, 2001). This information is detailed below.

A range of values of k was tried. When $k=5$, five clusters were identified that were reasonably homogeneous and with well-defined boundaries. The clusters are shown in Table E.1.1 along with a measure of each country's distance from its empirical cluster centre. So, for example, the UK appears as an outlier in cluster 4. Table E.1.2 shows the final cluster centres that indicate how each variable contributes to discriminating between the clusters. Thus the financial situation, material possession and housing circumstance indicators are all important in cluster 5, whereas the material possession and housing circumstance indicators are less so in clusters 1, 2 and 4.

Table E.1.1   Distance from cluster centre

Cluster	Country	Distance
1	Portugal	0.000
2	Italy	0.000
3	Greece	2.472
3	Ireland	1.764
3	Spain	2.728
4	Belgium	1.854
4	France	1.561
4	Germany	1.199
4	**UK**	**2.437**
5	Denmark	1.491
5	Luxembourg	1.599
5	The Netherlands	1.599

Table E.1.2   Final Cluster Centres

Indicator	Cluster				
	1	2	3	4	5
Financial	9.00	3.33	7.33	6.00	9.00
Material	2.00	1.67	8.00	2.50	15.00
Housing	3.00	1.33	3.00	2.75	14.00
N'bourhood	6.00	1.33	2.67	3.50	4.00
Social	5.00	2.00	1.00	1.50	4.00
Physical	1.00	3.67	1.67	3.25	4.00
Mental	1.00	1.00	1.33	1.25	1.00

Appendix F   Proportional Disadvantage Index algebraic formula

The most conventional and valid way to measure social exclusion across countries is to use a relative approach as it ensures that social exclusion is measured against a standard that has social relevance in each country involved in the analysis. The Proportional Disadvantage Index (PDI) approach combines information on individual and population levels of the possession of resources (or participation), at a country level in this case, to create a direct measure of disadvantage. This allows a range of information to be used according to its relative importance in each country, therefore providing valid comparative measures between countries.

The PDI approach selects a number of items to form an indicator to represent a particular domain of disadvantage. To each item is assigned a weight that gives more importance to the form of disadvantage considered significant by larger groups of the population. The score on the PDI is therefore the outcome of the number of items a person (or their household) possesses (or participates in) and the specific weight assigned to each item according to possession (participation) of the item in the population as a whole.

In algebraic terms, the formula for the calculation of each population member's disadvantage score, μ_j, is:

$$\mu_j = \frac{\sum_{i=1}^{I} w_i X_{ij}}{\sum_{i=1}^{I} w_i}$$

where I is the total number of items for which information is available w_i is the proportion of the population living in accommodation with material possession i and X_{ij} a variable that takes the value of 0 (1) if the dwelling of individual j is privileged (disadvantaged) with household economic resource i (adapted from Tsakloglou and Papadopoulos, 2002).

Index